Civic Symbol

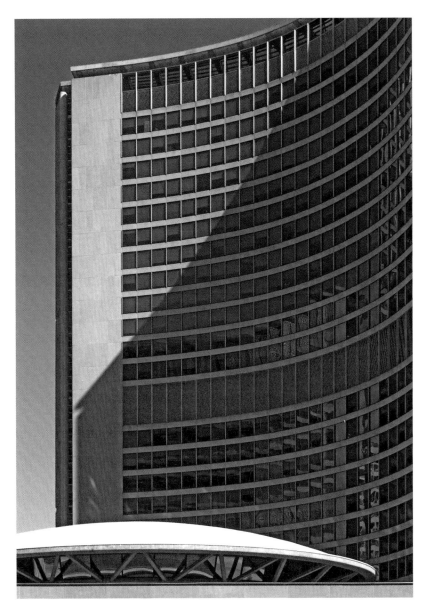

Civic Symbol

Creating Toronto's New City Hall 1952–1966

Christopher Armstrong

UNIVERSITY OF TORONTO PRESS

Toronto Buffalo London

ISBN 978-1-4426-5027-5

Printed on acid-free paper.

Publication cataloguing information is available from Library and Archives Canada.

University of Toronto Press acknowledges the financial assistance to its publishing program of the Canada Council for the Arts and the Ontario Arts Council, an agency of the Government of Ontario.

 Canada Council Conseil des Arts
for the Arts du Canada

 ONTARIO ARTS COUNCIL
CONSEIL DES ARTS DE L'ONTARIO
an Ontario government agency
un organisme du gouvernement de l'Ontario

University of Toronto Press acknowledges the financial support of the Government of Canada through the Canada Book Fund for its publishing activities.

Contents

Illustrations

Foreword

It is rare that a government with the aspiration for a project that will be "a source of pride and pleasure to its citizens" comes close to realizing such a noble goal. But Toronto's New City Hall more than meets that promise. It is entirely appropriate that this book begins by quoting the intention of Mayor Nathan Phillips in the words set out above.

And it is even more amazing that the aspiration survived the extraordinary twists and turns, the immense hurdles, and the sometimes odd opinions of those holding positions of power, all of which is described fully here, and found lasting form.

The vision comprised the square and the new city hall. The way each is conceived and executed enhances the other, and most Toronto residents see them as part of a very successful and beloved whole.

The square designed by Revell quickly became the city's outdoor room. Before it was created, the citizens of Toronto didn't have a recognized civic space that was both significant and meaningful. There was a mean and narrow strip in front of the old city hall where public events sometimes occurred, but it was overwhelmed by a war memorial and there was no space for sustained human interaction. There may have been streets where parades and processions were held, but there was no outdoor area where people could express their lives together as citizens. Revell created something Torontonians didn't realize they needed or would even have a use for.

The most remarkable features of the square are its edges, its boundaries, and its views out into the city. At its head is New City Hall, Revell's visible signal that the city had dressed up in new clothes. There is pride in the austerity of the design, its modesty, its sense of proportion, its relationship to its surroundings. To the east, the old city hall peaks over the colonnaded edge of the city's room. The old and the new co-exist, rather than the new overshadowing and belittling the old. Osgoode Hall and the old law courts – some of the oldest structures in the city – are to the west and they too get fair respect. An unfortunate large and unimaginative structure looms on the south edge, but that is also part of the real life of Toronto. As Robert Fulford wrote, "it was a Finnish architect's belief in urban life that gave shape to generations of dreams and provided the city's focal point ... this is where the new Toronto was born" (*Accidental City*, 8).

Once completed, the square and New City Hall immediately created a sense of civic culture for Toronto. Dennis Lee locates "Civil Elegy," his famous poem about Canadian citizenship, here. It was written in 1968 in the square, and when published with other poems in 1972 was honoured with the Governor General's prize for poetry. The reverie of the poem keeps returning to the square and the harmony exhibited by the towers of New City Hall. And so began the flowering of the city's new cultural expression: not only Dennis Lee but also Margaret Atwood, Gwendolyn MacEwen, Matt Cohen, Paul Thompson, Rick Salutin, and many others writing about what it meant to live in Toronto. They all fed on Revell's inspiration.

The square became a key political space. It was the locale of demonstrations against the Spadina Expressway, against nuclear war, against urban renewal. This was the space for civic engagement and the expression of public opinion. I remember one sign from 1971 with a big photo of Revell's New City Hall and the slogan "City Hall belongs to the people." Indeed.

The square was the place of celebration in the way no street could ever be – for royalty, sport champions, popular singers, heroes like Terry Fox as his great run across Canada for cancer research made its way through Toronto. It was also a place of public sorrow and commemoration. When Jack Layton, leader of the Official Opposition in Parliament and a former member of Toronto city council, died in 2011, the square was filled with sadness as citizens scribbled with chalk their support for Jack's vision of public life and duty on every square inch of concrete in the square. The public letter he wrote just before his death fitted perfectly with the mood of the square: "My friends, love is better than anger. Hope is better than fear. Optimism is better than despair. So let us be loving, hopeful and optimistic."

It was also a place for fun: skating in the winter, art shows, farmers' markets, greeting the New Year. The square institutionalized the idea of mixed uses for the city and made it perfectly clear that the best well-designed space could be used for a whole range of different functions.

New City Hall itself emphasized the sense of civic engagement. In the old city hall, the public were relegated to a distant balcony in the council chamber as they watched the city fathers (less frequently a mother or two) do the city's business. Revell changed all that. He placed the city council in the middle of the chamber,

carefully surrounding its members with citizens in the hope of making the elected representatives captive to the public interest. The city's business was now under careful scrutiny, and the generous number of seats allocated to the public in the council chamber – almost 300 – meant that the public voice was sure to be heard.

The mayor's office was lined with glass and fronted on the square so the mayor could look out and, more important, the public could look in. It is little wonder that only a few years after the building and the square were opened, the first voices of civic reform were heard on city council, and the Reform Council was elected in 1972, ushering in Toronto's golden years. The Reform Council, led by Mayor David Crombie, institutionalized citizen participation by establishing powerful working committees of local people to address a myriad of city issues. It committed itself to protecting neighbourhoods rather than seeing them fall to the developer's hammer. It began an ambitious replanning of the downtown to introduce housing among the office towers, as well as requiring a mix of uses in the centre of the city and an urban form that emphasized rather than denigrated street life. The Reform Council commenced a program to build new affordable housing, strengthen neighbourhoods throughout the city, and ensure that heritage structures were protected.

I was one of the voices of reform at that time and served on city council from 1969 until my election as mayor in 1978 for a two-year term. Before my election I was a community organizer pushing hard for the residents of the Trefann Court Urban Renewal area which city hall wanted to demolish. We held many demonstrations in the square and carried them into the committee rooms in New City Hall. I am convinced that the changes that we made in the 1970s could not have taken place in the old city hall. The spirit of Revell's city hall was critical to neighbourhood voices being heard. The square was ours, and city hall was open to the expression of our interests.

Nathan Phillips Square and New City Hall are very clearly the symbol of the Toronto we know today. I believe the spirit of the place seeps into the psyches of the political leaders who now practise their craft there, leavening their fierce views, asking them to do better, urging them to embody in their actions the fine values embodied by Revell in these wonderful structures.

John Sewell
April 2015

Preface

When researching my book on the development of modern architecture in Toronto, *Making Toronto Modern: Architecture and Design, 1895–1975* (2014), I encountered the discussions about a new city hall from the beginnings through the design competition in 1958 and the lengthy construction period. September 2015 marks the fiftieth anniversary of the building's formal opening, and I decided to write this monograph to mark the occasion.

The City of Toronto Archives holds two extensive series of records concerning the competition and the construction which provided invaluable detail. I discovered that Professor Eric Arthur, the professional adviser to the jury, had deposited a collection of papers in the Baldwin (now Baillie) Room at the Toronto Reference Library, mainly documents dealing with his unrealized plan to write a book about the architectural competition. I was also fortunate to make contact with the family of Viljo Revell, the winning architect, whose daughter Tuula (herself an architect) welcomed me on a visit to Helsinki and arranged for me to examine her father's papers both in her personal possession and also on deposit at the Finnish Museum of Architecture. I also owe special thanks to Tuula's husband, Veli Rahala, who not only drove me to and from the museum's distant suburban repository but translated some of the correspondence from Finnish into English. These records provided me with the information about the whole project that forms the basis of my text.

Any book about architecture would be enriched by illustrations, and I was fortunate to find that the city hall project was extensively documented in photo-graphs, a large selection of which have been included in the book. The city had commissioned Panda to take a series of photographs documenting the judging of the design competition and the construction of the building from start to finish. The originals of these pictures are held at the Canadian Architectural Archives at the University of Calgary. Linda Fraser has been extremely helpful (as she always is) in supplying copies of these images; archivist Diana Doublet responded promptly to requests for higher-resolution scans. I also discovered that the Toronto Public Library had commissioned its staff photographer, Wallace Bonner, to take pictures of about four hundred of the almost five hundred architectural models submitted by the entrants into the competition. Moreover, in 1958 the library microfilmed the elevation drawings submitted along with a selection of a small number of other drawings in each case, a total of more than twenty-five hundred microfilm frames. This film had been shelved uncatalogued and forgotten until I mentioned the matter to Katherine Vice and her colleagues, who discovered the box of reels and allowed me to make use of them. With the library's permission, several images in its collections have been reproduced in this book.

In the 1950s colour photography was something of a novelty, but I was happy to find that Eric Arthur had commissioned a number of such photographs for his planned book along with shots of such events as the formal opening of the building in 1965. These are also to be found in the Baillie Room at the Toronto Reference Library, as part of the Reed Collection, and some are reproduced here. I was particularly fortunate to make contact with Anthony Rolph, one of the architecture students at the University of Toronto recruited by Arthur to lay out the hundreds of models and drawings to be assessed by the jury. Tony Rolph is a talented photographer and in 1958 he took two rolls of colour slides of the models that appealed to him most. He gave me these pictures (which in many cases are the only colour images of several of the models) and granted permission for their reproduction here; without his generosity, black-and-white photographs would have been even more heavily predominant in the book.

Len Husband, the history editor at the University of Toronto Press, enthusiastically supported the publication of the manuscript, for which the copy editing was most capably done by Curtis Fahey. John Sewell, who has supported the idea of such a book throughout, willingly agreed to contribute a foreword. My old friend and collaborator, Viv Nelles, read an early draft of the manuscript and provided many useful suggestions.

The look of the book owes a great deal to Mark Fram. He is an assiduous collector of historical images of Toronto, and he found many interesting pictures of the city and the building for inclusion; he was able to improve and enhance many of them for publication. Moreover, he undertook the design of the book for the press with highly satisfactory results.

Any errors are, of course, my own responsibility.

Introduction

PREVIOUS PAGE
0.1
Presenting
New City Hall:
published in a 1962
advertisement
for Atlas
Steels, a major
construction
supplier, with the
caption "Coming
up ... one of the
world's finest city
halls."

In 1957 Toronto Mayor Nathan Phillips announced the intention to hold a competition for the design of a new city hall. Prospective entrants were advised that what was sought was a building that would be "a symbol of Toronto, a source of pride and pleasure to its citizens." It would stand upon the great square at Queen and Bay streets in the midst of downtown whose creation the ratepayers had approved a decade earlier. The ensemble of building and square was intended to become "a most important element in the life of the city."[1]

Phillips got what he wanted. Over the next eight years the building designed by Finnish architect Viljo Revell[2] rose at the north end of the square (named after Phillips). The curved twin towers cupping the circular council chamber did indeed become a symbol of Toronto, its best known and most recognizable structure, as evidenced by the fact that its stylized outline remains the city's official logo in the twenty-first century. This book tells the story of how the idea of a new city hall became a reality, truly the civic symbol that the mayor had sought.

Yet the process of creating the building also revealed another long-standing aspect of Toronto's urban political culture. This might be symbolized by the double-headed eagle of the Hapsburg banner: while the eye of one bird was firmly focused upon the future and the exciting changes it might bring, the eye of the other looked back towards the past. In any such debate one side was composed of a shifting alliance of intellectuals, architects, artists, and urban planners aligned with some ambitious local politicians. Yet any time a proposal was made which would have an important impact upon local life, in areas like city planning, public transportation, or urban design, there quickly emerged a strong adverse reaction. Sometimes it was costs that aroused alarm: city aldermen wondered if the public would support some new-fangled scheme. Many taxpayers believed that they were already over-burdened with the high cost of local government and were reluctant to take on new debts. Couldn't Torontonians make do with what already existed with only a few incremental, low-cost, changes? Or fears were expressed that the citizenry would resist a highly radical idea like the embrace of such new dogmas as modern architecture or abstract art. And there was always the instinctive clench of local protectionism: surely local people were capable of doing what was best for the city without adopting the embrace of outsiders (or worse, foreigners). So the proposal to create a new city hall in the 1950s unleashed tendencies familiar to Torontonians and deeply laid in the political and aesthetic culture of the city. Phillips desired to revitalize an aging infrastructure and capture the attention of the wider world by commissioning a building that could become a "civic symbol," but many people resisted. How this debate unfolded, and the somewhat surprising triumph of the modernizers, are examined in this book.

The need for a new city hall in Toronto had become increasingly apparent since the First World War, and by the 1950s most city politicians and officials were ready to support action. Yet the first response was protectionist: to commission a trio of well-established local architectural firms to come up with a design. In 1955, however, the ratepayers voted down their highly traditional proposal.

Mayor Phillips seized upon the opportunity to promote the idea of an international design competition, and in 1956 the voters approved spending $18 million on a new building. Though the architectural profession sought to restrict entrants to Canadians, the mayor was able to persuade a majority of the city council to approve the international competition.

Eric Arthur, a professor of architecture at the University of Toronto, was chosen as the professional adviser for the competition and set out to draft the conditions and to recruit an international jury. By the end of 1957, hundreds of architects from all around the world had paid the required $5 entry fee. In the end about five hundred models and designs were submitted from over forty different countries, leaving the jury to select the eight finalists in April 1958. Finalists were permitted to refine their proposals before the final selection was made the following September. Viljo Revell's winning design was so radical that even Mayor Phillips seems to have been a bit dumbfounded when it was unveiled. The public, however, responded quite positively to the plans.

Once the competition was over, progress slowed. Revell associated himself with the large Toronto firm of John B. Parkin Associates, but the drawings had to be considerably reworked because of concerns that the building would cost far more than the city council could be induced to approve. And doubts about the structural stability of the towers necessitated changes. Meanwhile, the chair of the regional Municipality of Metropolitan Toronto ("Metro") blew hot and cold about whether to lease space in the building, suggesting that something

more like the conservative 1955 plan (which looked a lot like an ordinary office block) would be quite satisfactory. In the end, however, the bid from contractor Anglin Norcross Ontario came in at less than the estimated $25 million; city aldermen were so elated that they readily accepted Phillips's proposal that an additional floor be added to each of the towers even though the cost involved was not at all clear.

Revell, who had moved to Toronto with a team of associates, resisted some of the proposed changes, but in the end he agreed to live with them. He was also unhappy about the amount of the fees that flowed to him, a concern exacerbated because the Finnish and Canadian tax authorities were proposing to tax him at a rate which would have exceeded 100 per cent of his earnings on the project. By the end of 1962, the architect had ceased to be a resident of Canada. He returned from time to time in the following months, but by the end of 1963 he had suffered a stroke while on a visit to Mexico. Though he returned to Finland he did not visit Toronto again except for one brief visit in the autumn of 1964, when the building was still far from completion. Within a few weeks his illness recurred and he died at the age of only fifty-four. Winning the competition for Toronto's new city hall was thus a rather bittersweet experience.

Construction got under way in the autumn of 1961 but proceeded slowly as the completion date was steadily pushed back. City bureaucracy proved demanding to work with as pieces of paper wended their way from place to place, but the real problem lay with the city council. Matters were approved in principle but then changed or left to languish for months without the necessary by-laws being approved. A particular bugbear was whether to instal a costly restaurant atop the taller eastern tower or a windowless cafeteria in the basement, either of which was certain to entail expensive changes in the plans. The officials fell to squabbling with the architect and the contractor until finally in early 1963 Anglin Norcross threatened to suspend work completely unless the plans were finalized and an agreement reached upon how the numerous alterations were to be paid for.

Nathan Phillips was defeated as mayor in the elections at the end of 1962, depriving the project of its most influential political backer. His successor, Donald Summerville, though he had been council's budget chief, claimed to have known little about the seriousness of the problems creating the delays. In the spring of 1963 he decided to instal George Bell, the city's commissioner of parks and recreation, a man known around city hall for getting things done, to oversee the whole project. Bell was instructed to keep a close eye on progress and to report on the financial situation regularly. By November, the idea of a restaurant had finally been abandoned though costly alterations would be required for the cafeteria. Bell's other great problem was to get the north end of the parking garage underneath the square completed so that the foundations of the southwest corner of the building could be laid. Summerville's sudden death in the autumn of 1964 led to the installation of Controller Philip Givens in his place, a man who became a firm supporter of progressive change. At long last it was clear that the public areas of the new city hall and the council

chamber would be sufficiently complete to schedule a formal opening in the autumn of 1965.

One persistent problem that hovered in the background was the choice of furnishings to be installed. Viljo Revell believed that his victory in the competition carried with it a commitment from the city to give him a separate contract to carry out a complete program of interior design including the furniture and the wall coverings. Whether or not this would occur hung unsettled for years and allowed for a display of the penny-pinching and reactionary views that all too often characterized decision making in Toronto's urban politics. For the first three years after 1958, the city dragged its feet on the ostensible grounds that it was not even clear that it could afford to construct the building. Once the construction contract with the architects had been signed in the autumn of 1961, Revell expected that his deal for the furnishings would soon be forthcoming but still nothing was done. He complained to his partner John B. Parkin that Toronto officials really did not understand that his building would never be what he had envisaged. Once George Bell had taken over direction of the project, he decided in the autumn of 1963 that a separate competition should be organized with the winner to be chosen by a Furnishing Design Committee (FDC), which Revell would be invited to join though he refused all entreaties to participate. Bell, like many Torontonians, was convinced that it was unnecessary to pay the Finn a separate fee to design or choose from among exotic and costly European styles when Canadian suppliers could produce perfectly adequate chairs and desks. In the best tradition of protectionism, local manufacturers did their best to convince the city to use their products. The new competition was arranged, and in the spring of 1965 the FDC chose Knoll International. It was quickly discovered, however, that its products would cost considerably more than Bell had budgeted for. Some alderman demanded that the lower-cost entrants should be given the job, but Knoll pointed out that the competition conditions had not specified a maximum price and after an anguished debate the city council very narrowly approved Knoll's proposal. With scant weeks until the formal opening, the furnishings were installed in the public spaces.

As mayor, Philip Givens proved to be an enthusiast for the city hall project. He did his best to get the Knoll furniture approved. He led the preparations for the opening of the building in September 1965, which was celebrated with suitable pomp and ceremony, including, in an effort to involve the local citizens, music and dance celebrations in the square outside. The general reaction to the new city hall seems to have been enthusiastic.

There remained one more obstacle to the completion of Revell's original vision that had to be overcome. The architect had become acquainted with the sculptor Henry Moore, and after discussions the two agreed that one of the Englishman's monumental bronze abstractions would provide a fitting embellishment to the square. In February 1966 a piece was offered to the city for $150,000, sparking an immediate outcry from locals convinced that any welder could have produced something similar to this "monstrosity." Givens did his best to persuade city council to approve. The debate reprised all

the themes of anti-modernism and local protectionism that had surfaced so regularly throughout the creation of the new city hall, and the purchase was rejected.

Fortunately, a group of civic-minded Torontonians decided to set up a fund-raising campaign, and in the end Moore agreed to accept the $100,000 they were able to offer. Three-Way Piece No. 2 (The Archer) arrived in the city in October 1966 to be formally unveiled. Even that ceremony sparked controversy when a group of local architecture students paraded through the crowd with a junk sculpture which was destroyed when the police intervened. The kind of "civic symbol" envisaged by activists like Nathan Phillips, Eric Arthur, and Viljo Revell was complete at long last, but right to the end the process revealed the city's underlying currents of backwardness and timidity.

Beginnings

When Nathan Phillips was elected to the mayoralty at the end of 1954, he brought something new to Toronto's municipal scene. At first glance the shock of white hair and neatly trimmed moustache above his well-cut suits showed him to be the successful lawyer and prominent member of the Conservative Party that he was, a man who had first been elected to city council in 1926.[1] Leslie Saunders, the man he defeated for mayor, was, like every previous holder of that office, a Protestant.[2] Also like many of his predecessors, he was a prominent member of the Orange Lodge, and soon after taking office he had offended some people by writing a letter on the eve of the well-attended Orange parade on 12 July, using his official stationery to celebrate William of Orange's 1690 victory at the Battle of the Boyne over Roman Catholic James Stuart as being of similar importance to the defeat of Nazism. Phillips was a Jew, the first one to become Toronto's mayor, and despite the continuing prevalence of anti-Semitism, some voters evidently responded positively to him for that very reason: as a politician who was neither Protestant nor Catholic, he was seen to be above the city's endless sectarian rivalry. Phillips proved to be a skilful and ebullient politician who lost no opportunity to remind everyone that he was the "mayor of all the people."

Phillips was one of a growing number of Torontonians who had become convinced that the city's downtown had become tired and dilapidated, lacking in excitement visually or architecturally. Along the shore of Lake Ontario lay a thick skein of railway tracks with a vast yard south of Front Street filled with locomotives puffing black smoke. This barrier to the lakefront would soon be reinforced by a high-speed, limited-access "superhighway" just south of the rail corridor. On Bay Street stood a line of office towers constructed in the 1920s, but most of the rest of the central business district consisted of Victorian commercial buildings increasingly grimy from coal smoke and looking more and more outdated. The streets were clogged with automobile traffic dodging around the trolley cars, though a new subway under Yonge Street had opened in 1954. The most imposing public buildings in the city, like E.J. Lennox's city hall, were heavy red-sandstone piles in the Romanesque Revival manner popularized in the United States by H.H. Richardson.

For somebody growing up in Toronto in the 1940s and 1950s, the centre of the downtown seemed to be located at Queen and Yonge. To the northwest stood acres of buildings owned by the T. Eaton Company department store (while across Queen to the south was its lesser rival, the Robert Simpson Company). One could draw up to the corner of Albert and James streets just beside the city hall and hand over a car to Eaton's parking service to take away to a lot west across Bay Street. Inside the main store lay floors and floors of almost everything under the sun, from women's purses to domestic appliances like washers and dryers of the "Viking" house brand (though not cigarettes in deference to the founder's hostility to tobacco products). Atop the building was the Georgian Room restaurant to refuel a tired shopper. Down in the basement was the grocery department, where one could order all kinds of food to be packed into wooden boxes and delivered to one's home by the vast fleet of blue and

1.2
City hall, 1899: the
building completed
but the clock not
yet installed.

red Eaton's trucks. From there one could enter the tunnel that ran diagonally under the Albert-James intersection, passing the ever-fascinating doughnut machine where a nozzle dropped a steady stream of batter circles into a gently flowing current of sizzling oil from which the golden treats emerged at the far end. Beyond lay Eaton's Annex for bargains and seconds. North and west of the store stood huge red-brick buildings where the company manufactured and stored its thousands of stock items, which could be dispatched anywhere across Canada to the avid readers of the annual mail-order catalogue.

To the west of Eaton's main store the city hall occupied an entire block stretching as far as Bay Street. Across that street lay a curious zone of parking lots, lumber yards, and rundown buildings that the city of Toronto was in the process of expropriating to make way for the eventual creation of a great civic square. Also on the west side of Bay was Shea's Hippodrome Theatre, one of the largest auditoriums in North America, once a vaudeville house, now used for showing first-run movies like Walt Disney's *Bambi*. Westward, about the only architectur-

ally impressive building to be seen lay off in the distance to the northwest, the large Ionic temple housing the city's Registry Office. Two summers working there in the Land Titles section during high school gave me the task of walking through the area each morning carrying a canvas bag containing thousands of dollars worth of cash and cheques to be deposited in the Province of Ontario Savings Office at Bay and Richmond streets. The walk along the south side of Queen opposite the eventual site of the civic square offered no architectural delights from a line of low dilapidated shops, but it was enlivened by the Casino Theatre, Toronto's only burlesque house, with tempting posters of strippers and well-known American musical acts. Heading down Bay one passed the row of skyscrapers erected in the 1920s that housed the trust companies, banks, legal offices, and stock brokerages which reflected the city's importance in the country's mining industry.

Toronto then hardly seemed a serious rival to Montreal, which remained the largest city in Canada, the metropolis where the banks, railways, and insurance companies had their head offices. Torontonians interested in architecture and urban planning had begun to feel that time was passing their city by, and that something needed to be done to revitalize it. After viewing the annual show mounted at the University of Toronto's School of Architecture in 1948, a reviewer in the student newspaper complained, "Toronto has no architecture and … the only distinctive aspect of her public buildings is their incomparably hybrid design." Looking at photographs of reputed local gems, the writer concluded that they were really eyesores, a message that appeared so persuasive by the time he reached a picture of Victoria College's Richardsonian pile that "it needed no caption to make me guffaw openly that such a monstrosity should have been thought worthy of preservation in any era."[3]

By the 1950s, the ideas and concepts of the modernist movement, founded in Europe thirty years earlier by the likes of Le Corbusier, had some strong proponents within the local architectural profession.[4] Peter Dickinson, a talented and prolific designer trained at the Architectural Association in London, arrived in Toronto in 1950. He later wrote of downtown Toronto, "These are the buildings of modern Europe fifty years ago. They are contemporary inasmuch as a Russian Communist building is contemporary." He grumbled that the most lucrative jobs kept flowing to outdated designs from a few old-line architectural firms: "I feel that nothing can come of our collective or individual efforts if this mutual admiration society continues, in which the man who gets the highest commission is regarded as the finest architect."[5]

Nathan Phillips was among those who believed that the rejuvenation of Toronto's downtown could be sparked by the construction of a new city hall to stand at the head of the large civic square on the north side of Queen Street just west of Bay. Moreover, he took the view that the best way to elicit a truly innovative and exciting design would be to hold an international competition, open to architects from around the world. When Phillips won re-election to the first of three two-years terms in 1956, he found himself in a better position than any of his predecessors to carry out long-range planning.[6]

The need for new municipal office space had long been apparent. E.J. Lennox's massive reddish sandstone structure with its tall, slender clock tower closed the view northward up Bay Street. The earlier city hall on Front Street at Jarvis (behind which lay the city's public market) dated from the mid-1840s and by the end of that century had long been the subject of complaints about overcrowding and poor sanitation. The council approved expropriation of the site at Bay and Queen in 1884, but (after an international architectural competition) construction took fifteen years of wrangling before the building was ready for occupation in September 1899. In the face of continued public grumbling about cost overruns during the decade-long process of building the grand new edifice, Mayor John Shaw defended the project at the opening: "Why people will spend large sums of money on great buildings opens up a field of thought. It may, however, be roughly answered that great buildings symbolize a people's deeds and aspirations. It has been said that when a nation had a conscience and a mind it recorded the evidence of its being in the highest products of the greatest of all arts. Where no such monuments are to be found the mental and moral natures of the people have not been above the faculties of the beasts."[7]

The city hall was not the only municipal improvement proposed in the early twentieth century. After a disastrous fire destroyed much of the central business district in 1904, agitation from local architects, artists, and businessmen spawned a "City Beautiful" plan for Toronto. In 1911 a Civic Improvement Committee (CIC) proposed that a broad ceremonial avenue be constructed

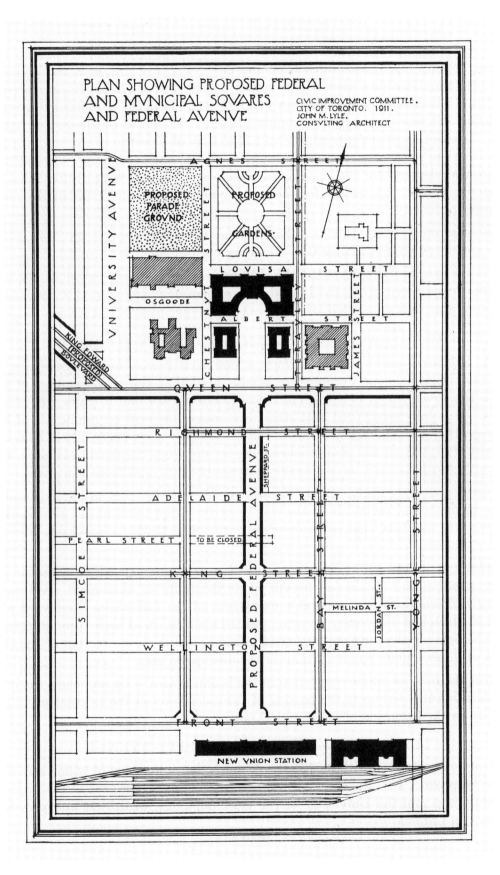

1.3
Civic Improvement
Commission,
"Plan Showing
Proposed Federal
and Municipal
Squares and
Federal Avenue,"
1911, by John Lyle:
this continued to
be part of the civic
vision for decades.

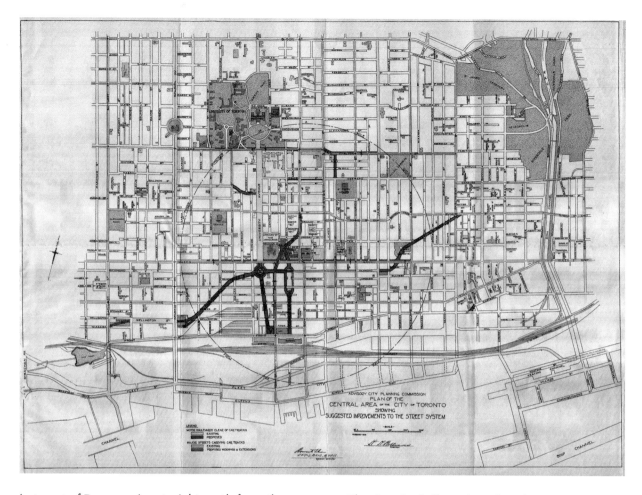

just west of Bay, running straight north from the new Union Station planned by the railways on Front Street up to Queen just west of the new city hall. The CIC's consulting architect, John Lyle, envisaged the demolition of a large swath of the rundown buildings in "the Ward" (St John's), north of Queen between Bay and Chestnut, just east of historic Osgoode Hall. A grand square would be created around which would be arrayed monumental buildings including new space for city offices. To the north would be a further open space extending as far north as Dundas Street (then called Agnes).[8] Municipal parsimony, the onset of a recession in 1913, and the outbreak of war the following year ensured that the only concrete product of this scheme would be a large Neoclassical building for the city's Registry Office located near the northwest corner of the proposed square which opened in 1917. Nevertheless, the idea of such a civic square proved remarkably long lasting.

The 1899 city hall was large but the western section, about one-third of the building, was reserved for use as courtrooms and judicial offices. By the 1920s, municipal employees were already finding space scarce, even the attics having been brought into use before the war. Though no longer practising actively, Lennox drew up plans in 1925 for an eleven-storey block to be inserted into the central courtyard of his existing structure, but this idea was never even presented to the city council. A few years later, architect Alfred Chapman proposed to duplicate the Registry Office with a new courthouse on Bay at Albert Street, the two serving as pavilions on either side of a central city hall block from which would spring a tall domed office tower. The aim was to create a Neo-classical ensemble like the Los Angeles city hall, which was currently under construction. Again nothing resulted.[9]

In 1928 an Advisory City Planning Commission composed of prominent local businessmen was appointed to

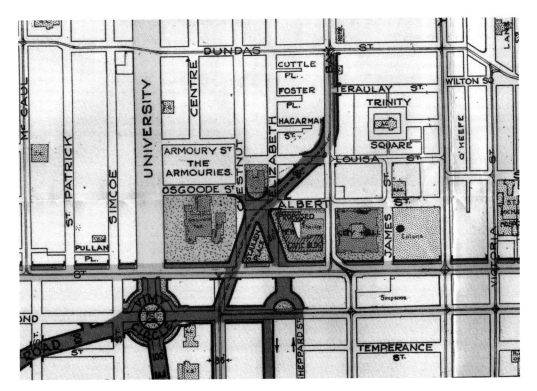

1.5
Detail of Figure 1.4.

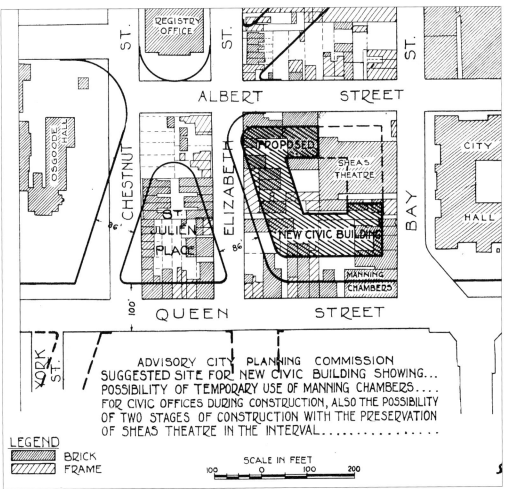

1.6
Overlaying
the proposed
improvements
onto the existing
blocks, with the
triangular St Julien
Place.

consider laying out new streets downtown to improve traffic flow. Its report suggested reviving Lyle's idea of a street running north from Union Station flanked by prestigious office buildings up to a civic square on Queen where a new municipal building would adjoin the Registry Office.[10] However, the voters rejected the candidate favouring this plan in the mayoralty election of December 1929, and the deepening economic depression and later the outbreak of war ensured that no action would be taken for more than a decade.

In 1943 the recently created City Planning Board reported that more open space was required downtown and again suggested a new square, following the model proposed by Lyle many years earlier, west of the city hall north from Queen all the way up to Dundas Street including the site for a new municipal building. The following year, the planners recommended that locations also be reserved on the square for a courthouse and police headquarters. In 1946 the Planning Board discarded the idea

of the huge square extending all the way from Queen to Dundas and proposed a northern boundary about halfway at Hagerman Street but including a four-level underground garage. Property Commissioner G.D. Bland reported to Mayor Robert Saunders that every square foot of usable space in the 1899 building was now occupied, offices being located even behind elevator shafts and in the corridors. A number of departments were expanding, often separating some branches from others and creating serious inefficiencies: "It is utterly impossible to effectively cope with the situation under existing circumstances." Department heads were complaining constantly, and the city was already spending considerable sums renting space in a number of buildings elsewhere, but by that time the entire city was facing an acute shortage of office space with the post-war economy booming so it was almost impossible to find additional premises. The situation was both costly and wasteful, and the need for "definite action" was imperative.[11]

The chair of the Ontario Association of Architects (OAA) expressed enthusiasm for the Planning Board's scheme: "This is the first time for many years that an architectural programme worthy of the size and dignity of this city has progressed so far, and it is hoped that no picayune consideration will now be allowed to interfere with its progress or reduce its scope." The association's executive committee recommended that an expert committee be created to serve as unpaid volunteers to advise the city on the layout of the square and the design of any buildings facing onto it. After consultations, the mayor proposed that architects F.H. Marani, A.S. Mathers, and Harland Steele should be recruited along with landscape architect H.B. Dunnington-Grubb and engineer A.E.K. Bunnell. Preliminary sketches of a layout were prepared.[12] In the autumn of 1946 city council passed a by-law ordering a vote at the municipal election on 1 January 1947 seeking approval to acquire or expropriate all the properties north from Queen between Bay and Chestnut streets up to a line running about 460 feet to the north (or roughly along the line of Hagerman Street). The assessed value of these lands was about $2 million, but city officials calculated that the area was largely vacant, and many of the existing buildings, owing to their dilapidated condition, accounted for only about one-quarter of the total assessed value, making it desirable to acquire the land before redevelopment greatly increased property values. The voters assented by a vote of 27,671 against 18,761, and a few weeks later the provincially appointed Ontario Municipal Board (OMB) gave the necessary approval for the issuance of city debentures to fund these purchases. Including streets, the lands totalled ten and one-half acres, the intention being to erect at the northern edge a new city hall and another building for police headquarters and magistrates' courts. Realtor W.H. Bosley was commissioned by the city council to begin negotiations with owners as soon as possible.[13]

1.8
Aerial view from the west of the future location of the city hall and square: the beginning of demolition south of Queen Street (1930) for the University Avenue extension, with the then-new Canada Life building.

In an effort to remedy the acute need for more office space in the short term, the city also moved in 1947 to expropriate the privately owned Dominion Building on the northeast corner of Albert and Bay streets behind the city hall. Attempts were made to clear out any other tenants (including several departments of the federal government) as quickly as possible, though this proved difficult since much of the space was leased for fixed terms and leaseholders refused to move because of the shortage of space elsewhere in downtown Toronto. Gradually the city gained control of most of the building (renamed the "City Hall Annex" in 1950), which made the accommodation crisis less acute in the short term.[14]

Meanwhile, efforts to acquire the lands for the square continued in a rather leisurely fashion despite increasingly vehement complaints from judges about the dirty and dilapidated state of the courtrooms in the 1899 building.[15] A conference of court and municipal officials in the autumn of 1949 agreed about the urgent need for both more office and courtroom space but this produced no action. In June 1950 the heads of all the civic departments concluded that, if the courts moved out, the city hall and the Annex together would only accommodate the current municipal workforce, leaving no room for expansion. They therefore recommended that the 1899 building be handed entirely over to the courts and a whole new city hall built.[16]

In the spring of 1951, city council voted to ask the Civic Advisory Council composed of prominent citizens and headed by lawyer Roland Michener to study the matter further. University of Toronto architecture professor H.H. Madill was retained to advise on technical matters, and widespread consultations were undertaken. The Advisory Council refused to be rushed, and it was not until the autumn of 1952 that it reported. The old building's 130,000 square feet were deemed too small for a city hall and impossible to expand, but it was concluded that it could be renovated, air-conditioned, and sound-proofed to function satisfactorily as a courthouse. Only 30,000 square feet should continue to be occupied by the city for the council chamber and offices for its members. Fewer than one-third of the properties required for the square had yet been acquired, but any usable buildings could be converted to municipal offices for the time being. An added complication was that discussions were now under way about the possibility of amalgamating the city with the dozen or so small suburban municipalities ringed around it. Toronto politicians tended to favour the idea while suburbanites resisted any such takeover. The Advisory Council concluded that any new city hall ought to remain downtown to be highly accessible, and that a 350,000-square-foot structure should be erected on the civic square to allow space for future expansion. Architects Marani and Morris should be retained to design a police building at the eastern side to mirror the Neo-classical Registry Office to the west (as in Chapman's plan from the 1920s), between which a low wing including a council chamber with an office tower behind would link the two pavilions together. These recommendations were released to the public with great fanfare at a dinner in December 1952.[17]

1.9
Queen St West
in the 1950s,
looking east from
Chestnut, towards
the 1899 city hall.

Critics were not impressed with the design proposed by Marani and Morris, and public protests led by the architecture students at the university produced an angry exchange of correspondence. Professor Eric Arthur of the university's School of Architecture observed that the difference of opinion showed the "contrasting philosophies of a die-hard architectural minority and the current students."[18] To avoid the construction of some rather tired Neo-classical pile of the sort favoured by prominent local architects like Marani and Morris, suggestions were heard for the first time that any design ought to be chosen through a competition. Several architects immediately wrote to Mayor Allan Lamport to press for the idea, one observing that the type of design most suitable for the site would be something like the modernist box of blue-green glass just completed for Lever Brothers on Madison Avenue in New York by Gordon Bunshaft of Skidmore, Owings and Merrill, which had attracted much attention. The mayor's executive assistant replied that there had already been internal discussions about the possibility of a competition open to any architect in Canada, but that any decision would ultimately rest with city council.[19]

Another element in the plan for the square remained the inclusion of a huge underground garage at its south edge. The city had recently created its own Parking Authority to construct and manage new space in the increasingly congested downtown. The mayor's executive assistant reported that while in San Francisco he had made enquiries about a similar garage under Union Square. Private businesses had complained about a decline in economic activity owing to a lack of parking, and to prevent an exodus the city had built the garage and leased it to a private operator. Either following this example or allowing the Parking Authority to undertake construction and management itself could have a "very beneficial effect" while producing a healthy stream of revenue for the city. An added attraction was that the garage could function as an air-raid shelter for thousands of people in the event that the Cold War turned hot.[20]

A committee composed of the city's commissioners of finance, works, buildings, planning, and property, along with the city solicitor, was set up to consider these proposals. A new element was the Toronto Transportation Commission's plan to build a subway line along the north side of Queen, which would have to be integrated into the design for the square and the underground garage.[21] In January 1953 the Toronto chapter of the Ontario Association of Architects submitted a brief to the city recommending a design competition for a city hall on the grounds that it would attract the widest range of submissions: "The professional competition is the surest method of attaining the optimum quality of buildings and square." Assured by the executive assistant to the mayor that he shared this point of view, the OAA sent a delegation to repeat its call for a competition when the city council took up the matter in April.[22]

Before council could formally approve a plan, however, a familiar form of local protectionism reared its head. In June 1953 the committee of officials concluded that it would be too time-consuming and costly to draw up the conditions and stage a competition. Moreover, it might require the expertise of architects from the United States to manage such an undertaking. Instead, the bureaucrats recommended giving the job to a consortium of local firms, Marani and Morris, Mathers and Haldenby, and Shore and Moffat, all of whom had undertaken "large important works" in Toronto, a decision that later led somebody (probably Eric Arthur) to scrawl the word "Calamity" on a memorandum. The city council allowed itself to be persuaded and confirmed the recommendation in the belief that a new city hall could be ready in no more than a year and a half. The city solicitor set to work

drafting a preliminary agreement with the three firms, which was signed in March 1954.[23]

These architects were just the kind that Peter Dickinson had in mind when he complained in his article that same year about the entrenched system "in which the man who gets the highest commission is regarded as the finest architect." Marani and Morris were responsible for rather dull Neo-classical designs for buildings like the Bank of Canada on University Avenue and Mathers and Haldenby for a similar headquarters for Imperial Oil on St Clair Avenue West; Shore and Moffat was then less well known, having been founded only in 1945. The failure to include the firm of Page and Steele in the consortium ensured that Peter Dickinson, their new star, would not be involved.[24]

By that date, the need for a large new municipal building had become all the more urgent. While Toronto's architecture seemed firmly stuck in the past, the structure of its municipal government had undergone a radical makeover to enable it to cope with the problems created by a rapidly growing population. The twelve small municipalities ringing the city proper were not to be annexed by the city of Toronto, but in 1953 the provincial government of Ontario decided on a restructuring. The municipalities would remain in existence with responsibilities like policing, fire, and social services, but a new Municipality of Metropolitan Toronto would be created with regional responsibilities, principally for matters like water, sewers, the construction of major roadways, and the operation of public transit. The new "Metro" bureaucrats would need office space and a chamber was required for Metro council meetings.

That council, composed of elected officials from the constituent municipalities, came into existence in April 1953, and the new government would begin to function on 1 January 1954. City officials were quick to realize that, if Metro could be persuaded to purchase the old city hall to house the courts and to agree to share space in a new building, it would greatly lessen the financial burden of a new city hall upon the taxpayers of the city proper. Whereas the mayor and the city council were often closely divided, Frederick Gardiner, the first Metro chair, proved to be a skilled politician with a formidable talent for carrying his council with him. Gardiner's views about when and where a new city hall would be built thus became a crucial consideration.

While the work of the three architectural firms commissioned by the city was just getting under way in the spring of 1954, there suddenly came a bolt from the blue. A firm of developers from Chicago arrived in town and put a proposition before Mayor Allan Lamport and Metro's Gardiner: the Americans offered to buy the old city hall, tear it down, and build a fifty-one-storey office tower costing up to $75 million in its place. The city would lease twenty floors, Metro ten, and ten would be used for the courts, still leaving twenty to be rented out to generate income for the developers, with the city having the right to reacquire the building after twenty-five years. The colonnaded entrance to the city hall on its second floor would be reached from the west by means of a vast staircase bridging over Bay Street and tying it to the proposed square with its parking garage underneath. The proposal was presented to the Board of Control but does not appear to have been formally dealt with, because it aroused a storm of protest at the very idea of Toronto's city hall being owned by a bunch of Americans; it was allowed to die though Mayor Lamport argued privately that the sale-leaseback deal had "many advantages."[25]

In June 1954 Metro council appointed a special committee to undertake liaison with the city on the creation of a new municipal building for both. City officials recommended that an offer be made to rent Metro office space in a new building and to sell the old city hall for $4.5 million to Metro for use as a courthouse. At the end of the year, Metro agreed in principle to rent space in a new structure. By February 1955, the consortium of Marani and Morris, Mathers and Haldenby, and Shore and Moffat had submitted their preliminary design for the building, which had a three-storey colonnaded Stripped Classical pavilion running east from the Registry Office towards Bay to house the council chamber with a twenty-storey office block behind for staff. To the north a separate building would be built for police headquarters and the magistrates' courts.[26] L.E. Shore of Shore and Moffat announced that the design of a new limestone-clad city hall was inspired by the United Nations building in New York, though in truth the ensemble looked much like Chapman's 1927 scheme.[27]

By the time this tired proposal was made, Nathan Phillips had been elected mayor. When shown the preliminary plans, he studied them for five minutes and then remarked that the central block looked like "the Grand Hotel with the longest balcony in the world. All it needs is a swimming pool."[28] Meanwhile, the whole project was thrown into doubt when the architects Craig and Madill reported to Metro council that the purchase of the old city hall for a courthouse was not a wise idea. There was simply not enough space in the 1899 building to allow for anticipated future expansion, something rendered difficult and expensive in any case because the load-bearing walls could not be tampered with. Moreover, all the mechanical systems would have to be replaced to allow air-conditioning and sound-proofing, and the staircases must be enclosed to meet the current fire code. The suggestion that a new structure might be inserted in the courtyard was vetoed as impractical. Fred Gardiner quickly declared that he could not support the acquisition of a building that might cost up to $6.5 million when a new courthouse could be erected for less, a decision endorsed by Metro council. Since the city was counting on the revenue from selling the old building to help finance a new one, the future looked dark. In an effort to keep the project alive, Phillips floated the idea that the city might use the building as its police headquarters or sell the site for "a large modern hotel or other suitable building."[29]

Nothing came of that idea but Phillips remained determined to keep up the pressure for a new city hall, preferably with an international design competition. The four members of his executive Board of Control took the unanimous view that a commitment already existed to the three architectural firms and refused to endorse any competition.[30] Faced with this roadblock, Phillips encouraged the architects to get on with a final design, since the new city hall and the square were "one of the most important matters" facing his administration. He was promised more detailed sketches by the autumn. F.H. Marani asserted that a satisfactory new building could be erected at a cost of $18 million over the next twenty-eight months. Eventually the architects produced sketches showing a design very similar to Marani and Morris's 1952 proposal, with a three-storey colonnaded wing for the council chamber. Behind this would stand a large tower that appeared identical to the building that Mathers and Haldenby was erecting for Imperial Oil.[31]

City council decided to ask the ratepayers at the December 1955 election to approve capital spending of the $18 million estimated by Marani on a new building. When more detailed renderings of the proposed structure were unveiled in time for the vote, architecture students at the university authored a joint letter which denounced the proposed layout as "a funeral home of vast dimensions" and a "monstrous monument to backwardness." Always ready with an opinion, Frank Lloyd Wright pronounced it a "cliché already dated." That giant of modernism Walter Gropius declared it "a very poor pseudo-modern design unworthy of the city of Toronto."[32]

These criticisms and the lèse-majesté shown by a bunch of undergraduates led the president of the Ontario Association of Architects to commiserate with Phillips on the eve of the election about "public statements … in such vein as to imply incompetence of the retained architect with a recommendation for his dismissal."

1.10
The 1955 city hall proposal that set the stage for an unprecedented international architectural competition.

Obviously, the students were not being given proper "training in ethical conduct." The three firms involved were "among the most prominent in Canada ... internationally known and respected," and their advice ought to be accepted. Yet on election day the voters turned down the proposal by a margin of 4,000 out of 60,000 ballots cast.[33]

This rejection may have been sparked in part by the parsimony of local taxpayers who balked at the city taking on such a large additional debt. The controversy, an architectural history of the city has observed, stemmed "less from the design itself than from the dissatisfaction felt by many people in the Toronto arts community at the extremely slow acceptance of modernism and its forms in Toronto. The design's stripped-Classical monumentality and conservative inspiration seemed to typify the 'Old Guard' that dominated painting, architecture, and the other arts in the city." Safely re-elected, Mayor Phillips himself later observed that the decision of the voters was a "godsend" since it kept alive the possibility of a future design competition.[34]

Immediately after the election, John C. Parkin, an increasingly visible figure in the city's architectural community, wrote to Phillips to try and insert himself into the discussion (no doubt with a view to gaining involvement in the design). Parkin observed, "There would appear no doubt that the electorate was confused, in some measure, by the large number of letters to the press and certain editorials therein, decrying what was claimed as a 'timid' design. You may be aware that the School of Architecture apparently organized some strong

opinion against the design as presented, in the belief that the architecture of the proposed City Hall was not consistent with the aspirations and ideals of a progressive and growing metropolis." The architect asked for a meeting with the mayor to discuss some of the reasons for this "widespread and unfavourable reaction" to the design. He offered the view that, if a competition were to be held, the selection of jurors would be critical, suggesting that the mayor himself would be a good choice as a member.[35]

Phillips believed that the need for a new city hall remained abundantly clear, and that its proponents had fallen down on the job in 1955. He contended that if a design competition, even one open only to Canadians, had been promised, rather than presenting the voters with a single proposal, they might have approved spending $18 million.[36] In the meantime, with Metro sticking to its refusal to buy the old city hall, the mayor approached John David Eaton, head of the department store located just to the east, to see if he could be persuaded to acquire the building as part of a larger redevelopment, but failed to elicit any interest.[37] In February 1956 Fred Gardiner did announce Metro's willingness to share the council chamber and to rent office space in a new city hall, though he wanted "a strictly functional building" which would be economical to construct. He suggested that the Crown Life building up on Bloor Street East near Church, another dated layout by Marani and Morris, would be a good model. He approved the old idea that a duplicate of the Neo-classical Registry Office should be erected at Bay and Albert streets, with an office tower in between looking like either the Crown Life or the Bank of Canada building (by the same firm). A joint city-Metro committee was established to discuss future needs, and the management consulting firm of Woods Gordon was retained to draw up definite space estimates for a new building, the lack of which had long plagued any detailed planning.[38]

Meanwhile, the city Planning Board proposed a whole series of studies of the proposed civic square.[39] For instance, the city Parking Authority's ramps for cars and stairwells for parkers would have to be incorporated into any design. In the autumn of 1956, the Authority recommended that a three-level garage with 1,280 spaces be constructed under the southern part of the square at a cost of $3.6 million. A second stage with about 1,000 more spaces could be added later to the north just in front of a new municipal building. City council approved the first stage in November 1956, with work to begin the following spring for completion in 1958.[40]

In May 1956 the joint city-Metro committee concluded that the old city hall could be successfully converted into police headquarters and magistrates' courts, and Gardiner now threw his support behind the idea.[41] A formal offer by Metro to purchase the old city hall for $4.5 million was made in July, and the Metro chair endorsed the demolition of the Registry Office building to free the entire site for redevelopment. Metro would build a new structure to house the higher courts on University Avenue north of Osgoode Hall; this would stand on the site of the huge red Romanesque Revival Armouries built in 1891 if the federal government could be persuaded to sell. Now Gardiner was keen for quick decisions so that city

voters could be asked to approve the necessary expenditure at the December elections.[42]

In September the city decided to terminate its contract with the three firms of architects to design the new city hall. Each one had been at work on the project since June 1953 and early in 1955 had consolidated their activities. A joint drafting room had been created under A.S. Mathers which produced the sketches and the more detailed renderings laid before the city's ratepayers at the 1955 election. Though that proposal had been rejected, the architects continued their work during 1956, and discussions went on until August about the idea of adding to the design an eastern pavilion matching the old Registry Office. At that point, however, the Board of Control directed the city solicitor to terminate the contract. He sought to persuade the architects to accept a fee of $30,000, but their lawyers insisted that they should be paid $96,000 for work done up to December 1955. The city then raised its offer to $50,000, but, faced with the threat of court action, it finally agreed to pay the full amount. The agreement was formally terminated in June 1957.[43]

The decision to dismiss the local architects gave Mayor Phillips the opportunity to revive his plan for an international design competition. He had always argued that the previous design had been "rejected because it was presented in the wrong way and urged that the new hall be a building "in keeping with the importance of the city," a view strongly endorsed by the recently founded periodical *Canadian Architect*.[44] Somewhat surprisingly, Fred Gardiner, who had previously insisted upon a low-cost, bare-bones office building, now agreed to the idea

1.11
The site for the
civic square and
city hall, seen from
the west.

1.12
The beginning of
the development:
the southern
part of the
underground
parking garage.

of a competition though he wanted entries restricted to Canadians. He and Phillips believed that the voters would approve if asked to authorize the city to spend up to $18 million for a new building[45] (including the $4.5 million to be received from Metro for the old hall). The balance of the funds would be raised by the city issuing $13.5 million in thirty-year debentures to be amortized with the rent received from Metro for office space. In addition, the city could expect to receive about $4 million from the sale of City Hall Annex on Bay Street when it was no longer needed, and an agreement had been reached with the provincial government to purchase part of the lands of the municipal jail farm, located on Yonge Street at Langstaff out in the suburbs. These funds could help to defray the cost of the lands being acquired for the civic square, which would now comprise about twelve acres on Queen Street between Bay and Chestnut extending as far north as Hagerman.

In October the city council approved the inclusion of the spending proposal for a new city hall on the ballot for the elections on 3 December 1956. The ratepayers were merely asked to approve the necessary borrowing to build a new city hall at a cost of $18 million and the rental of office space to Metro; there was no mention of the sale of the old city hall or of how a design was to be selected. However, in his successful campaign for re-election to the mayoralty for the first of his three two-year terms, Nathan Phillips made it quite clear that he intended to ask the new city council to approve an international design competition. The voters approved the expenditure by a vote of 31,814 to 26,811, only a slightly larger margin than had rejected

the previous proposal a year earlier.[46] Finally, it looked as though Toronto would get its new city hall.

Nathan Phillips wanted a new city hall facing on to a grand square because he thought that this would begin the process of revitalizing a downtown that had become old-fashioned and dilapidated. And he believed that the design of a new building should be the result of an international architectural competition which aimed at a layout that was noteworthy and eye-catching, a symbol of the city's ambitions for wider recognition. The campaign for a new building, however, also produced a response that symbolized the way in which municipal affairs were normally conducted in Toronto, namely with a reflexive conservatism and traditionalism that focused upon the risk and the cost of undertaking any dramatic initiatives.

The need for more space to house the city's employees was eminently clear by 1950, but the first response was to create a blue-ribbon panel of worthies who predictably recommended that the design work be handed over to one of the city's old-line architectural firms which could be relied upon the produce a conservative proposal. Even the notion of staging a design competition was rejected as too costly and complex. In the end, a trio of local firms was granted the design job, but in 1955 the ratepayers rejected spending $18 million on such a structure. Mayor Phillips seized upon this rejection to promote an international competition.

Competition

Eric Arthur arrived in Canada in 1923 to join the architecture faculty at the University of Toronto. Born in New Zealand in 1898, he was shipped to Britain by the army right at the end of the First World War. There he pursued his architectural education at the University of Liverpool, where the curriculum closely followed the Beaux-Arts model. During the 1920s he displayed a cautious conservatism, but in the later 1930s he brought many of the famous names from the modern movement to Toronto and introduced his students to their views and writings. Becoming the editor of the *Journal* of the Royal Architectural Institute of Canada (RAIC) in 1937, he vigorously promoted modernist ideas in his editorials.[1]

In 1940 the RAIC declared that design "competitions are appropriate in cases of important public buildings and those of a novel or special character." Eric Arthur became a keen promoter of such competitions. In 1951 he submitted a brief to the Royal Commission on the Arts, Letters and Sciences urging that competitions be held for major projects, a suggestion that the commissioners endorsed in their report. Juries could opt for a safe but dull choice, but in the RAIC *Journal* Arthur editorialized that "it is fair to assume that the modern jury will not be lacking in courage or foresight. Our only reason for saying so is that we have passed the stage when a jury could hide behind a façade of archeology on the grounds that it was safe or tried. Creative design has to have meaning even to the 'man in the street.'"[2] In 1952 he acted as professional adviser to a competition open only to Canadian architects for the design for a new National Gallery in Ottawa (which was never realized). Later, Arthur wrote:

In general there are three kinds of architectural competitions. There is one where a selected group of architects (perhaps six) is asked to submit designs for a public or private building ... The success depends entirely on the wise selection of competitors, the competence of the jury and clarity of the printed conditions from which each architect works. A more common procedure is where the competitors are limited to those practicing in a city or state ... Finally, there are national and international competitions which require no definition as to scope. While all competitions are exciting for the architects involved and for the public who eagerly await the result, the international competition is in a class by itself.[3]

Arthur was a wit and a gadfly, though some people thought him more an amusing talker than an effective actor. The administrators at the University of Toronto were certainly careful not to allow him or the modernist acolytes among his colleagues to design a building on the campus, preferring the more sober-sided Mathers and Haldenby. Only in 1959 did he receive the commission for a women's athletic building in the modern manner. He did undertake the task of preparing a redevelopment plan for the university-affiliated Victoria College in the early 1950s, where he was able to express his dislike for the Romanesque Revival main building by recommending that it be torn down. That was too much for the Victoria people, but Arthur designed the modernist Wymilwood student centre, which opened in 1953 to considerable acclaim.[4]

Over the years Arthur came to know Nathan Phillips well[5] as a lawyer whose practice involved many real-estate matters. So it was no surprise that the mayor concluded that Arthur would be just the man to act as professional adviser if the city council could be persuaded to approve an international competition for the design of a new city hall. In that role he played a critical part in shepherding the project to completion between 1957 and 1965, helping to move it forward when progress threatened to stall.

The idea of holding a competition to produce a design for Toronto's new city hall was first raised in 1952 and endorsed by the Toronto chapter of the Ontario Association of Architects the following year. But the profession soon had a change of heart, and in 1954 the Toronto chapter chair, E.C.S. Cox, argued that the commission should go to some well-known local architect.[6] In 1953 the city council endorsed the idea of retaining the consortium of three local architectural firms to prepare a design and eventually a contract was signed. Nathan Phillips might favour an international competition, as did the Toronto *Telegram*, but, as one commentator put it, Phillips and the paper's editor often seemed but two voices masquerading as an army by shouting as loudly as possible. The *Star* opposed such a competition, while the *Globe and Mail* had once suggested simply hiring a recognized star like Le Corbusier or Eero Saarinen. Architect Forsey Page (of Page and Steele) tried to put paid to the idea of an international competition by asking what would happen if such a contest was won by a Communist Chinese.

Phillips brought the idea of an international competition before the four-member Board of Control in September 1956. Despite support from a joint city-Metro "Committee Regarding the Development of the Civic Square," the motion passed by the narrowest of margins with only Phillips and Ford Brand in support and William Allen opposed, the other two controllers having already departed the meeting for home. When the matter came before the full council, Allen renewed his objections but the city council approved the idea of an international competition by a vote of 14 to 5.[7] City Planning Commissioner Matthew Lawson[8] was directed to discover from the Union internationale des architectes in Paris how such an international competition should be organized and what it would cost. The secretary general of the union supplied the necessary information and suggested that a jury should consist of three to five members including a couple of Canadians.[9]

Even before the voters approved spending $18 million on a new city hall in December 1956 the president of the OAA got in touch with Phillips to suggest a meeting with the city Planning Board concerning a competition. Arthur was asked to join the delegation and sent Matthew Lawson a copy of the competition conditions that he had drafted for the National Gallery of Canada, expressing particular pride in a clause that he had drafted, which permitted "the young genius" to win while protecting the federal government against an inexperienced architect and at the same time preventing the "genius" from being forced into an association with an older architect who might attempt to subvert the chosen design.[10]After the meeting, the OAA council reiterated its support for a Canadian-only competition. At the same time it emphasized the importance of choosing as the professional adviser a person of outstanding reputation. Association president George Masson wrote to Eric Arthur to urge him to accept this task despite his other obligations. Perhaps the university could be persuaded to grant Arthur time off, especially if the association called for him to be drafted for the task. In the meantime the OAA council voted unanimously to appoint a liaison committee to work with the city on a competition to be chaired by Arthur along with E.C.S. Cox and George D. Gibson.[11]

The year 1956 saw the mayor, aldermen, and controllers elected for the first time to a two-year term of office, 1957–9, during which Mayor Phillips hoped there would be time to bring the city hall project to fruition. The OAA continued its opposition to an international competition in a letter to the mayor even before the first meeting of the new council in January 1957. Masson insisted that Canadian architects had no reason to fear "superior talent" among foreign entrants, since they had already been recognized by awards for their designs in many other countries as far away as Pakistan. Yet Canadians might suffer a "psychological reaction" when faced with rivalry from a large number of Americans and other outsiders. He noted that the recent announcement that a Canada Council for the Arts was to be created to promote national cultural development made it "odd and contradictory" to allow a foreigner to handle such a prime assignment. And there were practical considerations: seventeen hun-

dred architects and their employees and dependants represented a "not inconsiderable segment" of Canada's population. Moreover, foreigners (though presumably not Americans) would be able to produce their entries at bargain prices for labour and materials while Canadians would have to put up between $3,000 and $5,000 for their models and drawings. Building techniques and climatic conditions were admittedly not unique to Canada, but it seemed "more satisfactory" to have local residents produce designs. Masson concluded by observing that the president of the Royal Architectural Institute of Canada, Douglas Kertland, heartily endorsed his letter.[12]

The next day Alan Jarvis, director of the National Gallery, told an OAA luncheon that its members should be delighted to take part in an international competition, but his argument apparently won few converts. Over the following months the OAA president continued to grumble about the competition since the city was "insistent that it be open to architects in all parts of the civilized world, and this includes Russia."[13]

Planning Commissioner Lawson hastened to prepare a report for the new council, noting that the appointment of the professional adviser for a competition was crucial. The planning staff supported the choice of Arthur, described as a man "with a lively mind conditioned by a lifetime of academic classicism." Despite the OAA's opposition, city council lost no time in approving the recommendation for an international competition on 21 January 1957.[14] Yet the admission of foreigners remained highly contentious. In April the Toronto *Star*, which continued to oppose the idea, discovered that the rules of the

Union internationale des architectes required all competition judges to be professional architects or planners. Weren't such people likely to select a "faddy design" that looked like a 1937 automobile, asked the paper? "Modern" architects were certain to favour a modernistic design, but the judges need not share the same point of view or lean towards an "eccentric style." In response the *Telegram* argued that no self-respecting architect would enter a competition without confidence in the integrity of the judges. If a Canadian won then he would secure a worldwide reputation, while a foreign winner would guarantee Toronto international attention.

Meanwhile, Eric Arthur had begun thinking about the conditions that should govern the competition. Now officially professional adviser, he reportedly brought what was for him an uncharacteristic air of "intelligent calm" to organizing the event. City council provided no detailed specifications for the project, but it was clear that the civic square should be an attractive gathering place for local residents. While nothing had been said about including pools or other water features, it was evident that such a thing would be desirable especially if a skating rink could be created in wintertime. With so much open space there was room for other buildings like a library, a museum, an information bureau, restaurants, shops, and perhaps a bandshell. A skilful designer would want such additions to humanize the layout, but care must be taken since the subsurface garage being built underneath would limit the size of such structures to a couple of storeys and restrict the planting of tall trees. Arthur had already concluded that it would be unwise to make a proposed second stage of the garage larger than five hundred spaces so as not to constrict the new buildings, and that, after all the dithering, the Registry Office at the northwest corner should be demolished to permit the entire square to be planned as a seamless unit. All the streets that currently crossed the site should be closed up to make a pedestrian compound. As for the lands bordering the square to north and south, current Ontario legislation would make it almost impossible to enforce stringent design controls, so the city would have to live with piecemeal private development governed only by zoning regulations.[15]

Gradually a consensus emerged from a lengthy series of meetings involving Arthur, the city planners, and the people from the management consultants, Woods Gordon, retained to estimate the space requirements of a new building. By mid-March, a set of recommendations was ready. The streets crossing the square as far north as Hagerman should be eliminated, though both Bay and Queen would be widened around the margins. The Registry Office would be torn down. The new building would have to include space for the land registry and a branch library. Metro and the city would share a council chamber surrounded by offices for the politicians, and Woods Gordon would be asked to make allowance for the expansion of other city space requirements for the next decade. On the square a pool or other water feature (which might double as a rink) should be required.

The two-stage competition would be open to all registered architects, with a short list of eight finalists who would receive financial assistance to produce detailed drawings. The decision of the jury would be final, the finalists each receiving $7,500 and the winner getting a $25,000 advance on fees. The city would start construction as soon as possible, but if the project was eventually aborted the winner would get a further $25,000. Without Arthur's prior knowledge, someone leaked the news to the press that his fee as professional adviser would be $5,000. He pointed out to Lawson that this was the same amount as he had received in 1952 for doing the same job on the National Gallery competition, even though that building was far less complex and entry was open only to Canadians. Since the task would probably take more than a year, Arthur complained to the mayor that he thought $7,500 would be more reasonable but agreed to take the lower amount in order to avoid embarrassing Phillips.[16]

In January 1957 Arthur also pointed out that the provincial Architects Act might render a non-Canadian winner impossible. Only British subjects domiciled in Ontario and residents intending to become citizens could be registered as architects, though citizens of the British Commonwealth could be granted temporary licences. If a person from another country were to win, it would be almost impossible for him to supervise construction unless the legislation was speedily altered to permit an outsider to form an association with an OAA member. In the hope that the city would change its mind, the association's secretary pointed out to Mayor Phillips that it still favoured a national competition. But the mayor stuck to his guns: city council had endorsed an international contest and the law must be changed, so the OAA had better

get busy and support new legislation. There was intense debate within the association, but under this pressure the OAA's Registration Board (chaired by Eric Haldenby, whose firm had just been dumped by the city as part of the previous design consortium for a city hall) eventually agreed in March to an amendment to its regulations to permit a successful competitor in an international competition to link up with a local practitioner.[17]

Within a week of the city council giving approval in principle to holding a competition, Matthew Lawson began to sound out possible jurors; his first feeler went to American Eero Saarinen, an architect much in the news on account of his dramatic designs for the swooping TransWorld Airways terminal at Idlewild (later Kennedy) airport in New York City and the Ingalls Rink at Yale University (nicknamed "The Whale"). Saarinen was well known to Canadians, having already served on the juries for the National Gallery, an opera house in Vancouver, and a convention hall in Windsor, Ontario, as well as for the Sydney Opera House in Australia.

Lawson confided to Saarinen that much of Toronto's downtown was "not very distinguished architecturally," so it was necessary to recruit high-profile jurors in order to inspire confidence among potential entrants. Preliminary discussions suggested a three-person panel including Professor Gordon Stephenson, a Liverpool University graduate who had left that institution to head the Department of Urban and Regional Planning at the University of Toronto in 1955 and had drawn up plans for both Perth and Fremantle in Australia.[18] If the other member was to be a North American resident, perhaps it should be Italian-born Pietro Belluschi, who had recently closed his practice in Portland, Oregon, and become dean of architecture at the Massachusetts Institute of Technology. If a Briton was to be included, Leslie Martin, formerly chief architect for the London County Council and now heading a new architecture school at Cambridge University, would be a good choice. If a continental European was needed to inspire the confidence of the profession there, Swiss-born architect and designer Max Bill, trained at the Bauhaus and now at the Ulm School of Design in Germany, should be considered. Both of the latter were well-recognized exponents of modernist trends in architecture.[19] Saarinen (who was personally friendly with Eric Arthur from the National Gallery competition)[20] was receptive to the idea of becoming a juror, provided that the Torontonians would not feel that he had been involved too frequently in previous Canadian competitions; it was agreed that Lawson and Arthur should come to Detroit, where Saarinen practised, for consultation, and a meeting was arranged in April.[21]

Arthur was especially keen to get Saarinen to act because he believed that would persuade others to agree to participate. He wasn't all that keen on having somebody from Britain, but, as he wrote ruefully to a British friend at Harvard, "I suppose we must have an Englishman to give confidence to the troops over there." Knowing the penny-pinchers at city hall, Arthur initially hoped to avoid involving anyone from continental Europe in order to save money on the two visits to Toronto that would be required to choose the finalists and then the winner. Perhaps Walter Gropius could be

enticed to come from his post at Harvard, which would give the required European flavour without entailing so much expense.[22]

Gropius was sounded out and found to be "very willing" provided the dates did not clash with another jury in Berlin, but in the end nothing came of this. Leslie Martin of Cambridge declared he would also be very happy to participate but only out of term time, which seemed to make this impossible in practice. He suggested the noted town planner Sir William Holford, trained in Liverpool and teaching at University College, London, who was currently working on the layouts for three national capitals, in his native South Africa, in Rhodesia, and in Australia.[23]

Holford accepted along with Gordon Stephenson (who could after all count as both British and Canadian). In the end a five-member jury was decided upon,[24] and Ernesto Rogers, professor of the theory of architecture at Politecnico di Milano and a prolific writer and publisher of the influential periodical *Casabella*, was added.[25] The Canadian slot was filled by Charles E. ("Ned") Pratt, a 1939 Toronto graduate who had joined the Vancouver firm of Thompson, Berwick, Pratt. He was known to be sympathetic to modernist design in the "West Coast" style and was already the focus of much attention for his nearly completed headquarters building for BC Electric in Vancouver.[26]

Eero Saarinen thought that Arthur had done a pretty good job in his recruiting, regretting only that Martin had refused. If the addition of somebody from Britain could have been avoided, Saarinen had suggested that

that the famed Finnish architect Alvar Aalto might have been approached, but in general he applauded Arthur's choices. All the younger architects who had talked to Saarinen had agreed that including somebody like Ernesto Rogers was a "first rate" idea.[27]

By now, the city bureaucrats had fallen to wrangling about the amount of space recommended for allotment to various departments by the management consultants at Woods Gordon. In late June, Eric Arthur protested to Planning Commissioner Matthew Lawson that, until the amount of floor space needed was settled, he could not finalize the conditions of competition to go out to entrants, noting that "when criticism falls on us, as it must, I shall be the one to be blamed." Lawson pointed out to the politicians that there were also other recommendations made by Arthur about which council had to make definite decisions, such as whether a branch library and a restaurant should be included in the building. One of the thorniest matters was whether more effort should be made to secure suggestions from the competitors about the form of development beyond the boundaries of the square proper. In the end, Lawson's advice was accepted that current legislation made such prescriptions pretty much impossible beyond zoning regulations, and that controls were likely only to arouse protests about interference with the rights of private property owners.[28]

A month later, the Board of Control approved most of Arthur's recommendations. The aim was to have the competition program ready by September. Arthur drafted an introduction to be signed by Mayor Phillips, calling upon the best architectural talents to enter and create a plan to show off Toronto as "a great and growing world city." Council authorized the formal announcement of the competition and the payment to Arthur of $3,000 of his $5,000 fee for serving as professional adviser. On 23 September 1957, having been approved by the Royal Architectural Institute of Canada and the Union internationale des architectes in Paris, the competition program was ready for release to the press, to Canada's embassies, and to the professional journals.[29]

City Hall and Square, Toronto, Canada, Conditions of Competition was a hefty printed pamphlet.[30] The Foreword by Nathan Phillips, which Arthur had drafted, proclaimed that the people had decided to approve this project as a "most important element in the life of the city, a symbol of Toronto, a source of pride and pleasure to its citizens." The architects of the world were invited to enter, an eminent jury would choose the winner, "and the City will accept its decision."

In his Introduction Arthur provided a potted description of the site of Toronto and then sketched in the physical surroundings of the new square, describing Lennox's 1899 building to the east and historic Osgoode Hall to the west. He politely described the rather dilapidated buildings on the south side of Queen Street and the jumble of Chinatown to the north of Hagerman Street as being composed of small, old residences converted to stores. The twenty-three items in Part II of the competition conditions provided general information about southern Ontario including its climate and weather. Also included were photographs of the buildings that currently surrounded the square. The amount of space required by each municipal department of both the city and Metro was enumerated but no limit was placed upon the size of the building. Moreover, Arthur decided not to specify a maximum cost on the grounds that architects in faraway places could hardly estimate the cost of a square foot of construction in Toronto. Instead the conditions merely observed that "while extravagance cannot be entertained, competitors will use their discretion, submitting a design of the character and dignity one associates with a building that is the seat of municipal government in the capital city of the Province of Ontario." Also included with the conditions was a sleeve of white prints which depicted the area bounded by Yonge, Richmond, Dundas, and University Avenue and a more detailed view of the square showing the underground garage on which only two-storey structures could be built.

The organization of the competition was set out in the thirty-eight items in Part I. Any recognized architect willing to pay a $5 fee could enter. The professional adviser would answer any relevant questions submitted in English. The nature of the models and drawings that might be included was definitely specified. In order to save costs, a two-stage process would be used: on 18 April 1958 the jury would choose the eight finalists, each of whom would be paid $7,500 to develop their proposals further before the winner was selected the following September. No total cost for the project had been fixed, but the standard fee of 6 per cent of construction costs would be paid to the winner who would receive an immediate advance of $25,000 on fees to undertake the detailed drawings and specifications. The city would accept the

jury's decision as final. Should an act of God or financial problems render the project impossible, after a period of three years the winner would receive an additional $25,000 in full payment for services rendered.

The response from architects was enthusiastic. By the end of September, Eric Arthur was already reporting an impressive geographical spread of enquiries. Writing to Toronto *Globe and Mail* columnist Lotta Dempsey, he suggested that she give the competition "a shot in the arm." The public might be amused at its humorous side: letters had come in addressed to Arthur at "Townville, Canada," others styling him a "Most Learned Professor" or "Right Honourable," and these, he said, did not even originate in China. Mrs Marian Fowler, the secretary overseeing his office in the old city hall, had already worn out one paper-cutter opening envelopes. He suggested that Dempsey should pay them a visit since "we are having a lot of fun, and you may like to see the little office in operation." On a more serious note, Arthur added that he had been a little disappointed that the press had not analysed more closely the requirements for landscaping the square and including a pool: "I have mentioned ancient squares and modern ones where the public can promenade to music and perhaps to orators. It strikes me that that is very important. I can't tell the competitors what I think it should be like as I could be wrong, but I have said several things that they should know about its character."[31]

By the end of October, 731 enquiries had been received and a month later two printings of the conditions totalling 1,400 copies had been exhausted and another 600 ordered. As a result, the deadline for entries was extended to 31 December 1957 though the date for submitting questions to the professional adviser still remained fixed at 6 December.[32] Naturally, the wide publicity brought a few people of dubious mental stability out of the woodwork. A consulting geologist from Ottawa expressed outrage when his entry was returned to him because it did not meet the terms of the competition (as open only to architects) and forwarded it to former Ontario lieutenant governor Ray Lawson. The conditions gave the jury arbitrary powers to exclude almost anybody, but he magnanimously offered to let the city council decide on his admissibility. He told Mayor Phillips that if he won he wanted only 20 per cent of $1 million as his fee, but Phillips replied that he had failed to meet the conditions of the competition. An unhinged Parisian wrote several letters to demand that the revolutionary building system that he had invented should be considered, because it eliminated the need for most foundation work by suspending two large wings from a central tower that could be as tall as three hundred metres. Ignoring this innovation would be like neglecting the ogival arch or the use of concrete and steel and would deprive Toronto from entering a place in architectural history like Athens or Rome. However, the mayor's executive assistant ended that correspondence by simply replying that the jury had already made a decision about the finalists.[33]

Eric Arthur worked to prepare his answers to the questions submitted by prospective entrants in time for release on 1 January 1958. His printed letter ran to thirty-two pages that covered all manner of subjects, showing the kind of detailed preparations necessary by a professional adviser in order to run a successful international competition. First came a series of technical issues about the "Presentation of Drawings and Models" that specified, for instance, that all drawings should be in pencil. Then "Rooms, Departments and Department Heads Needing Definition or Clarification" explained the layout of the council chamber, the functions of committees like "Adjustment," and what constituted a "washroom." "Department Relationships" detailed the responsibilities of the city and Metro departments. "Construction and Bylaws" set forth regulations about fireproofing, stairwells, and the cost of materials in Toronto. The need for a design to include room for "Future Expansion" totalling about 25 per cent over the next decade was reiterated. "General Considerations" indicated that facilities like a bomb shelter were not required. The retention of the old city hall as police headquarters and magistrates' courts was part of "Externals, Zoning, Etc." A "Miscellaneous" section included answers to eccentric enquiries from Britain, one explaining that there was no need for doorkeepers or "beadles" because their functions would be handled by an information desk in the lobby. Nor did there need to be special accommodation for "a lady mayoress." (One shocked Briton had even written, "Is this a city hall in the true sense of the word when it has no banquetting hall?")

More practical was an enquiry about whether the 54.6 inches of annual snowfall occurred all at once. The answer was that an accumulation of more than twelve inches of snow at one time was rare. It took considerable research to discover how much dust fell on downtown Toronto annually, the answer being between twenty and forty-six tons per square mile on average.[34] Arthur's secretary, Marian Fowler, also had to cope with problems like how to decipher a telegram in Polish, and what to tell an entrant from India who proposed to send his fee as a bag of rupees since he could not obtain foreign currency.[35]

By early 1958, Arthur was starting to worry that the competition might be too attractive. He confided to Matthew Lawson that the "unprecedented interest" shown might generate as many as 1,700 entries. In an effort to estimate the actual number of submissions, Arthur sent out prepaid postcards to the hundreds of recipients of the conditions asking them if as "architects and gentlemen" they really intended to submit. He received only six responses.

Arthur still fretted that as many as 1,000 schemes might be submitted. How much time would it take to check to see if each entry met the competition conditions: even fifteen minutes apiece would require a week and a half. Jury member Gordon Stephenson, a colleague of Arthur's at the University of Toronto, told him that he was following "the worst of North American journalism" in predicting so many entries, but he remained concerned that two and one-half miles of wall space might be required to display all the drawings. Arthur warned the jurors that it would probably take about eight days rather than the five initially predicted to do the preliminary judging, so city council had to be persuaded that the basic stipend of $1,500 would have to be increased at the rate of $150 each day for the extra time.[36]

Eero Saarinen, the most experienced competition juror, was unconcerned at the prospect of such a flood of entries: "Assume a thousand competitors; assume also that among those thousand competitors 700 will be so ugly or ridiculous that under no circumstances would one want to give them any kind of mention." He envisaged a "fairly economical" method of proceeding: before the jury arrived in Toronto, Arthur should pick out about one hundred reasonably competent-looking entries and have them checked against the competition requirements. When the jurors showed up they could familiarize themselves with the mandatory features by looking at the chosen hundred.

This will give us a fairly good idea of what can be expected, and then with that much of a preliminary survey we can go through and eliminate the bulk of the material. It is important to spend as little effort as possible on eliminating those which under no circumstances would be eligible for prizes because of their sheer ugliness. In other words, we only have to glance at them [and] their models would not have to be placed in the master model. This procedure would probably take the group down to about 50. I would imagine at that time we could divide the group into two sets, and one could be checked while we studied the other. It might be desirable to have two or four helpers who keep putting drawings up and taking them down. It occurred to me that actually wheel chairs might be the best kind of seating for the jury.

2.2
The rush of
entries in the last
week before the
deadline.

I see no reason why we need to have a hall large enough for all the drawings on the wall, particularly if the helpers can put up new ones at night. I should think that if we had a hall large enough for a hundred that would be ample. One of the big problems in logistics will be to keep a set of drawings and its model together. A continuous shelf below the tackboard space might help this somehow.

One thing they did in Sydney which I believe was quite impressive to the public and which was liked by all the competitors was that at the close of the competition the exhibition included all the projects in the competition. I do not recall whether this is possible, but I think it might be a possibility. We can talk about that later.[37]

Despite Saarinen's sanguine view, Arthur arranged to rent the large Horticultural Building on the grounds of the Canadian National Exhibition for two weeks from mid-April at a cost of $4,000. He filled the floor with scaffolding on which to lay out "ten-test" panels on either side of six-foot-wide aisles to hold the models, with wires above on which drawings might be hung. Another pesky problem that had to be dealt with was to reach a deal with the federal government's Department of National Revenue to permit the free importation of models sent from overseas which were normally subject to an ad valorem duty.[38]

Finally, the competition deadline arrived on 18 April 1958. Among the 540 entries, Arthur had to disqualify eight from the Soviet Union because they failed by some

hours to arrive in time (though he was careful to point out that he had also ruled out some from Britain on the same grounds). The only waiver for a late entry that arrived after the judges had started work was granted when he received a late-night telephone call from Montreal to say that a box addressed to him had been recovered from the freighter Damtor which had gone aground in the harbour; he agreed to pay the express charges on a rather damp model and set of drawings. As Arthur pointed out later, had this entry gone on to be a winner it would have been a romantic tale for the ages, but it was not to be.[39]

In the 32,000-square-foot Horticultural Building, ten architecture students whom Arthur had retained took ten days to lay out the entries (almost 500 of which

were accompanied by models), labelled only by numbers to preserve anonymity. A heavily annotated typescript "List of Competitors" notes 513 entry numbers, names, and addresses, but there are several blanks plus a few notations on this document that one entry duplicates another, so that a precise tabulation of the exact number of competitors seems impossible. However, they did come from addresses in forty-two different countries, which indicated widespread interest within the architectural profession. Not surprisingly, residents of the United States led the way with 132, following which were Canada with 75 and Great Britain with 65. Then came Japan with 25. France and Germany generated 17 each, with 16 from both Italy and Poland, 15 from Czechoslovakia, 14 from Australia, and 11 from

Mexico. Brazil produced 10, India 8, Argentina, Holland, and Switzerland 7 each, Spain and South Africa 6, and Sweden 5. Romania had 4 and Belgium, Denmark, and Uruguay 3 each. Another 19 countries like Finland generated only 1 or 2 entries each, but their range demonstrated the unprecedented international interest in the competition. A newspaper columnist reported that there were 19 female entrants.[40]

When the contest was first approved, the secretary general of the Union internationale des architectes had advised Arthur that the competition for the Palais des Nations of the League of Nations in Geneva had attracted about 400 entries in the early 1920s, the Haupstadt Berlin 393, and the Chicago Tribune building 263 in 1922. Trailing far behind were the Cologne's cathedral with 122, the

2.4
The New City
Hall competition
jury: left to right,
Arthur, Pratt,
Saarinen, Rogers,
Holford, and
Stephenson.

Arizona Solar house with 113, the Syracuse Basilica with 100, the Karachi mausoleum with 57, and the new Aleppo museum with only 31.[41] The Sydney Opera House competition in 1957 attracted 217 entries.

Not everybody harboured high expectations about the likely results. Dr Francisco Villagram visited the city and, after a look around, predicted that no Mexican architect would win because their work was "too advanced for Toronto." Others labelled the likely outcome "Nathan's folly."[42]

Some of the entrants were well-known people like American I.M. Pei, while others were dark horses such as a team of architectural students from Harvard headed up by Australian John Andrews whose instructors had shown little enthusiasm for these activities.[43] One final-

ist claimed to have spent just $15 on preparation while certain American firms invested as much as $10,000 in a model and drawings.[44]

The jury gathered in Toronto as soon as the deadline passed to begin the task of winnowing out possible winners from the no-hopers. William Holford admitted to a newspaper reporter that, when he first saw the three miles of drawings mounted in the Horticultural Building above the hundreds of models, he was "blank terrified," but that a closer look left him feeling "terrific elation." Even Eero Saarinen, who had been so sanguine about the process of judging, admitted to the press that looking at the massed entries gave him a sense of "horror."[45]

Arthur had devised a system that he hoped would facilitate decision making; the judges were each given a packet of squares of differently coloured paper and directed to leave a square on models in which they had no further interest. He roved about and, when he saw a model with three or four rejection squares, would call the jurors together for a discussion. Usually that entry was relegated to the discard list, but on several occasions the defenders of a particular design put up a convincing enough case that the paper blackballs were removed and the entry reserved for further discussion. The process went fairly smoothly, though, with about six thousand linear feet of tables to display the models, the jurors were grateful that Eero Saarinen's suggestion that each of them be given a wheelchair in which to rest their feet had been adopted. Arthur recalled one coffee break at which he and the jurors sat in the chairs in a circle like "tired old men at a Florida resort."[46]

In various documents the jurors later laid out the considerations that had guided them in their deliberations.[47] First of all, a city hall was a particular type of building; not only should it be the centre of the downtown, but its layout ought to express its functions and suggest the importance of the democratic traditions and activities that operated within it. It should be accessible to members of the public who must visit to pay taxes, obtain permits, and so forth, and to observe the city council in action. In the old city hall the council chamber was in an awkward and undignified location and ignored the need for both politicians and citizens to come and go with ease.[48] City halls usually remained in use for long periods of time so that some features might become obsolete, which made it necessary that there be a certain flexibility to the layout to permit it to be changed. Some administrative units would shrink and some expand over time so that interior alterations must be possible. The conditions did not specify a maximum cost, but each design should make allowance for the possibility of a 25 per cent expansion of floor space within ten years. Nothing specific was said about the materials to be used in construction, but use of materials must be sensitive to initial cost and ease of maintenance and well adapted to the wide annual variations in air temperature and the severity of winter conditions.

An important part of the competition was to lay out the vast civic square to the south of the building where the underground garage was already being constructed, so that no tall structures could be erected on top of it though in places up to three feet of soil could be added. The conditions called for the square to be attractively landscaped to provide a forecourt for the city hall and to encourage people to gather there. A shallow pool was to be included, perhaps with water jets, to be used as a skating rink in winter. Other features might include gardens, covered ways, and locations for open-air exhibitions of sculpture, but the exact configuration of paved areas, walls, and level changes, as well as the colour of plantings along with the interplay of sun and shade or floodlighting at night, was left open. However, in view of Toronto's grey winters, the inclusion of some evergreen vegetation seemed advisable. The objective was to create an ensemble that would attract people to the square in all seasons and at all times so that it did not become a dead zone after the office towers in the downtown emptied of workers.

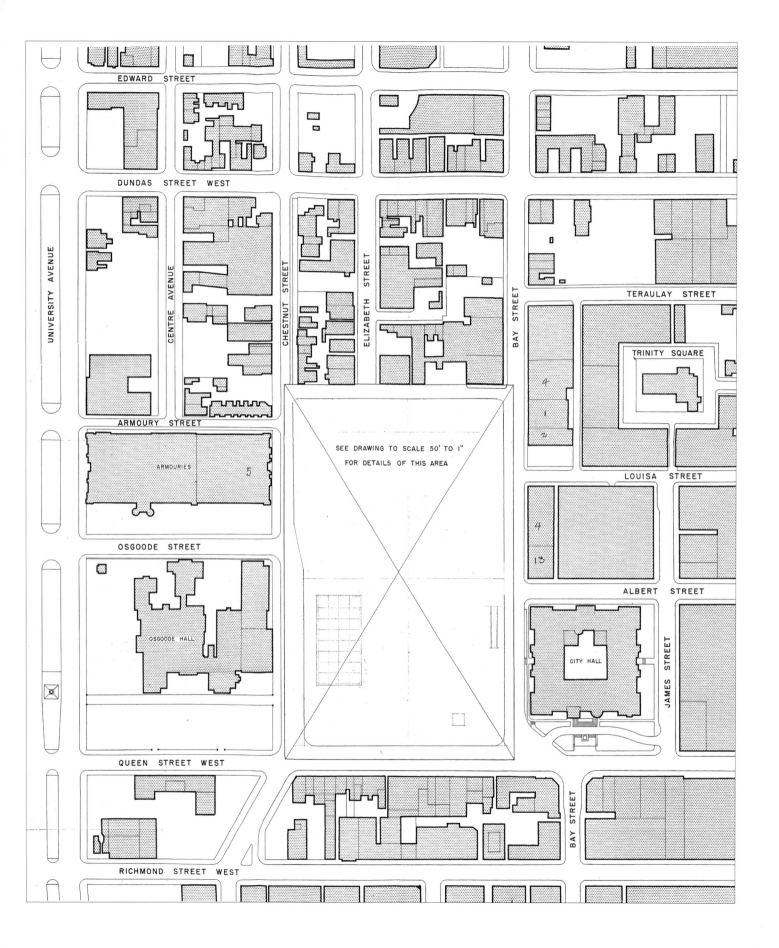

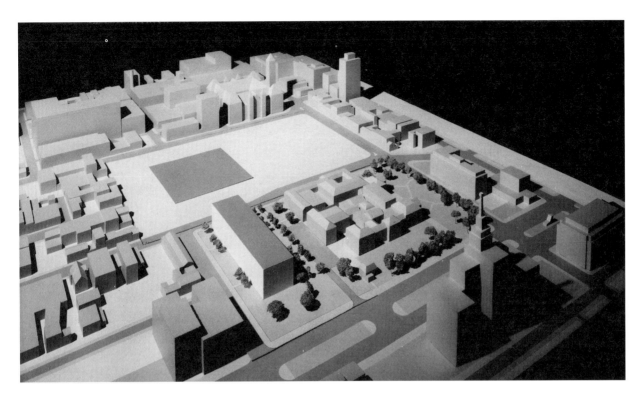

FACING PAGE
2.5
The map of
the site and its
neighbourhood,
included in the
competition
instructions.

LEFT
2.6
One of the context
models into which
competitors'
models were
placed, viewed
from west-
northwest (see
Figures 1.8 and
1.12).

2.7
The judges, their
assistants, and the
architects' entries.

The jury also was careful to consider the surroundings of the square and their relationship to the new building. It was pointed out that the facade of Lennox's 1899 building was a "rich design of high quality" which would be enhanced by the new structure and its square to form an important element in the final composition. To the west, with a generous setback from Queen Street, lay Osgoode Hall's "fine landscaped garden" behind its handsome wrought-iron fence. The eastern side of the historic building was somewhat jumbled but would make an adequate flank for the square and provide a "satisfactory foil" for the new city hall. Most people would reach the square from its southeast and southwest corners on Queen Street, so that no other prominent entrances would be required along that street. A link between the square and

University Avenue to the west, north of Osgoode Hall, should be considered. If a new Metro courthouse was constructed on the site of the Armouries, a landscaped mall should be left to its north or south to provide a sightline from University to the square and hall.[49]

Viewing the models and drawings laid out in the Horticultural Building, "the jury, at this stage, looked primarily for designs that have architectural quality coupled with imagination." What they sought were "original solutions to this difficult problem. In other words, they looked for ideas." Their aim was to be receptive to as wide a range of ideas as possible and to ignore preconceptions about a "correct" solution to the design challenges. Their "exciting, but also exacting" task was to select the finalists, although aware that the successful competitors

would have the right to submit "a completely new design for the final competition."[50]

Space does not permit a detailed stylistic analysis of the approximately five hundred entries here.[51] Reflecting on the entries after the competition was over, Eric Arthur concluded that "if any world leader in architecture could be said to have a following in the competition it would be Mies van der Rohe." He observed that it was just as well that neither of the era's most famous architects, Frank Lloyd Wright or Le Corbusier, had been jurors. If either had been, Arthur was convinced that many proposals would have deliberately been designed in a manner aimed to please the great man. As it was, there were a couple of entries from India, where Le Corbusier's work in Chandigarh was well

FACING PAGE/ABOVE
2.8
Details from Figure 2.7: On the facing page, Viljo Revell's drawings hang on the panel at the left (behind Ernesto Rogers), and Revell's model sits in context atop the white box. On this page, above, other finalists are getting their last calls; John Andrews's model is faintly visible on the table where Stephenson, Saarinen, and Pratt are deliberating.

2.9
Dobush and
Stewart of
Montreal: a
Canadian entry
in the strictly
International Style
as refined by the
German/American
Ludwig Mies van
der Rohe.

known, which were obvious imitations of the French-man's style.[52]

An examination of the drawings and the photographs of the models reveals genetic materials drawn from the work not only of Mies van der Rohe, but also of Wright and Le Corbusier, as well as Neo-classical layouts that might have looked fresh around the time of the First World War and Soviet-style palaces that would have gladdened the heart of any Stalinist. While some lay-outs were entirely conventional and dated, some were as futuristic as rocket ships. A few layouts were highly idiosyncratic, like the one devised by an Armenian named Kaplan living in Aleppo, Syria. He proposed a round tower whose ground floor consisted of a dance floor with space for an orchestra and a bar, an idea that would have amazed most Torontonians in 1958 though if realized it might have transformed the life of the city.

Arthur later expressed some surprise that so few tall towers had been proposed by Americans though some had been put forward by architects in Czechoslova-kia, Israel, and India. Nor were there many structures clad with transparent glass-curtain walls despite their growing popularity in the United States, Canada, Brit-ain, and other parts of Europe. The largest number of entries featured low designs, many arranged around courtyards, perhaps as a result of professional adviser's discouragement in the competition conditions against seeking to build the tallest tower in the vicinity, surely bound to be outstripped before long by surrounding office buildings.

2.10
Cass Gilbert, Jr,
from New York
City, echoing his
notable father's
very early-
twentieth-century
historicist look and
feel.

2.11
Very much
in the Soviet
manner, from the
Stockholm office
of L. Kurpatow.

2.12
A different modernist approach – the antithesis of the sober Miesian blocks found in so many entries – from Zareh Kaplanian Kaplan, a practitioner in Aleppo, Syria.

2.13
Kaplan's plan, encouraged by some of the competition instructions, if oblivious to the official mores of 1950s Toronto, placed a serpentine bar, orchestra, and dance floor at the very centre of its ground-level public space, with side entrances to Bay Street.

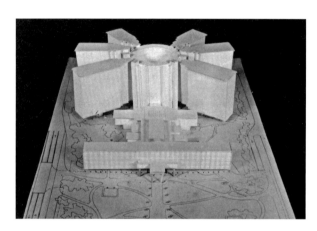

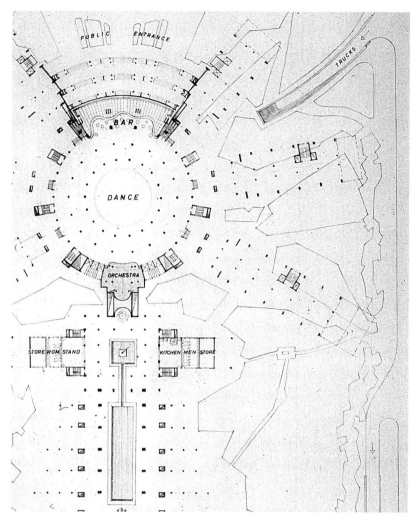

2.14
A.P. Kanvinde, from New Delhi, heavily influenced by Le Corbusier's recent work.

2.15
Balkrishna Doshi, from Ahmedabad, with another take on Le Corbusier.

2.16
Kenzo Tange, a Tokyo architect of international repute, employing very modest geometrical twists to his otherwise rectilinear blocks.

2.17
R.C. Smith, a Londoner with classical Egyptian tastes.

2.18
Philadelphia's H.W. Peschel seemed to propose a rocket-launching facility.

2.19
D.R. Dobereiner
of Urbana, Illinois,
offered an eighty-
one-storey spire,
in defiance of
Arthur's position
on tall towers.

2.20
Vancouver's
Christopher
Owtram
developed, in this
and other designs,
a reputation for
unusual shapes.

2.21
P. Hamilton and
J. Bicknell of
southwest London
enabled official
vehicles to drive
to the top of the
building.

2.22
H.G. Egli, a
Pennsylvanian,
proposed a square
courtyard within
an extremely
cantilevered
perimeter, made
out of massive
interlocked
trusses.

2.23
Enrique Casteneda Tamborel of Mexico City proposed an office tower that widens as it rises.

PUBLIC AREAS PERSPECTIVE

SOUTH ELEVATION

2.24
Casteneda Tamborel: the drawing shows that the model photo is not an optical illusion; the tower really does splay outward as it rises above the especially curvaceous public hall.

2.25
The competition
judges thought
Tekne (an
architectural
firm from Milan)
had produced
a distinctively
Japanese design.

Later, when the anonymity of the entrants had been stripped away, it became clear to Arthur that there were no clear similarities in the plans submitted by practitioners from particular countries. A perceived uniformity among the twenty-five Japanese entries was later attributed by him to the fact that all of them were beautifully executed in wood, though they did display some homogeneity in their treatment of the square. As always in architectural competitions, the jurors spent considerable effort on guessing as to the authorship of particular models, and (as usual) eventually finding out that almost all their hunches were mistaken. One design featuring a series of square boxes stacked upon one another convinced the jurors that it must be of Korean, Mexican, or Japanese origin, engendering considerable surprise when it was revealed to be the work of an Italian firm, Tekne, whose offices in Milan lay just a few blocks from Ernesto Rogers's base.[53]

As Eero Saarinen had predicted, the jury took only a short time to reduce the possibles to about two hundred in number and eventually to about twenty or thirty serious candidates to haggle over. These models could be placed in an eight-foot-square mock-up of the buildings surrounding the civic square to provide a sense of context. After eight days of deliberations, the jury was ready to announce its decision on 25 April 1958. The eight finalists chosen included one Canadian, a Danish partnership, a Finn, and five Americans. Two entries most clearly reflected the influence of International Style modernism: the Danes Halldor Gunnlogson and Jorn Nielsen proposed a glass-walled tower and the American William B. Hayward a slab rising upon columns (like the pilotis popularized by Le Corbusier). There were five horizontal structures of the sort that the jury had identified as particularly attractive. Canadian David Horne offered a low, square building on pilotis around a central courtyard.[54] American Frank Mikutowski proposed a somewhat similar though higher structure. I.M. Pei devised an office building perched on top of the council chamber, and Perkins and Will a square block with an open centre atop high legs, also with the chamber below. Australian John Andrews and his fellow Harvard students suggested a honeycomb-like roof covering a plaza for winter use, with the open square beyond for the summertime.

The most unusual design, highly distinctive in both form and materials from its surroundings, was submitted by a Finnish architect, Viljo Revell. And around that entry hangs a remarkable tale. After the first day and a half of their labours, the jurors had agreed on which entries were to be eliminated from further consideration. At that moment, however, events took an unexpected turn. Eero Saarinen, who had been absent from

the deliberations to that point, finally showed up in Toronto and made an immediate demand to the other jurors: "Show me your discards." Irritated though they must have been, they gave way – and then accepted Saarinen's argument that at least one of the rejects was worthy of reconsideration: Revell's entry with its two curving towers of unequal height cupping a rounded council chamber balanced on three legs containing staircases. The jurors agreed to add Revell's unusual layout to the shortlist of eight finalists.[55]

Saarinen's conduct in this regard seems to have been a reprise of the Sydney Opera House competition in Australia, where he had also resurrected Jorn Utzon's striking design from among the rejects.[56] His fellow jurors in Toronto were apparently sufficiently impressed by the reputation Saarinen had earned from his recent projects to give way to his imperious demands.

The jurors also designated two alternates, presumably in case any of the finalists decline to participate in the second stage though in the event none did so.[57] Ronald Zellner of Chicago proposed a square International Style tower of about thirty-five floors with pools on either side, and to its north a four-storey block with two internal courtyards spanning the entire width of the square where the council chamber would presumably be located. Bruno Lambert of Dusseldorf envisaged a square three-storey building surrounding a courtyard, from the north side of which would rise a transparent glass slab of twenty-eight floors. A broad bridge over a pool led to a projecting ceremonial entrance into the lower building, and the library branch was placed in a separate two-storey structure near the southwest corner of the square.[58]

The competition conditions granted each of the eight finalists $7,500 for work during the next four months during which they could expand upon or revise their submissions completely.[59] In their report upon the first stage of the competition, the jurors set forth the general considerations that had guided their choice of the finalists, and they expressed gratitude to the competitors for the "unusual expenditure of care, thought, and time – to say nothing of cost." Among the hundreds of entries they had sought out projects capable of producing an original

2.27
Perkins and Will,
final model.

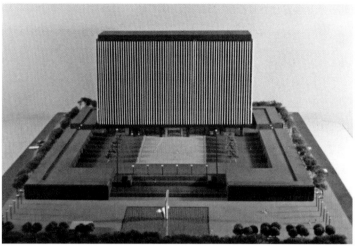

2.29
William Hayward,
final model.

2.28
David Horne,
final model.

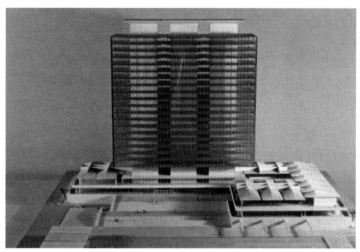

2.30
Gunnlogson and Nielsen,
final model.

2.31
Frank Mikutowski,
final model.

2.32
John Andrews,
final model.

2.33
I.M. Pei,
final model.

2.34
Viljo Revell, under
review. The judges,
persuaded by
Saarinen, had
liked Revell's first
design well enough
to send it to the
finals, and the
revised scheme
retained most of
its qualities.

city hall and square. Or, as they put it, they had "looked for ideas." The choice of finalists did not reflect "preconceived" views since the eight selected were permitted to produce entirely new designs in the second stage. By not opting simply for formal efficiency, they hoped to avoid ruling out a layout that would distinguish the city hall from an ordinary office tower and a civic square from a mere open space.

The jury added half a dozen specific suggestions to the finalists, really warnings about matters they considered of particular importance. Obviously, the significance of the council chamber should be stressed by providing a suitably impressive space easily accessible to the public (though at the same time allowing separate access to elected officials). The municipal offices should be laid out in such a way as to permit alterations as needed, but no major elements should be placed below grade without daylight. Since more space might eventually be needed, competitors were warned that jurors were not enthusiastic about proposals for vertical additions joining new to old structure; only in "special circumstances" would such expansion be appropriate if it did not appear to detract from the "unity and character of the original design." An unobtrusive new wing or building to the north of the city hall, perhaps even extending across the existing right-of-way of Hagerman Street, would be preferable. Two of the recommendations concerned access to the new civic square. There was no need to provide a special central gateway on the north side of heavily travelled Queen Street, but a mall extending to University Avenue north of Osgoode Hall seemed particularly desirable, making

the new building more visible and providing a passageway to what was supposed to be Toronto's most impressive north-south artery.

The final list of specifications from the jurors to the finalists concerned the crucial issues of size and cost. All competitors were aware of the findings of the management consultants at Woods Gordon about the amount of space required for municipal offices, but nothing had been said concerning the amount of space to be occupied by the council chamber and the public areas of the building. Arthur believed that it was in the design of those facilities that an architect could "throw his weight around and incidentally produce a great piece of architecture or an indifferent one."[60] At this point, however, the finalists were advised that the total enclosed space should be 700,000 square feet with a margin of variation of no more than 10 per cent up or down. And the eight were reminded that, while the original competition had fixed no maximum cost of construction, a reasonably economical structure should be proposed. Finally, they should keep in mind the severity of Toronto's climate, with its large temperature variations even within a single day. The external cladding of the building must take account of the need for economical maintenance and upkeep in view of continuing air pollution.[61]

Before leaving town, the jurors also issued a series of warnings to the city about problems revealed by studying the competition entries. The streets north of Hagerman up to Dundas Street were lined by many old, rundown buildings which would soon require replacement. In view of the importance of the area to the square, the

Planning Board should immediately get to work on a comprehensive redevelopment scheme which might include additional public buildings. That area and the east side of Bay Street north of the old city hall, much of which was owned either by the city itself or Eaton's department store, should also be redeveloped in an appropriate manner. Of equal concern was the "unworthy" appearance of many buildings facing the square on the south side of Queen. Leaving them would be "disastrous," and the city ought to make a comprehensive plan since pressure for changes would quickly arise. One way to make that part of Queen a fitting complement to the square would be to require a uniform facade stretching all the way from Bay to York which should not exceed ninety feet in height with a continuous open pedestrian arcade running underneath. To achieve this, the city would have to alter its zoning and planning regulations or expropriate the entire area.[62]

The Board of Control promptly requested the Planning Board to report on the redevelopment of the lands around the square. Another study should also be made of the hoary issue of whether to retain or demolish the 1917 Registry Office at the northwest corner of the square. (Arthur had recommended demolition to the city in the spring of 1957 so as to avoid interference with the design of the square, but, as so often in the saga of the new city hall, in July the Board of Control approved keeping the Neo-classical structure as part of the square.)[63] Now it

was suggested that perhaps the building could simply be moved northward to a less prominent location. City officials reported that the building was worth about $2 million, and that if a pathway could be cleared it could be shifted for about $750,000, an expense that might be justified by the cost of a replacement.[64]

The other issue of importance was whether the federal Department of National Defence would agree to sell the Armouries north of Osgoode Hall to Metro as a site for a new courthouse. Fred Gardiner had sought unsuccessfully to clinch a deal by 1957, but he was now hopeful that his strong ties to the Conservative Party would persuade the recently elected federal government to reach an agreement. The vast red-brick castle, enclosed by a barbed-wire fence around a huge truck parking lot, he deemed quite out of keeping with the plans for new square, but the Metro chair was concerned that a quick agreement on the Armouries was the "last shot at this proposition" since otherwise Ottawa might decide to sell to a private bidder at too high a price.[65]

The designs from the finalists were to be received by 19 September, with the winner to be announced on 26 September. The original intention was to keep the names of the finalists secret until the winner was announced, but by the end of April the *Globe and Mail* had revealed that David Horne, a young Toronto resident, was among the eight, so Arthur decided to release the names of the others. He, however, was the only person who knew

After long years of negotiation, the site of the Armouries, at the left side of this aerial view in the 1950s from the southwest, became part of the civic complex, in part as a pedestrian concourse, that passes beneath a wing of a new provincial courthouse.

Competition **59**

which architect had produced which design so that the jury could not be charged with bias.

Once selected, the finalists began to pepper the professional adviser with further queries; Arthur took most of May to prepare responses to sixty different questions. The largest number of answers concerned the materials and presentation of the final entries themselves, such as a ban on the inclusion of photographs. Other questions dealt with details of the arrangement of particular spaces (like interview rooms for the use of city council members) and the layout of the council chamber. There were a number of enquiries about the square and its surrounds. Was there a master plan for the whole area? What were the future plans for the lands north of the new building up to Dundas Street? The answer was that the Planning Board had just commenced a study of that area. Did the revised designs have to include a mall from University Avenue to the square north of Osgoode Hall as recommended by the jury? Arthur admitted that the city had shown little interest in this proposal so that was not mandatory. Pedestrian bridges over Queen Street at the southeast and southwest corners were not required, but the ramps to the parking garage under the square were already under construction and could not be altered.[66]

Just as the first stage of the competition ended in the spring of 1958, Eric Arthur began working on a book on the subject. The suggestion came from Sigfried Giedion (author of the much-admired book *Space, Time and Architecture*), who wrote to him to point out that, with the exception of the compendious book on the 1922 competition for the Chicago Tribune building, there had been little documentary study of other design contests. The one held in 1927 for the Palais des Nations in Geneva had produced "important schemes which were not brought to the attention of the jury" and eventually resulted only in "a small paper-backed book containing a few of the schemes presented." Wrote Giedion:

Your competition is for me one of the most important of recent times for many reasons. It has come at the right moment in the development of urban design, when – after a generation of hesitancy – urban renewal has attained maturity. This is of course why your competition proved so popular and why you received entries not only from the younger architects working single handed, but also from men who have long since made their name, from large firms normally only interested in remunerative work and from members of architectural faculties ...

The publication of this Toronto competition would, I feel sure, come as an astonishment to the general public and open their eyes to the high level which has now been achieved in the design of urban centres. This volume would remain a tribute to the noble initiative of the City of Toronto in taking the first great step towards reestablishing the dignity of a democratic community spirit as well as giving the world an account of the present state of contemporary architecture, and in some way recompensing the sacrifices offered to you by architects from throughout the world.

And Giedion added, referring to the recent competition for the design of the new city of Brasilia: "I would like to stress how much the world has appreciated the attitude of the City of Toronto, in not limiting its competition to Canadian nationals in contrast to another recent competition for a capital city whose results were far from satisfactory."[67]

Knowing that such sentiments would be music to the ears of the mayor, Arthur hastened to write a "Dear Nate" letter to pass along the idea with the suggestion that the city might like to underwrite the cost of a book. He also immediately approached the University of Toronto Press about the project.[68] Though he promised that he would seek no remuneration for his work in preparing a book that would surely bring valuable worldwide publicity to Toronto, the city council showed no interest in putting up any funds to subsidize publication. The Board of Control did, however, agree that Arthur could take on the task with the understanding that any sponsorship for a publisher must come from others.[69]

In January 1959 Arthur reported to Giedion that he was well launched on the project, which would include photographs of about one hundred of the entries that the jury had designated as "typical, very good or (mile high) very strange." Giedion readily agreed to provide an introduction for such a book. Discussions with the University of Toronto Press dragged on for years. Without funds from the city, the press calculated in 1964 that a high-quality book would have to be sold for about $75 to recover costs, which would severely reduce the number of likely buyers. Only a hefty subsidy would reduce

the list price of a book to somewhere below $20. That autumn Arthur approached the recently created Centennial Commission preparing for celebration of the anniversary of Confederation in 1967; he asked for $10,000, but, after lengthy foot-dragging, the response was not encouraging. Arthur then unsuccessfully sought funding elsewhere.[70]

Nevertheless, Arthur continued to work on the book. He drafted an outline, noting which documents he had already collected along with photographs of the one hundred selected entries. He composed an introduction to the book that emphasized the merits of competitions: "The designs submitted in an international competition form an ideal base for a study of architectural trends of the time. All the competitors work to the same size and floor area. They know something of the client, his city, his finances, and his ideals (insofar as these can be expressed in the conditions of the competition), and they are pinning their faith on a jury of unquestioned reputation and integrity … The buildings in these pages do represent the architecture of our era frozen, as it were, in a moment in time. The good and the strange are there; the highly imaginative may lie side by side with the traditional and the derivative."[71] In addition, Arthur wrote by hand fifteen pages of text for the book to supplement the millions of words already in print to provide "facts concerning the competition that have not been published."[72] He also had produced a series of typescript accounts of various aspects of the competition, some of which contained extensive quotations from the documents already mentioned above, that he wished to include in the book.[73] In the end, the necessary subsidy could not be found, and the project was abandoned. The effort did, however, galvanize Arthur to draw together material he had been collecting for over a quarter of a century on the architectural history of the city from the late eighteenth century to the end of the Victorian era in a book that appeared in October 1964 under the title *Toronto: No Mean City*. In his Epilogue to that work, he observed that "nothing humanly predictable could delay the completion of the City Hall by 1965 ... a portent of greatness to come."[74]

With the deadline for the decision about the competition winner looming in September 1958, Arthur busied himself with arranging suitable publicity for the final announcement. He collected biographical information on each of the finalists.[75] One problem that arose was precisely how to credit them. Arthur had advised that the only names mentioned would be those that appeared on the original register of applicants for the competition conditions. Thus, the large firm of Perkins and Will would be credited as a finalist while the name of the actual partner-in-charge, J.D. Lothrop, was never formally mentioned. However, as the moment of truth approached with all the favourable publicity involved, the American finalists in particular tried to expand the list of names in case they won. I.M. Pei wanted eight of his associates included, but Arthur turned him down for "overdoing things" and insisted that he would follow the register and show Pei's name alone.[76]

At the end of August, Arthur pointed out to Mayor Phillips that no plans had been made to bring the win-

ner to Toronto at the time of the announcement, but that CBC producer Vincent Tovell had proposed a half-hour television program on 28 September, a couple of days after the decision was made. Arthur persuaded the network to pay the travel costs of the finalists if the city took care of living expenses. He told the mayor that "I am gambling my reputation" that the jury would reach a decision by 25 September, so that the announcement could be made first thing in the morning the following day. Within a few days the College Street branch of Eaton's department store would display a show of models by the winner and the finalists as well as one hundred of the best entries, and stage a gala reception in its restaurant for up to five hundred people when the mayor formally opened the exhibition. The Ontario Association of Architects offered to hold a dinner for the jurors, to be followed by an informal discussion of the competition.[77] The Board of Control was sufficiently impressed by all the work that Arthur had done that it was decided to raise his fee as professional adviser to $10,000.[78]

As the final entries began to arrive in September, Arthur tried to make sure that no unauthorized persons could see the models and drawings laid out in a room on the top floor of Old City Hall. Only two members of the Planning Board staff would be involved, and, as he told Matthew Lawson, "naturally I am asking no friends, no Controllers, no aldermen, no press, and no mayor." The large eight-foot-square model of the buildings surrounding the civic square was again set up, into which each entry could be dropped to allow the jurors to see its impact upon its surroundings. Finally, the jurors settled down to make their decision. The debate was hot and heavy. With the announcement to be made by Mayor Phillips at 8 a.m. on 26 September, the jury was still debating at 3 a.m. before a decision was finally made. The exhausted jurors could not agree about what to say in their final report, so Lawson was called in to draft a document which they could sign.[79]

The final report of the jury included a detailed analysis of each entry.[80] The two Danes, Gunnlogson and Nielsen, were praised for the layout of the square and the monumentality of a building which would likely have a very long life. Still, the main-floor council chamber was no more than satisfactory in its layout, particularly for ceremonial events. J.D. Lothrop of Perkins and Will had provided a fine setting for public gatherings with a council chamber in a courtyard surrounded by a pool. Yet the building seemed less accessible to the general public since those doing business like seeking a permit would be forced to enter below grade. John Andrews and his associates produced a "tour de force" with its double plazas for summer and winter. Pierre Berton, of the Toronto *Star*, who seemed to have good sources, claimed that this "curious building that seemed to have [a roof that had] been basket woven" was the one that all the jurors initially liked best of all.[81] In the final report of the jury, however, doubts were expressed about how much use the below-grade winter plaza would actually receive. The final design was little changed from the original entry that had so attracted the judges though it still seemed to take up too much space on the east-west axis. I.M. Pei's design impressed the jurors with its abstract beauty and

the serenity of its landscape plan, but the building's exterior lacked the simplicity and monumentality of the interior. The council chamber was well placed and beautifully laid out, but there was no expression of its presence on the outside.

Canadian David Horne also fell short, his design lacking a clearly designed central entrance from the square and placing some elements like the library in a separate structure which would require users to take a dreary tunnel or go outside. Still, the judges considered the results dignified and workable with faults that were "those of judgment rather than of taste." Less favourably received was Frank Mikutowski's layout since it was too little altered from the original submission, showing an unwillingness to re-evaluate certain elements to avoid offending the judges. He had included sunscreens all around the outside, which seemed unnecessary in Toronto's climate. Both Horne and Mikutowski were criticized for placing expansion space in vertical additions which the jury disliked and for including such thick tree plantings in the square that the area might attract "undesirable characters."

The winning design came from the Finn, Viljo Revell, the entry originally rejected until Eero Saarinen had persuaded his colleagues to reconsider. In the first stage of the competition, Revell had submitted a highly attractive model made of clear acrylic for transparency and supported only by a bare minimum of drawings. His highly unusual layout featured two curving buildings of unequal height whose glass inner walls cupped a clam-shaped council chamber supported only by three

2.36
The three phases
of Viljo Revell's
winning design:
here, as one of the
entrants in the
big hall; then, its
towers rearranged,
as the victor over
the other finalists;
and its triumphal
re-presentation
to the citizens
months later, after
some further
modifications, in
close to its final
form.

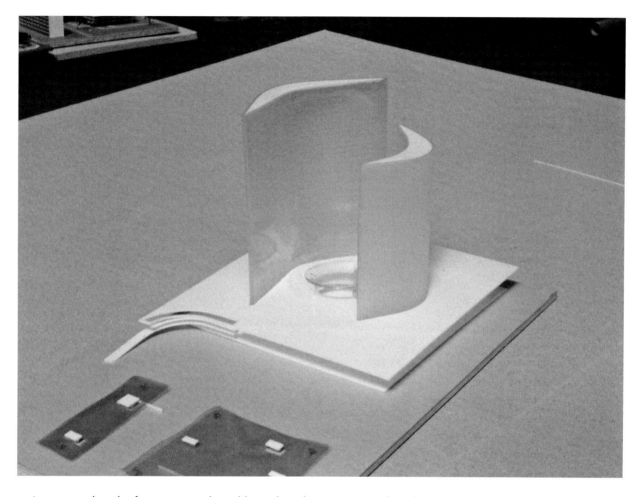

staircases, so that the focus was on the public, political functions of the building surrounded by tall office towers for the staff. The most evident change in Revell's design between the initial and final entries was that originally the taller tower had been placed to the west with a ramp leading up from beside Osgoode Hall to the ceremonial entrance to the central council chamber. In the final version the taller tower and the ramp had been shifted to the east along with the ramp while an elevated colonnade now surrounded the square. Revell's collaborators believed that this layout seemed to gesture more effectively to Lennox's Old City Hall across Bay Street while at the same time enclosing the square visually and defining it by cutting it off from the surrounding streets.[82]

In September 1958 the jurors debated long and hard about whether Revell should win because of serious concerns about how much such a structure would cost. His design included floor space totalling 770,000 square feet, the absolute maximum allowed. There were well-founded doubts that the building could be constructed for anything like the $18 million that the voters of Toronto had approved by plebiscite in the election of 1956. (Such doubts may have been one of the reasons for the original rejection of Revell's entry.) Yet in the end a three-person majority of the jury composed of Pratt, Rogers, and Saarinen carried the day for the Finn.

The majority argued that Revell's layout not only made excellent use of the square to the south of the building but also drew attention to Lennox's existing city hall to the east and the open space in front of historic Osgoode Hall to the west, just as the jury had specified in its report after the first stage of the competition.

The towers constituted a superb aesthetic statement, while the distinctive shape of the complex would make it a landmark on the city's skyline. The square was surrounded by an elevated colonnade forming a walkway around the vast paved space, with the reflecting pool at its south edge aligned with the old city hall across Bay Street.[83] Matthew Lawson later recalled that one of the jurors (whom he declined to identify) had told him that he had supported Revell's design because it was so striking even though he did not like it all that much.[84]

The two dissenting jurors, Holford and Stephenson, were convinced that some of the other finalists had submitted outstanding designs that could be built more economically. They joined in acknowledging the originality of Revell's conception but in their minority report they made some pointed criticisms. The unusual boomerang shape of the two buildings and the circular council chamber almost guaranteed budget overruns. The cost of construction was bound to be high since each of the floors in the towers was to be cantilevered from the outside walls rather than using simpler framing which would be cheaper to construct. Internal circulation was complicated, with long corridors on every floor plus the need for staff to navigate from one tower to the other. The curving outside walls of these buildings were windowless from the east and west, showing nothing but blank expanses of concrete which would hardly welcome future development around a square that was itself rather stark. Pierre Berton soon got wind of the division within the jury and reported that Holford and Stephenson had considered resigning; he claimed they were talked out of the idea by the other three who argued

that Toronto needed something innovative, a position with which Berton heartily agreed after a walk down "Tombstone Alley" (University Avenue).[85]

Matthew Lawson claimed that, when Nathan Phillips was shown the winning design fitted into the larger model of the surrounding buildings just before the 8 a.m. announcement on 26 September, the planning commissioner was immediately summoned to the mayor's side. Phillips confided gloomily that he supposed they were just going to have to live with the results. Lawson counselled him to tell the press that the design would make a "wonderful symbol" for the city, but Phillips could not contain himself from making "numerous snide remarks" about a design he really disliked. The planner concluded that the politician was afraid that the voters were not going to take to the exotic

proposal and would blame him for saddling them with paying the costs.[86]

A live broadcast of the half-hour CBC program "Explorations" took place two days later on 28 September. Hosted by Harvard faculty member Jacqueline Tyrwhitt,[87] who looked rather like a deer caught in the headlights, it began with an interview with Eric Arthur on the background to the competition. Then Viljo Revell was shown looking reflectively at the large model. Arthur would later observe that the number of entrants from so many different countries had created anxiety among the city aldermen that the winner might come from Communist China, Ethiopia, or Patagonia. He went on to claim, "I must say, on behalf of my fellow architects, that the prospect of welcoming such exotic persons into the rather conservative bosom of the

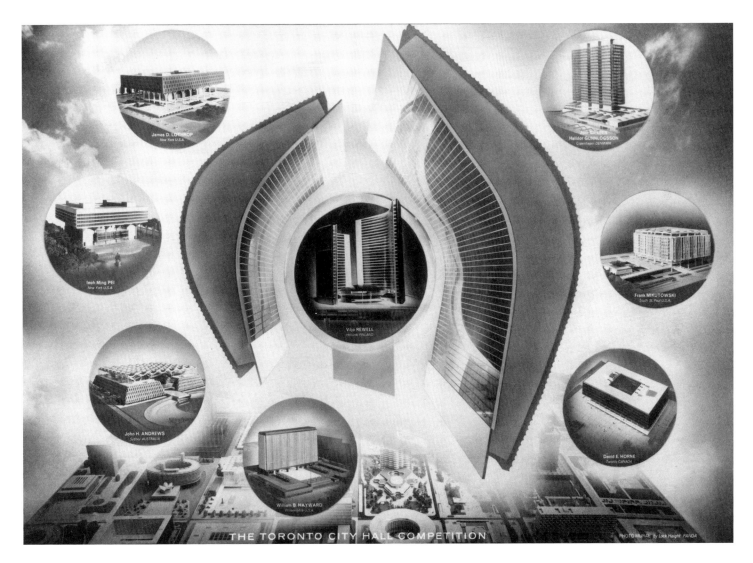

THE TORONTO CITY HALL COMPETITION

Ontario Association of Architects never arose as a matter of serious concern. I think we hoped he might have a word or two of English, and our relief was great when the winner turned out to be a charming, handsome, or shy Finnish gentleman with a reasonable command of English."[88] In the television broadcast Revell was certainly reticent to a fault, replying to Tyrwhitt with as few words as he decently could. Asked if preparing the entry had taken a long time, he simply said, "No, it was very fast, it was teamwork, you see." She then asked the five members of the jury for their observations and Revell made a few more brief comments of his own before the program drew to a close with a trailer about the following week's

episode where leading Canadian businessmen would be interviewed about how they had got to the top.

The public seemed generally enthusiastic about Revell's plan: thousands of people flocked to Eaton's College Street for a look at the winning design and a selection of the other models. Press coverage was overwhelmingly favourable, since even those not seduced by Revell's plan concluded that the project would give Toronto's cultural development a long-overdue shot in the arm. Praise also came from professional quarters: *Canadian Architect* eventually ran an article by Sigfried Giedion publicly repeating his congratulations to Toronto for holding an international competition and resisting the

2.39
The montage "announcing" the winner and runners-up.

Competition **67**

2.40
The public
exhibition at
Eaton's College
Street after the
competition,
including the
finalists and Eric
Arthur's selection
of roughly a
hundred other
models.

temptation to restrict entry to local citizens as had been done for the new national capital city at Brasilia. He noted that the concentration of focus by Revell upon the council chamber in an inner courtyard reaffirmed an old tradition while the solid exterior walls of the two towers provided an interesting context. Jacqueline Tyr-whitt later declared that Revell had shown skill in providing zones for different activities in the square and allowing for ceremonial access to the council chamber by automobiles through the provision of a ramp leading up to the council chamber at the colonnade level.[89]

Arthur himself joined Matthew Lawson in issuing a rather self-congratulatory report on the competition. They applauded Nathan Phillips for having persisted in seeking an international competition despite criticism from the architectural profession and the local press. The nearly five hundred entries represented the best brains

and brought world attention to Toronto. Gradually opinion had swung behind the notion that architecture "was as important in our society in Canada as it ever was in Europe at the height of the Renaissance." In a cityscape once dominated by soaring churches, it was appropriate that the municipal government should be housed in a notable structure. Visitors would be impressed as they entered from the square and looked up three storeys at the dramatic view of the convex underside of the council chamber, which was the "jewel framed by the curved arms of the operating floors which rise above it."[90]

Naturally, carping about the design continued in some quarters. Always ready with a pithy quote, Frank Lloyd Wright glanced at a drawing and declared, "You've got a headmarker for a grave and a future generation will look at it and say, 'This marks the spot where Toronto fell.'" Local critics compared the towers to a couple of pieces of broken sewer pipe standing on end. George Rolland, who planned to be a candidate for Board of Control in the 1958 election, immediately issued a pamphlet saying, "I respectfully condemn the proposed city hall as handed down to us by the 'Judges and Architects,' on the grounds that if such a building is constructed it would appear more like a vegetable market or an oversized filling station than a city hall." With its high, thin walls it would be unable to withstand windstorms, sandstorms, or snowstorms and might topple over even before it was completed. If ever built, it would become a target for bombs in wartime and any explosion would send concrete flying in all directions. He demanded that the city council refuse to accept the design as "very ugly," "very unsafe," and "completely unacceptable." In a letter to the Planning Board, Rolland added that the plan looked like a "Mexican hotel" which would quickly become the object of hatred and insisted that the voters ought to be permitted to pronounce upon any design at the next election.[91]

Another self-appointed expert raised the old argument that the competition should have been restricted to Canadians to show people they were not ashamed of their home-grown talent. No wonder university students went off to the United States to study since everyone assumed that foreigners were superior. Patiently, Mayor Phillips reminded him that in 1956 he had told the voters plainly that if they approved a new city hall there would be an international competition for the design.[92]

Others registered their admiration for the choice. New Yorker Thomas Creighton lectured the Ontario Association of Architects about the "New Sensualism"; designs like Le Corbusier's chapel at Ronchamp, Saarinen's Trans World Air terminal, and Revell's city hall rejected "geometric precision and proportional niceties" and appealed directly to the emotions. Donning his other hat as editor of the Royal Architectural Institute of Canada's *Journal*, Eric Arthur pointed out that only a minority of the five hundred entries had adopted the rigorous International Style of Mies van der Rohe. Just one of the finalists had opted for a transparent glass-curtain wall. Toronto architect Eberhard Zeidler claimed that the austere rectilinear forms and restricted choices of material common to early modernism were already being replaced by more exotic shapes like Saarinen's hockey rink at Yale University, whose curving roof suspended from above had earned it the sobriquet "the Whale." Somewhat immodestly, Zeidler made similar claims about innovation for his layout of a new church where the roof was formed by overlapping two parabolic arches which created a clerestory at the ridge line of the roof.[93]

Revell had won the competition, declared Arthur in a later speech, because he had paid careful attention to the emphasis placed in the conditions on a layout clearly expressing the various functions that the building would serve. Many other entries had also aimed for a "sculptural" form, but Revell had been the "most representative" of the group. Arthur suggested not only that his conditions pointed to a sculptural solution, but that by 1958 a worldwide reaction against the "mechanical precision and cubism of Mies van der Rohe" was beginning. Only one of the eight finalists had proposed a multistorey office building clad in glass. At the same time, Le

Corbusier's chapel at Ronchamp had become a mecca for architects and theorists, reflecting a new interest in more plastic forms.[94]

The interest created by the competition outside Canada was evident from a number of enquiries that arrived once it was publicized in the *Architectural Record* in November 1958. The person charged with planning a new capitol complex for the U.S. territory of Hawaii asked Matthew Lawson for his confidential assessment of the process.[95] Lawson prepared an aide-memoire in which he declared, "I'm sure we are convinced that generally the competition was an unqualified success. In confidence it might be said that the disagreement among the jury was unfortunate but not by any means disastrous – rather the result of democratic voting. Obviously the pros and cons of a democratic vote can constitute a lengthy epistle! If the local press can be used as a measure of the public's reaction we also are assured of success, especially if it is assumed – and I think it must [be] – that objectors are more inclined to put pen to paper."[96] Lawson advised the American that the competition had been "very successful" in attracting architects from around the world because the jurors had been carefully chosen so as not to represent "any particular school of design." The conditions had been drafted to ensure "there would be few possibilities of misunderstanding or bungling at a later date." Revell's design had been chosen by a narrow vote, but differences of opinion were almost inevitable among the members of a balanced panel. An alternative was to seek a single design from a local hand, and indeed the city of Toronto had sought to do this in 1954 with a consortium of three firms. The voters, however, had refused to pay for the proposed result. Some critics of the international competition had complained that all the entrants could not be fully familiar with a site and its context, but Lawson observed that outsiders had produced just as good designs as the local entrants. If there was a brilliant candidate at home or abroad for the Hawaiian commission, then that firm could be retained and paid, but if not then a competition was the best solution.[97]

Boston was also in the throes of planning a new city hall. One architect there was keen to see a competition, and in order to convince the local politicians he asked Mayor Phillips to produce a public endorsement. In reply, Phillips chose to highlight his own role in carrying the day for an international contest: "I argued that intelligence, skill, and ability were not regulated by artificial geographical boundaries and that Toronto should have the best design that the architectural world could produce. I emphasized that this would not cost any more than a national contest." As for the results, "design, of course, is a controversial matter and while acceptance has not been unanimous I can say that the preponderance of public opinion favours the design submitted by Mr. Rewell [sic]. The international competition was notice to the world that Canadians were willing to compete against the best architects in the universe and constituted an object lesson for other municipalities to follow." Perhaps a Canadian would win out in Boston.[98]

Totting up the costs of the competition revealed that a total of $113,000 had been spent. Though Eric Arthur's formal duties as professional adviser had been completed, he quickly offered his friend "Nate" assurances that he was happy to do anything more required to see that a building project that had made Toronto known around the world was carried to completion. As professional adviser, said Arthur, "I have occupied space like a cuckoo. I have always been made to feel that I was a very welcome cuckoo." Aware of how important Phillips had been in bringing about the international competition, when the mayor faced re-election for another two-year term in December 1958, Arthur wished him good luck: "You deserve it."[99] Without Phillips the push for the construction of the new city hall could still founder.

Arthur was justifiably proud of the way in which he had organized the competition though he did admit to a few minor problems. Each person seeking a copy of the conditions had been asked for $5, but he admitted that he had failed to add the crucial word "Canadian." As a result, the city treasurer ended up with a chest full of pesos, pesetas, kroner, marks, and indeed most of the world's currencies that had to be kept so as to be returned to entrants. Several architects had sent along copies of books worth more than $5, while one person who had no currency invited the professional adviser to come on a holiday in Hungary with him.[100]

Some entrants took little care with the packing of their models; a few arrived in flimsy boxes just stuffed with crumpled newsprint. One entry, Arthur admitted, was completely "shattered" in transit, and even one of the finalists' offerings had to be hastily repaired before the judging. In the end, some competitors had to be told that their models had arrived in poor condition and deteriorated during the judging so that the expense of returning them was not justified and they would be destroyed. Several people complained to the Royal Institute of British Architects that their returned entries had not been properly packed, one model being received so "completely disintegrated that even the smallest ancillary buildings made of solid wood and securely glued on had been removed." The secretary general of the Union internationale des Architectes agreed that these grievances were entirely justified.[101]

Arthur admitted that he had made some mistakes on practical matters. The parcels that arrived at city hall were sent to the Horticultural Building to be unpacked and laid out for the judges. (This process had taken ten people ten days to accomplish, and the city planning staff now thought it had been ill-advised to recruit architecture students for the task since they were "too interested in the architecture for this job.") After the finalists were chosen, the other entries were repacked and sent back to city hall, only to have one hundred of the best unpacked again to be displayed at Eaton's College Street store. Finally, all the boxes had to be reopened so that the drawings could be microfilmed, then once again parcelled up. All this made for a great deal of wear and tear on the delicate models from "too much handling" (which had helped provoke the protests from the Royal Institute of British Architects and the Union internationale des Architectes even though it had been done from "the highest motives"). To save money on shipping, local entrants, especially from Toronto, were encouraged to come and pick up their own models, which many did.[102] Even Sigfried Giedion, who was generally impressed with Arthur's preparation and management of the competition, complained privately to him that he had "heard from all sides that the scale of the model you required was too small, so that, in fact, an additional study model had to be made at larger scale."[103]

All of the jurors expressed keenness to see the project go ahead. In a formal report signed by the five, they declared that Revell's design was "the most original in conception." "Its monumental qualities are of a high order and it is a composition of great strength. Its shape is distinctive and dramatic, setting it apart from other structures in Toronto and from administrative and office buildings everywhere." They urged full support for the architect in carrying out the work even if some modifications were ultimately necessary.[104] Praise was heaped upon Eric Arthur as the professional adviser; Canadian Architect later remarked that the competition had come about only as a result of "much private manoeuvring and … in spite of much expert opposition." Gordon Stephenson later declared publicly that the jury had been prepared to leave many details to be worked out by Arthur, believing that his influence would make it easier to gain final approval from the city council.[105] Arthur did indeed prove to be a ubiquitous presence during the lengthy process of turning the winning design into a finished building over the next seven years.

Eric Arthur, like Nathan Phillips, was one of those bold Torontonians not afraid to press for dramatic change. During the 1930s he became an enthusiast for the modernist movement in architecture, bringing many of its leading figures to Toronto for his students at the university as well as a wider public. Given the opportunity to serve as professional adviser to an international competition, he oversaw the choice of Viljo Revell's entry.Yet Arthur's activities also uncovered that other vein of Toronto culture, traditionalism and conservative caution. His fellow architects wanted to restrict the competitors to design a new city hall if not to local practitioners then to Canadians alone. Some politicians like Fred Gardiner thought that a structure that looked like the headquarters of an insurance company would demonstrate economy and practicality. But Arthur supported Phillips's determination to admit foreigners, and the competition conditions that he composed allowed for inventiveness and radicalism. The members of the competition jury recruited by Arthur reflected a wide range of interests and a sympathy for modernism, and he received Revell's winning design with enthusiasm.

Winner

PREVIOUS PAGE
3.1
Apart from
the perimeter
structure, the
council chamber
interior is generally
unaltered from the
design.

Who was Viljo Revell? In an autobiography prepared at Eric Arthur's request when he won the design competition for Toronto's new city hall,[1] Revell recorded that he had been born in Vaasa in 1910 and lived there until he entered the Institute of Technology in Helsinki, Finland's only architectural school, during the 1930s. While still a student Revell and two contemporaries attracted notice with a plan for the "Lasipalatasi" (Glass Palace), a complex of shops, restaurants, and theatres near Helsinki's central station. When constructed this building was much criticized by the generally conservative Finnish public, but it was later recognized as among the first functionalist layouts that broke from traditional historicist models.[2]

Revell also worked twice as a junior colleague in the office of Alvar Aalto, in the period before Aalto had attained international fame, and his tasks there included work on the Finnish pavilion for the 1937 World's Fair in Paris. Having established his own firm, Revell served in the Finnish navy during the Second World War. Afterwards he returned to practice and acquired a considerable reputation for his work on a wide variety of projects in Finland, where, as he put it, "independent architects do not usually specialize in some special sort of buildings; in my opinion the general practice is better for the architect also in other respects."

Revell also explained to Arthur that by 1958 he was fully familiar with architectural design competitions, which in Finland had "an important position and old traditions." "In my opinion they have had a considerable significance in the development of our architecture. By

far the greatest part of those buildings that are important in view of the development of architecture are results of those competitions. I have participated in competitions for a couple of decades already, and so I have won nearly twenty prizes in them."

The best-known building that Revell's firm had designed was the Palace Industry Centre, a combined office and restaurant development that stood in a prominent place on the waterfront in Helsinki overlooking the busy harbour. Begun in 1949 and completed in 1952, it had a modernist look, standing on pilotis with strip windows.

Revell represented a new wave of modernist architects distinct from the founding generation, showing a particular interest in new materials and construction techniques, as in the use of concrete. He received a Fulbright Fellowship in 1954–5 and came to Mies van der Rohe's base at the Illinois Institute of Technology, but, finding the atmosphere too "Miesian," he moved on to the University of California at Berkeley. In the United States he became conversant with developments there. He was acquainted with Eero Saarinen, greatly admiring the plan for the concrete parabolic Gateway Arch destined to stand on the banks of the Mississippi River in St Louis that had been designed in 1948 though not completed until 1965. Revell's own work progressed from early functionalist designs to more free-flowing forms like those favoured by Aalto. When the news of his success in the Toronto competition reached him, Aalto wired Revell in Canada, "Seldom does a colleague feel so happy over another's victory."[3]

What did winning the Toronto city hall competition mean for Viljo Revell? By the 1950s, his firm was seen as a highly desirable place for a young architect. Those hired felt they learned as much in the practice as they had in their formal education, and a substantial number went on to become university teachers. A particular attraction was that, for important commissions, Revell formed teams of his junior associates and gave them wide responsibilities. Intrigued by the recent competition for the opera house in Sydney, Australia, won by a Dane, Jorn Utzon, Revell decided to enter the Toronto city hall contest and chose three men, Heikki Castrén, Bengt Lundsten, and Seppo Valjus, to work on the project.

Though he had no experience in building high-rise office towers, Revell applied for the competition conditions, and the team began tossing around ideas for the basic shape of a building. At a meeting where Revell was not even present, the three younger men hit upon the notion of a tall circular structure, then decided to split the circle into two halves that could stand apart from one another, with the city council chamber (on the prominence of which Eric Arthur's conditions placed much stress) to be inserted between them. They conceived the notion of shaping the walls of the towers as catenary curves such as a chain forms when suspended at each end, cupping a round council chamber.[4] When the three men presented this idea to Revell, he immediately grasped its aesthetic possibilities and set them to work out more details as a team, a concept often talked of in other architectural offices but not all that frequently adhered to.[5]

As the planning evolved, the idea of making the two towers of unequal height was hit upon. In the original entry the western tower was to be taller, with a ramp along the west side of the square next to Osgoode Hall leading up to the entrance to the central council chamber. When Revell was questioned by an interviewer about why he had adopted the curving shape of the towers of unequal height, he replied that architectural solutions generally sprang from intuition after investigation as one tried to give material form to an entity designed to serve a multitude of purposes. At a more mundane

3.3
FACING PAGE
The winning model
and its reflections.

level, he pointed out that he and his staff had realized that, when looking down from above, the proposed layout appeared like the round shade of an architectural draftsman's Luxo lamp, lit from on high, which created a shadow like the two curving shapes surrounding the central domed council chamber. In a self-deprecatory way, Revell added, "I do not invent anything; I am not in that 'position' in my office. If I would start inventing my assistants would most likely stop [the] inventing."[6]

The model originally submitted by Revell was an attractive translucent structure of clear acrylic in which the tripod-mounted council chamber seemed to float in mid-air between the two towers. In the final version the entry appeared little altered from the preliminary design except for a shift of the taller tower from west to east so that more sunlight could reach into the space above the council chamber. This change left generations of municipal employees in the upper floors of the east tower sweltering in the heat and glare of the afternoon sun. Bengt Lunsten said that this change had been approved by the Finnish consulting engineers who vetted the plan, they never having considered that the air-conditioning load would be too great on a summer day since Finland did not endure the same kind of scorching temperatures and humidity as Toronto.[7]

Once Revell's victory was announced on 26 September 1958, the most urgent task became the selection of a local architect with whom the Finn must be associated according to the regulations of the Ontario Association of Architects. Even before the decision, Eric Arthur had written to city Planning Commissioner Matthew Law-

son about the importance of the winner meeting some local architects while in Toronto: "If he is young and does not have the organization to carry out the job, partnership arrangements have to be made." The need for such an association was made clear in a column by Pierre Berton in the Toronto *Star*, noting that Revell still faced a "sticky problem." In order to reach a firm agreement with the city, he would have to make detailed drawings, perhaps as many as five hundred, so that a clear cost estimate could be reached. Including engineering services, each drawing might cost up to $1,000 to produce, and Berton pointed out that Canadian banks were unlikely to advance such a sum to the Finn in the absence of a contract. It would take months to prepare such drawings and then to translate them into tenders which could be handed over to contracting firms interested in bidding.[8]

After the announcement of his selection, Revell did not linger long in Toronto but returned to Europe. While in the city he did meet with several architectural firms to assess them as possible collaborators. By 2 October, Eric Arthur was writing to advise that he was already being "pestered" by architects seeking this association, and promising that he would forward any letters even though they should be ignored. One of the most persistent suitors, G. Everett Wilson, who also happened to be the president of the Ontario Association of Architects, approached Revell directly. Wilson and Newton was a small firm of just seven architects which was admittedly facing a dearth of commissions owing to the economic recession into which Canada had slid. Not only was the firm experienced with using reinforced concrete,

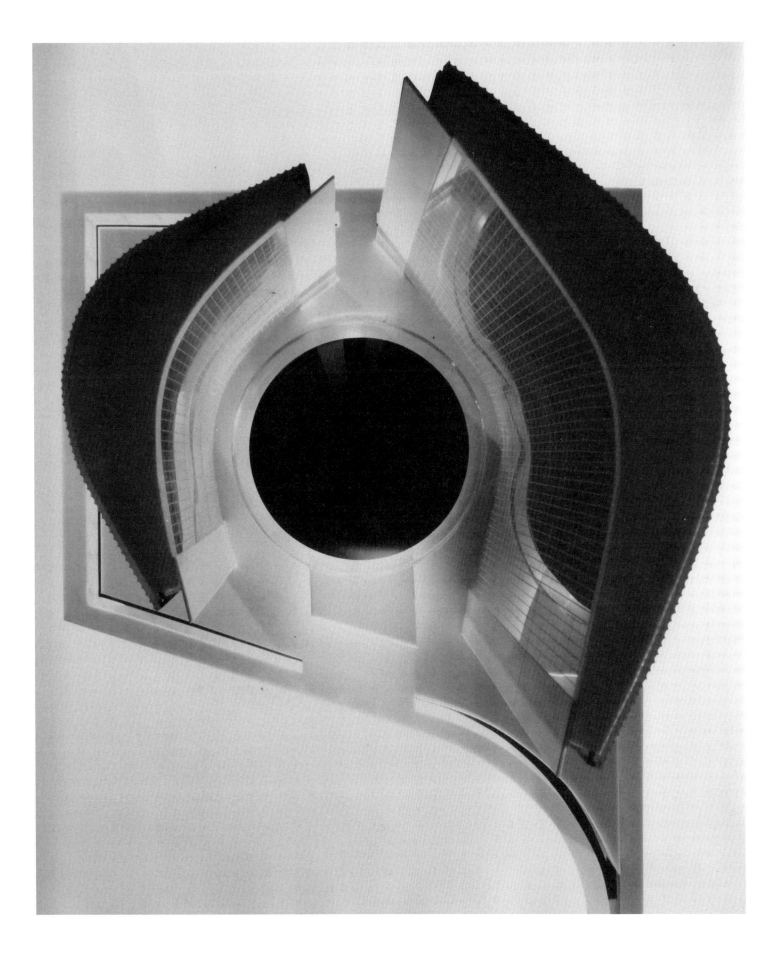

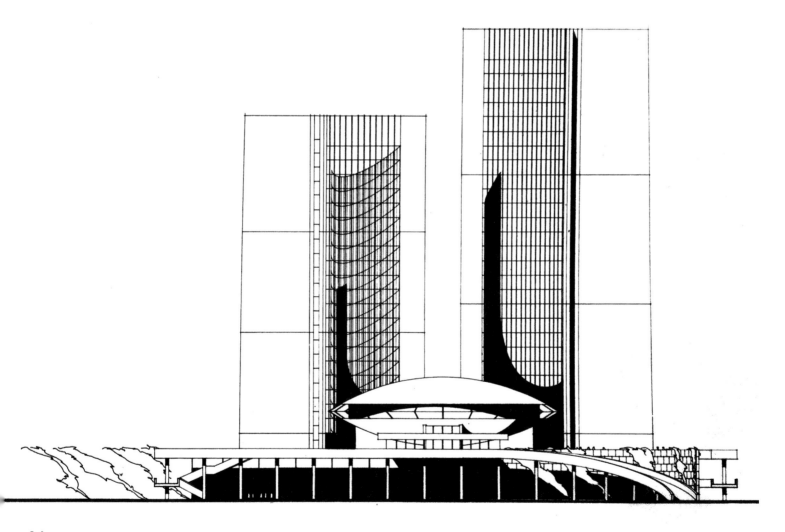

3.4
The "unequal"
towers, embracing
the council
chamber.

but Wilson warned Revell that "as you must realize the elected personnel you will be dealing with are liable to change and are always willing to capitalize on any opportunity to appeal to the voters." He added, "I have excellent contacts with the City of Toronto officials."[9]

Arthur advised Revell that the number of architects who were "a) congenial & would understand what you are doing and b) be capable of carrying out the work is small – perhaps 4." Wilson was clearly not among them in Arthur's mind, but he warned Revell that he must be treated diplomatically since as OAA president he could be "very helpful in getting you established professionally. And if you send out two of your boys he can help them" if they wanted to register as architects.[10]

John C. Parkin, who was always on the lookout for ways to propel himself and his firm, John B. Parkin Associates, into participation in any prestigious job, made certain that he met with Revell during his stay in Toronto and put himself on first-name terms with the Finn. Arthur clearly decided that the Parkins were the best bet as associates, for one thing because they were a relatively large firm with an in-house engineering staff so that Revell would not have to spend time and money establishing a full-scale architectural office in Toronto. John B. Parkin (partner but no relation to John C.), whose firm had already completed a large number of projects like schools, was likely to be listened to respectfully by the city council. By 9 October, John C. was writing to "Dear Viljo" to report that he had lunched with Arthur, who had asked him to have the Finn draft a letter announcing Revell's choice of the Parkin firm so that the professional adviser could send it to the OAA and the RAIC for their imprimatur. As soon as Revell got back to Helsinki after carrying out a long-standing commitment to give a lecture in Moscow, he produced the requested draft, which he sent off to Arthur with thanks for his "personal kindness and understanding" and the hope that the Parkins reciprocated the confidence he had in them. He enclosed a draft agreement between the two firms and an application for membership in the OAA. Revell asked that the arrangement with the Parkins be kept confidential until its terms were finally settled.[11]

John C. Parkin sent along a sheaf of press clippings showing that local sentiment was running three to one in support of Revell's layout, a shift from the time of the announcement when the pros and cons had been more evenly divided: "Public opinion is crystallizing in a very favourable way, and those who seem close to city hall affairs tell me they do not anticipate any serious obstacles now in the way." Parkin was to appear on a panel discussion with various newspaper columnists, and the mayor would hold a public forum designed to create support for getting under way as quickly as possible.[12]

Meanwhile, Eric Arthur was working on his proposed book about the competition. He sent Revell a series of questions about why he had had decided to enter the Toronto contest. Was it because he had confidence in the jury or was it confidence in the city's capacity to carry out construction? Was it for the monetary prize or were the conditions attractive and in the architect's interests as well as the city's? Was it the challenge provided by the scope of the problem to be addressed? Revell answered all these questions (though he asked Arthur not to quote his responses directly but merely to paraphrase them). He had not been much concerned with the financial benefits. Rather, he considered the challenge interesting, and the structure of the competition seemed to show that there was a "real task" in solving problems with the expectation that construction would commence soon. He revealed that he had entered the competition for the Haupstadt Berlin but had withdrawn because Toronto gave him confidence that it seemed more "realistic" about what was being sought.[13]

Arthur also asked if Revell had any "quick sketches" done at the very outset of the planning, reminding him of the way that "La Corbusier" [sic] included such preliminary "doodling" in his publications. Such an illustration would show readers how the initial suggestions evolved into the final competition entry. Revell replied that his practice, like that of other architects, was to prepare finished renderings only in the final phase of a proposed design, but he did send one illustration of the reflection on the shade of the Luxo lamp in his office that showed the basic layout viewed from on high.[14]

By late November 1958, word of Revell's intention to associate himself with the Parkin firm had leaked out. Matthew Lawson insisted that he had had nothing to do with the leak but that the press had been very keen to discover the decision; he praised Revell's "wise, sensible move" in his choice of collaborator. Revell set down for John C. Parkin the issues that he regarded as most important in any agreement. The very first of these was his desire for "full control" of the design of the furnishings of the new building. Practical matters included compensation for the cost of at least two round trips from Helsinki to Toronto annually while the job continued. Revell also pointed out that neither he nor his three team members had ever visited Ontario, and that the cost of local excursions for each of them should be covered so that they might become well acquainted with the scene there. Finally, he tackled the possible ramifications of demands that the total cost of the building be reduced. If that was necessary, then decisions on changes should be taken right at the outset in order to reduce the time and expense needed to produce detailed drawings. As an example, Revell pointed to the competition requirement that the proposed design accommodate future changes to increase the size of the building by up to one-quarter, which had hardly seemed "topical" when he was in Toronto; he thought it better to leave any expansion plans for the future when a separate structure could be built to the north of the square, though he admitted that aesthetically he preferred making the towers taller from the start, which might be cheaper if allowed for at the outset. Parkin agreed that these issues seemed reasonable and suggested that they should form the first order of business when Revell arrived in the city early in 1959.[15]

The other issue that was to become of critical importance over time also surfaced: the tax implications for the fees earned by Revell on the project. Right from the beginning, he was concerned that he could not escape from very high Finnish rates even by becoming a full-time resident of Canada, since his practice in Helsinki would continue. As he told Kingsley Graham, Finland's

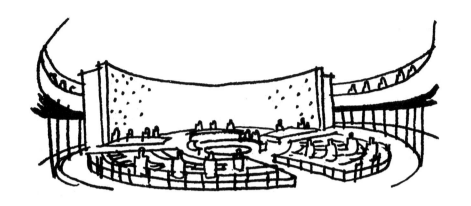

VIEW OF COUNCIL CHAMBER

3.5
Revell's early
design sketches,
April 1958;
he evidently
preferred
sketches and
models to finished
perspective
renderings.

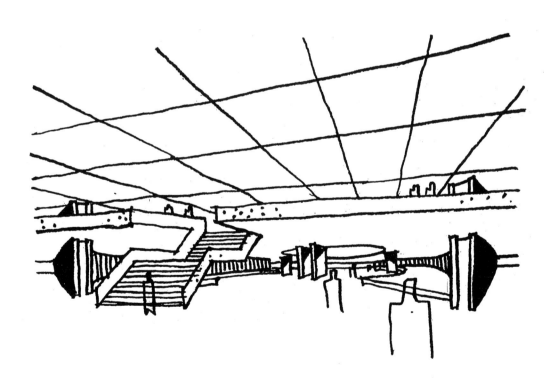

VIEW OF MAINHALL

consul general in Toronto, "currency regulations on Finnish citizens and their property abroad are highly inconvenient and restrictive." There was no tax treaty between Finland and Canada, and it was impossible to say when one would be signed though discussions were under way. Revell insisted that he wasn't seeking large monetary rewards for his work, only good working conditions for himself and his associates which would allow him to produce fine results.

Finnish tax rates were much higher than Canadian ones, and, while it was clear that some Canadian tax would be owed on the work performed there, Revell wanted to avoid "double taxation." Could the agreement with the Parkins be structured so as minimize this danger? He assured John C. Parkin that he was seeking not to transfer work properly done in Toronto to Helsinki but merely to make an efficient arrangement which might involve some of the furniture design and other work being undertaken in Finland: "It may be possible due to my other unfinished work I will be obliged to spend months in Helsinki, during which time I would like to develop some details and bring them to greater maturity here."[16]

December 1958 brought the good news that Nathan Phillips had been re-elected to another two-year term as mayor, a result that in Parkin's mind represented a "successful endorsement" of the plans for the new city hall as well as a guarantee that the strongest supporter of the project would be on hand to shepherd it through the city council.[17] There was even optimistic talk that the cornerstone could be laid by the end of 1960. Revell and

Heikki Castrén visited Toronto in January to look over the situation and work out the final terms of the arrangement with Parkin. It was decided that a Canadian firm called Viljo Revell and Company would be incorporated to enter into the partnership with John B. Parkin Associates as Revell-Parkin, which would sign the formal contract with the city.[18]

When Revell returned to Toronto in the spring of 1959 for his first extended stay, certain domestic details had been decided upon. He had always assumed that he would leave his family behind in Helsinki, but when he announced this there was a domestic revolt. His wife, Maire, and his three teenage daughters were adamant that they wanted to take up residence in Toronto, and he gave way to this pressure. At first the family rented two adjacent apartments in a building on Don Mills Road, not far from the Parkin offices at 1500. The parents lived in one flat while the girls shared another across the hall, an arrangement they found very satisfactory. In the meantime, Revell ordered a fancy Karman Ghia for himself while Castrén, Lundsten, and Valjus each got a standard Volkswagen; Maire Revell chose a flashier Ford convertible to get around town.[19]

The three associates each rented houses in suburban Don Mills where they would spend the next couple of years. When asked what their first impression of Toronto had been, Lundsten and Valjus said in unison, "Like the Wild West"; they explained that they were struck by the long lines of utility poles carrying great bundles of cables, which reminded them of the views of North America they had been treated to in Hollywood westerns. Toronto

3.6
Revell, at Parkin's
Don Mills office,
contemplating the
work to come.

seemed spread out for miles, especially in the suburbs, unlike the compact centre of Helsinki.[20]

The architects embarked on trips to places like Niagara Falls to familiarize themselves with North American society and design. One of their more exotic ventures was to meet with H.F. Johnson, Jr, head of the Johnson Wax company. He had advanced tastes in architecture, having commissioned a building from Frank Lloyd Wright at company headquarters in Racine, Wisconsin, in the 1930s. Johnson had become familiar with Finland, to which the company's products were exported, and decided that he would like to have a sauna designed by Viljo Revell at his cottage on Lake Owen in northern Wisconsin. "Wax" Johnson (as the Finns called him) seemed to fit the image of a North American tycoon, who took them aboard his private DC-3 aircraft and insisted upon playing poker as they travelled. The Johnson sauna became the only other building designed by Revell in North America beside the city hall, though it created endless problems for the Revell office during the early 1960s because the floor could never be laid so as to drain properly.[21]

In their own space in the Parkin offices at 1500 Don Mills Road in Toronto, the Revell team set to work preparing the Stage I drawings for presentation to city officials. Both Lundsten and Valjus remember the relationship between the two halves of the Revell-Parkin partnership as cooperative and agreeable, owing in part to the friendly presence around the office of John B. Parkin's father. They found John C. Parkin somewhat arrogant and preferred to deal with John B. if possible. Liaison between the firms was the responsibility of Par-

kin's Fred Smith and John (Jack) Mar, who also handled the contacts with the city staff with whom the Finns had little to do. Bengt Lunsten found both men satisfactory colleagues though it was sometimes difficult to know exactly what Smith had in mind.[22]

As an experienced architect, Viljo Revell knew that his plans would be modified as the work progressed. Nonetheless, the city proved a difficult and sometimes frustrating client. First of all, there was the laborious way in which municipal officials worked. Documents had to be drafted, referred to the legal department, sent to the Board of Control (if expenditures were entailed), and approved by council (which sometimes gave approval only in principle so an issue could be reopened later on), all of which could take months. Moreover, the aldermen were prone to changing their minds on matters such as whether or not to include food services in the building, which would be a costly business particularly if it meant adding floors to the towers or reallocating space to allow for it. Information wended its way from Revell's drafting tables to the Parkin offices and then downtown to the city officials and followed the same route back. Sometimes it must have seemed as though the chopping and changing might never end. Optimistic talk about laying the cornerstone by the end of 1960 came to nothing, though Nathan Phillips's re-election for a third two-year term as mayor at least guaranteed a strong political presence favourable to the project. Yet there were always those on council and elsewhere in Toronto who thought the whole building impractical and extravagant. Not until October 1961 was the formal contract with the general contractors approved so that actual work could begin on the site.

Three design issues proved particularly contentious. The biggest problem was overall cost; estimates were developed that showed that construction was going to be considerably more expensive than the city had anticipated, nowhere near the mythical (though oft-quoted) sum of $18 million. By July 1959, the architects reported that that figure was "in no way related" to the current plans. For one thing, the addition of space for the Registry and Land Titles offices and the inclusion of a branch library would entail an additional $2.25 million, and the square would cost $1 million more. Adjusted for inflation

to May 1959, construction costs alone would be at least $24.95 million.[23] So it was clear that the final total could be at least $30 million if one included the $4 million cost to the city for the land in the square, $1.5 million in architects' fees, and at least half a million dollars to furnish the new building.

A firm of American engineers produced studies which suggested that the cost of the basic structure of the two curving towers would be 25 or 30 per cent higher than a conventional rectangular shape also made of reinforced concrete and 15 to 20 per cent more than a building with a structural frame of steel girders. To adhere to Revell's plans would raise the final overall cost of the towers by between 5 and 10 per cent.[24]

The architects struggled hard to make changes in the design that would bring down construction costs to "a figure acceptable to the city." To do so demanded the "most resourceful and exacting planning" in order to scale down the floor area to a minimum still compatible with good design. The idea was to shrink the size of the towers and reshape their southern edges closer to the council chamber in a way that would be almost imperceptible. If the changes could be made during the preparation of the Stage I drawings, it would permit much greater economies than if the floor plans had to be revised later on.[25]

Eric Arthur later described the key alterations that were ultimately decided upon:

Reasons of structure and economy may [sic: made] quite serious changes in Revell's original scheme, the one which one [sic] the competition, but they were changes that did not in the least change the grand design of the central council chamber protected and embraced by the curving towers.

One can imagine an early meeting of Revell and his Parkin associates when a basic decision on cost had to be made. That obviously was a sphere where the Toronto associates were in a position to give some good & sound North American advice, however painful to the newcomer from Finland. The result was a shrinking of the whole program starting with the bringing of the towers closer together. That produced a chain reaction which first affected the area of the council chamber & the podium floors, and then inevitably the pattern and structure of the public space of the ground floor. We shall never know what we lost, if indeed we lost anything, but the Jury of Award certainly entertained visions of the central space that bear no relation to the dramatic space that we have today.[26]

One concern of the Finns was that the Parkin firm might come up with an alternative design that would cut construction costs considerably and persuade the city to accept it even without their consent. As the redesign process went on, rumours circulated around 1500 Don Mills Road that such an alternative was being planned by John Andrews, who had gone to work for the Parkins after his finalist entry in the competition had lost out to Revell. The fear was that behind closed doors Andrews was working on a building using a steel frame rather than

reinforced concrete, but the Finns were never allowed to see this proposal (if it really existed).[27]

The second problem concerned how to structure the council chamber. Revell's original plan showed a spaceship-like clamshell balanced upon three legs that contained stairs and lifts that would permit the public to enter directly from the plaza below through a glass wall around the outside. But the engineers from Severud–Elstad–Krueger of New York criticized the idea of piercing a round structure with three apertures as likely to destabilize the building. Paavo Simula, Revell's favourite structural engineer in Finland who had worked on the preliminary design for the Toronto building, came up with an alternative; he had recently built a water tower in Helsinki with a circular cap resting upon a single central column. The council chamber was redesigned along the same lines with a single massive trunk rising from the floor of the rotunda and branching out to form the floor of the chamber. Around the base of the trunk was a circular depression in the ground floor that would be developed as a Hall of Memory.[28] This structure would flare out into inclined diagonal struts to support a 14-inch thick cone surrounded by two post-tensioned ring beams. On top would rest a domed reinforced concrete roof 9 inches thick around the base and 4.5 inches at the top centre. The chamber was eventually integrated into the three-storey podium that ran between the two towers to provide them with more structural support.[29]

The third issue that proved much more contentious was Revell's plan for the shape and structure of the two

3·7
To hold up the
council chamber,
the trunk replaced
the tripod.

towers. The engineers in New York and at Parkin Associates pointed out that the curving inner faces of the towers with their pointed ends were shaped like the underside of an aircraft wing so that strong winds might produce severe lifting and twisting forces. Because of the different heights of the two towers (rising 290 and 225 feet above the podium), it was very difficult to predict the wind loads. It was decided that wooden scale models of the towers should be constructed and subjected to wind tunnel tests both in the United States and at the University of Toronto's Institute of Aerophysics. The results of the tests showed that wind velocities of 110 miles per hour at the top of the towers and 60 miles per hour at the bottom would produce pressures as high as 31 pounds per square inch and suction as high as 72 pounds per square inch.

This might result in enough force to strip the inner curtain walls right off the edges of the tower floors.[30]

Moreover, the Parkin engineers raised concerns about the interior structure of the tower floors. In keeping with progressive Scandinavian ideas about workplace equality, Revell had designed the flat floor slabs to be cantilevered from the solid back wall supported by beams that would taper from thirty-six inches at the rear to nine inches at the window, thus creating a clear open-space floor plan with secretarial offices near the windows and the executive offices located along the rear. The fear that wind forces might deflect these floor plates led the engineers to insist that a line of columns be inserted under the beams about sixteen feet from the rear walls so that the senior staff could be walled off behind glass parti-

The concrete structure of the office floors became more massive than the architects had hoped.

tions. The concerns about the wind forces also required that each tower be stiffened further by the central elevator service core and that the pointed ends of the buildings containing stair-service shafts be rounded and reinforced. The structural plan thus came to resemble more closely a conventional office building with each tower having a bulkier silhouette, particularly noticeable on the lower west tower which looked a bit like a squat cylindrical tank once its sharp fin-like ends had been shorn off.

Revell was apparently prepared to live with the blunting of the tower ends. As he told a reporter for the Toronto *Star* when he first saw the building nearing completion in the autumn of 1964, their look was somewhat different than he had originally envisaged but the result was

tolerable.[31] He was, however, furious with the Parkin engineers over their insistence on the insertion of the columns under each cantilever beam, since he remained convinced that his original design for the unsupported floors was quite sound.[32] For their part, the two Parkins, John B. and John C., felt somewhat aggrieved because the redrafting of a substantial number of drawings with Revell's reluctant assent had been done at a personal cost to them of $90,000, a price inflated by the need to get the task finished as rapidly as possible since the Stage II drawings and specifications had to be completed in early 1961 so that the city could prepare the tenders for the contractors.

Thus, as the planning process dragged on, relations between the two parties in the the Revell-Parkin part-

Winner **87**

nership sometimes got rather testy. In September 1961 Revell complained to John B. Parkin that the project was not bringing in enough revenue; the problem was compounded by the lack of correspondence between different sets of drawings as the city frequently insisted upon changes. The Finn thought the Canadian practice of making shop drawings had little purpose and consumed unnecessary time and money. Better to agree upon alterations in advance of making drawings. He suggested that Taivo Kappsi (a Canadian who was working in his Helsinki office) be brought in as chief designer to ensure coordination between the partners since Bengt Lundsten was returning to Finland.[33]

This suggestion produced an angry response from Parkin that he had "no further time available" for discussions but wanted to be sure "that your future course of action cannot lead to any misunderstanding which might prove to be against the best interests of the City Hall project ... I cannot agree with you that the City Hall commitment is economically less successful than originally anticipated." The architectural work was about in line with estimates, and he declined to comment on Revell's complaint about the wasteful duplication of drawings: "Unfortunately, I believe you are looking at this only from one point of view, and I think that the great success which has met the efforts of John B. Parkin Associates in connection with the political and economic aspects of this project indicate that, where at times you might have felt we were not cooperating because we were not wholly following your suggestions, we were, in fact, following what proved to be a wiser and more success-

ful course of action ... I am absolutely against introducing another chief designer to the project at this stage." It would be preferable for Revell to take someone from the Parkin staff to replace Lundsten so time and money were not wasted upon schooling a newcomer at needless expense.[34]

Revell refused to drop the financial concerns, insisting that the city hall had been much less successful than anticipated for him and his firm since his expenses had exceeded estimates and he had been forced to draw upon his company, which had also incurred expenses which could not properly be charged to it though a legitimate part of the project.[35] By this time, his concerns about the profitability of the job had been exacerbated by his problems with the tax authorities. He had raised this matter from the very outset in the autumn of 1959 and hoped that the Revell-Parkin agreement had solved potential difficulties. At the end of that year, however, his Helsinki lawyers had passed along an opinion that his tax liabilities rested upon the question of whether he had immigrated and moved his household to Canada. If he was still a resident of Finland and doing business out of his Helsinki office, he could hardly claim that work done on the Toronto city hall should be taxed only in Canada.[36] In the continuing absence of a tax treaty, both countries were claiming taxes upon the income earned on the job in Toronto. If he went back to Helsinki, the Finnish authorities would demand that he pay taxes on his Canadian income, which, compounded with what he had already owed Ottawa, would make for a total rate of over 100 per cent. It was suggested to Revell that he ought to relocate his practice to some more tax-friendly place like Switzerland as Alvar Aalto had done, but he refused to consider severing his Finnish roots.[37]

In the autumn of 1961 a possible means of escape from this fiscal disaster seemed available. Professor Lawrence Anderson asked him to come and spend a term teaching at the Massachusetts Institute of Technology (MIT) in 1962. If Revell relocated to Boston he could commute to Toronto for three days a week, thereby eliminating the Canadian taxation. He even asked MIT to consider paying his travel expenses, which would not then be taxable. Anderson advised that the university preferred not to cover the commuting expenses but offered to raise the stipend for the fifteen weeks of term from $5,000 to $7,200.[38]

Revell decided that he would not take up this offer in 1962. With his three daughters in school in Toronto, he was not keen to move his family to the United States. And he still felt attracted enough to Canada that he had purchased a lot on Post Road (in an exclusive area of the Toronto suburbs near to the offices on Don Mills Road) for $18,000 and drawn up plans for a house to be constructed there on which he calculated he would have to spend about $50,000.[39]

Furthermore, with the amount of work required on the city hall winding down somewhat, Revell had leased his own premises in an office building in the nearby Don Mills plaza. He had begun to plan an entry into the architectural competition for the design of a headquarters for the World Health Organization in Geneva. Bengt Lunsten and Seppo Valjus often left the Parkin offices at 1500 Don Mills Road late in the afternoon and went to the other place to work into the evening on the WHO project. Their impression that Toronto resembled the "Wild West" was reinforced one night when there was a knock on the door, and Lundsten, who was expecting Revell to join them, unlocked it to find himself confronted by two Toronto policemen with drawn revolvers. They said that they suspected the architects were burglars because their office was the only one in the building showing a light and threatened to handcuff the Finns before the confrontation was defused.[40]

By early 1962, however, Revell's financial situation had become extremely worrying to him. He sent Edmund Orlowski, the comptroller at Parkin Associates, details of his Finnish earnings for 1959 and 1960, observing, "I cannot overlook the situation but I very well understand it is bad enough."[41] The Canadian tax authorities were pursuing him for unpaid taxes. His Toronto lawyer advised that, as a resident of Canada, he must include as taxable all sources of income whether received from inside or outside the country. Compounding the problem, as he confided to Graham Tudor at Parkin Associates, was the fact that "the finances of the City Hall work are so weak especially from the point [sic] of Revell & Co." In January 1962 he sold a house that he had bought (the one on Post Road was never built), telling John B. Parkin that the taxation question had been finally decided with the worst possible consequences, and Viljo Revell and Company was in an "unbearable" position with no profits coming in from the Revell-Parkin partnership. He decided that he would accept MIT's offer in 1963. He told his lawyer, "I can in no case afford to be considered as a citizen [sic] of Canada during the year 1963. Please advise me how it is best to arrange our moving so that it is really watertight."[42]

In the midst of his tax troubles Revell also received some dispiriting information. At the beginning of 1962, he was approached by Toronto architect Robert Fairfield enquiring whether he would collaborate on preparing a plan for the redevelopment of the south side of Queen Street opposite the civic square. He told John B. Parkin that, if he had been asked about such a possibility in Finland, he would have refused outright on the grounds that he already had the city of Toronto as a client and ought not to take an active part as a consultant or judge in a related project in which the city would have a major say. Nor did he want to be in competition with Parkin Associates for a job. However, he asked Eric Arthur for advice on what to do since he was inclined (no doubt in part owing to his shaky finances) to enter to the collaboration if that was acceptable in Canada, provided that he was in agreement with the other architect on major questions of design.[43]

John B. Parkin replied that Fairfield had also been in touch with him and that Revell should be "extremely careful" about any discussions or commitments outside "our present arrangements." Still, only one proposal for the development of the south side of Queen would be chosen, and Revell-Parkin should do its best to be involved in any such scheme.[44] But discouraging news came privately to Revell from his lawyer, James Renwick, whom he had also asked about acting as a design consultant for this and perhaps other opportunities in Toronto. The answer was that the Finn might have a document stating that he was a member of the Ontario Association of Architects, but, having looked at the association's charter and the laws of Ontario, the lawyer advised that this was not the case.[45]

Way back in January 1957, when the city council had first approved an international competition, Eric Arthur pointed out to Mayor Nathan Phillips that the Architects Act required anyone registered to be a British subject domiciled in Ontario or to have declared an intention to become a Canadian citizen. Temporary licences were available only to residents of the British Commonwealth so that the legislation would have to be amended to permit a non-Briton to be licensed to practise. Arthur suggested that the act should be changed, something that could be done quickly and easily enough if the OAA supported the amendment. However, the Registration Board of the OAA simply altered its regulations to permit a foreigner who won an international competition to receive approval to practise provided that the person was associated with a bona fide Ontario architect.[46]

Renwick told Revell that, any document notwithstanding, the OAA had "no jurisdiction" over him or his activities, and that it would be an offence for him to hold himself out as an "architect" in Ontario. That would include preparing or offering to prepare any sketches or drawings for a proposed building or an alteration. Only if he was careful not to use the term "architect" and avoid preparing any such renderings could the Finn involve himself in a building project.[47] That, of course, put an end to Revell participating in any potentially lucrative Queen Street redevelopment scheme with Fairfield or any other architect, though the technical invalidity of his Ontario architect's licence seems never to have been revealed publicly.

In October 1962 Revell leased an apartment in Boston.[48] He would now commute to Toronto to consult about the city hall as required. Indeed, he soon received a request from the city's development commissioner, Walter Manthorpe, who had been placed in charge of the recommendations about the south side of Queen Street, to get together when next he was in Toronto. Manthorpe wrote, "I feel it is of primary importance to have the benefit of a talk with you regarding the general architectural characteristics which you would wish to see established in order to provide the fitting enclosure of the south side of the square." Revell arranged to meet with Manthorpe in mid-December and received thanks for his great assistance, because the commissioner felt he could play an "essential role" in assisting the city council in its decisions about the redevelopment provided that this had no adverse effects upon the Parkin firm. Manthorpe soon concluded that the only way to ensure a "finite" design for the south side of Queen was to recommend that the city expropriate the entire property, which was eventually approved with the lands to be leased to the successful developer.[49]

While teaching at MIT, Revell travelled to Toronto frequently in early 1963. His increasingly jaundiced views about his treatment by the city were captured by a letter in January to his associate Heikki Castrén back in Helsinki when he wrote, "Tomorrow I leave for Toronto taking with me a big bottle of nerve pills."[50] By that time, changes to the council chamber recommended by Revell and agreed to by city council back in June 1962 had led the contractor, who had originally predicted that no extra costs would be incurred, to demand more money. Revell explained to the city property commissioner (who was overseeing the entire project) that the alterations were necessary. The Stage II drawings had made the essential change to replace the three free-standing legs supporting the chamber to the single central shaft, which had been done at a late stage in great haste in order to allow the tenders to be prepared. As a result, not all the costs were carefully calculated. The elimination of the three legs had exposed the circular glass wall behind, which had produced an unfortunate effect upon the views of the council chamber from the square to the south; it became clear that reflections on the glass would create the appearance of a solid wall hiding the shape of the chamber and the shaft within. So after much study the architects had moved the glass wall and the entrances about eleven feet nearer the centre of the chamber, thereby reducing the wall's height by six feet but greatly improving its elegance and transparency. Council had approved the changes in June 1962 but, faced with additional costs, got cold feet in 1963 when presented with a letter from the contractor claiming an additional $250,000 on account of delays in providing drawings.[51]

The architects and city officials rejected this claim, and in March 1963 council voted 9–1 to refuse additional funds for the changes. City officials imposed a "freeze" on all "design changes."[52] Gradually work resumed though by then Revell was in Helsinki. Later on, city officials could discover no record of his presence in Toronto after mid-February 1963, though he may, of course, have continued to visit while teaching at MIT since the term would not have ended until late spring. By the summer, Revell was sufficiently disconnected to ask John B. Parkin for a report on how things were going because the Finnish newspapers were giving "a very strange picture of the situation." A month later, Parkin reported that the contractor had finally been persuaded to name a completion date for the building of December 1964, thirty-eight months after ground was broken. There seemed less and less need for frequent visits to Toronto by Viljo Revell.[53]

Though he was back in Finland, Ottawa kept pestering him about a previous balance of unpaid taxes owing of almost $2,000.[54] In the autumn of 1963 he visited Mexico but fell ill from a stroke that required a long convalescence. Eventually returning to Finland, he resisted all entreaties to come to Toronto on orders from his doctors. By early the following year, the accounting department at John B. Parkin Associates was reporting that the Canadian firm of Viljo Revell and Company had run a loss in 1963. Revell had been paid $1,920 in salary by the company but $1,850 of that had been used to pay off tax arrears from earlier years. Another loss was expected in 1964. The value of the Canadian company's shares depended entirely upon the commission to be paid for the city hall project, but that was unlikely to be collected for two or three years. The Revell-Parkin partnership had also run a loss in 1963, and a small profit anticipated in

1964 would have to go to offset this. National Revenue in Ottawa was still demanding $2,037.10 from Revell for tax arrears.[55] After early 1963, Revell made only a single brief visit to Toronto, in October 1964, to view his unfinished building. Within a week of his return to Finland, he suffered a heart attack and died at the age of only fifty-four.

Like other people who pressed for dramatic changes in the city, Revell encountered a variety of obstacles. His winning design was widely applauded at first, but fears about cost overruns necessitated changes in the design of the towers and the council chamber. With the help of Parkin Associates, he was able to produce alterations which overcame the fears of a majority of the aldermen, and the construction contract was finally signed in the autumn of 1961. But even then he was plagued by the dithering of council about whether or not to include costly additions like a restaurant or cafeteria. By the end of 1962, his tax problems had led him to move to the United States, and, though he continued to visit Toronto to consult, he ceased to be a permanent resident. His ill health in late 1963 led him to refuse even to visit until his final brief stay the following autumn. His building would become a symbol of the city, but his treatment reflected a familiar pattern for those who proposed radical new departures.

Construction

PREVIOUS PAGE
4.1
Ruination and
construction;
the Neo-classical
Registry Office
makes way for the
new building.

George Bell seemed an unlikely choice when it was announced in the spring of 1963 that he had been appointed to push the new city hall to completion in time for a formal opening in September 1965. He had never had anything to do directly with the city's real estate or buildings, and he was due to retire from the municipal service at the beginning of 1965, when he would reach the age of seventy, even before the building was finished. Yet Bell had a well-founded reputation around city hall for taking on and completing important projects. He had joined the ranks of city employees in 1919 upon return from serving overseas with the Canadian Expeditionary Force. His first job was to straighten out and index the old records that had accumulated in the attic of the city hall over the previous twenty years, for which he was paid $21 per week. Between the wars he rose through the ranks of the civil service, and in 1945 he was given the task of setting up a proper personnel department. One of his earliest acts was to rewrite the forms required from new recruits so as to eliminate questions concerning religion, lodge, and club memberships, something of a dramatic departure for Toronto where many policemen were Masons and the mayors all Protestants and often dedicated Orangemen.

The first department that Bell headed was the water-works, and in 1954 he was tapped to take over the Parks and Recreation Department, where he greatly expanded the city's facilities: park visitors were even encouraged to walk on the grass. For his energy and attention to detail, his admirers compared him favourably to New York's Robert Moses. He was experienced in the letting of contracts and in pushing projects to completion and had had extensive dealings with architects and contractors. In 1963, when the new city hall fell months behind schedule and threatened to bog down altogether under the management of Property Commissioner Harry Rogers, Mayor Donald Summerville backed him to take on the huge construction project despite the fact that, as an alderman, Summerville had previously become embroiled in a great row with Bell over the management of the city's High Park.

Everyone who has ever been involved with a construction job knows that it will not always run smoothly. Clients want to occupy their new premises on a certain date at the projected cost or under budget, but they along with architects and contractors are bound to find themselves at odds over design details, the cost and availability of materials, the quality of finished work, and a myriad of other unexpected problems. A public project like the city hall encountered more than the usual number of hitches. The building was large and complicated and the ultimate decision-making authority rested with elected politicians whose decisions were taken by majority votes. They, of course, were always looking over their shoulders for hints that the voters might consider plans ill-advised or extravagant, and elections could change the complexion of the city council so that what was already decided might be reversed – to the dismay of civil servants, contractors, and architects who were hustling to meet deadlines. Sometimes it seemed remarkable that anything at all got done in reasonable time and cost.

The city hall project seemed to start promisingly enough: the architects went to work and produced preliminary drawings. But soon there were serious questions about the cost of the project, and the designers were sent back to their drawing boards to seek economies. In the end more than almost three years elapsed until excavations began in October 1961. Work proceeded for the next year and a half but with constant complaints from all sides about the need to make changes and disputes about who should pay for them. Eventually, in early 1963, the contractors threatened to cease work altogether if not paid more, which the council refused to do. At that point, George Bell was brought in by the city to try and drive the job to completion by the autumn of 1965. He succeeded in time for the formal opening that September, seven years after Viljo Revell's design had been chosen the winner in the international competition.

Before any work could start, Revell and his partners at John B. Parkin Associates had to translate the Finn's imaginative entry into preliminary drawings so that the city council could approve a contract with the architects. Then came more detailed drawings and the costing of the project so that tenders could be called for the work to be done at a price that the city council would approve. Also with the goal of making the scheme financially viable, the Municipality of Metropolitan Toronto would have to agree to rent space in the building, a matter about which

Metro chair Fred Gardiner was prone to having second thoughts.

At the outset, the city had to define the exact area to be occupied by the new civic square. Meanwhile, the municipal Parking Authority was already at work on the underground garage at the south end of the square, and the second, northerly stage of garage construction had to be planned to mesh with the underpinnings of the new building. Every one of these factors had implications for the others, which made progress all the more challenging.

By the spring of 1959, Planning Commissioner Matthew Lawson, Property Commissioner Harry Rogers, and City Solicitor W.G. Angus had prepared a draft contract to be signed with the Revell-Parkin partnership which would make Revell and the Parkins jointly and severally responsible for the performance of their professional services, though the document "specifically indicates that Mr. Rewell [sic] shall be primarily responsible to the city for architectural and landscaping design and planning involved." On the city side, the project would be supervised by the Property Department, which would disburse fees equal to 6 per cent of the total costs: one-fifth ($255,000) payable when the preliminary drawings of Stage I were completed, $710,250 for the detailed drawings of Stage II, and monthly payments of $318,750, for a grand total of $1.275 million. In March, Mayor Nathan Phillips persuaded city council to pass a by-law approving the agreement for the Stage I drawings, with a detailed estimate of the total cost to be ready by November.[1]

There were already problems because, while in January 1959 city council had formally approved a deal to rent space in the new building to Metro, worries about spiralling costs led to a change of heart by Fred Gardiner. He complained that Revell's design resembled a "Taj Mahal" and reverted to his earlier view that "in his opinion a majority of the citizens of Toronto did not want a prestige building involving excessive expenditure for style but desired it to be a dignified functional building." He thought a conventional office building of 400,000 square feet could be built to house the offices of both the city and Metro at a cost of $25 per square foot or just $14 million over all. Nathan Phillips, fearing that if Metro backed out the new building would be economically unviable, did his best not to rush the negotiations because Gardiner might easily persuade his council to reject any agreement.[2]

Slow progress was the order of the day, as shown by a series of meetings in April 1959 between people from John B. Parkin Associates and a host of city bureaucrats. The civic square proved particularly contentious. The architects and the Planning Board wanted all the streets that crossed the site closed up to create a pedestrian precinct, but the traffic planners were determined to keep open Chestnut Street running up the west side next to Osgoode Hall, with a view to widening it to allow vehicles coming north from downtown on York Street to be diverted by a jog at Queen. And the traffic people also wanted the northerly twenty feet of Revell's building lopped off so that Hagerman Street could be widened from forty-four to sixty feet. Round and round

went the discussions, with the man from Traffic and Works demanding to know "what protection of their rights individual departments would have once the planning operation gained momentum."

Property Commissioner Harry Rogers, who had been appointed coordinator of the city hall and square project, declared that no decision on the precise boundaries of the square could be taken until it was known if Chestnut Street was to be closed and Hagerman widened. For the architects, John C. Parkin could promise only that there would be continuous liaison between his office and Rogers's people. On 2 April, Parkin announced that Revell had not yet settled permanently in Toronto but was expected in a day or two, though he does not appear to have attended any of these gatherings. Over the next month, nineteen meetings were held, mostly rehashing the same issues. Eventually it was concluded that the boundaries of the square ought to be Bay, Queen, the west side of Chestnut, and the north side of Hagerman, but Planning Commissioner Lawson reminded everybody that city council alone would make the final decision.[3]

Another particularly contentious matter was the space to be allocated to various civic departments in the new building. For the design competition, management consultants Woods Gordon had compiled the space requests of various units, both city and Metro, but now Metro officials submitted demands for an additional 10,000 square feet so it was decided to have the consultants review all these allotments once again. That led city bureaucrats to reconsider their requests and produced demands for 13 per cent more area. In the end, Rogers rejected these inflated demands and even ordered a reduction of 5,300 square feet overall though he did grant Metro its additional 10,000 square feet. Fortunately, Revell's design provided for 770,000 square feet of enclosed space, the maximum allowed under the competition conditions.

Soon some officials began complaining about the precise location of their departments within the building. Acting City Treasurer W.M. Campbell insisted that he was not opposed to the twin towers but registered his "deepest dissatisfaction" with his staff being placed on six floors of the smaller west tower separated in the middle by an equipment floor. Even the ground-floor wickets for the treasury staff were hardly adequate since they had to be visited three times yearly by large crowds of taxpayers, many of them "new Canadians." Campbell's efforts to seize space in podium from the Registry Office were rejected, but he made enough fuss that the plan now grouped his staff on four contiguous floors in the larger east tower. [4]

By the end of May 1959, the architects reported that the Stage I drawings had been completed at a scale of 1/32nd of an inch to the foot and they were ready to begin work on Stage II at 1/8 inch to the foot along with new models of the building and the square. [5] But not until October was it finally decided that Chestnut Street would be closed off. The proposal to connect to York Street was dropped, though this was not to be announced publicly since the city still hoped to acquire certain provincially owned land on the south side of Queen Street and did not wish to weaken its bargaining position. The boundaries of the square were now fixed at Bay, Queen, Chestnut, and Hagerman, subject to approval by the city council. [6]

The competition conditions had stated that the "city was not setting a limit to the cost of the project." By then it was clear that the oft-cited figure of $18 million was "in no way related to current plans." (That figure had originally been conjured up more or less out of thin air by F.H. Marani on the assumption that a building could provide about 600,000 square feet of usable floor space at an approximate cost of $30 per square foot.) In the autumn of 1959 one journalist applauded Mayor Phillips for turning to John B. Parkin and declaring, "Go ahead with Stage II; this is a very happy moment in my life," since it was only by such boldness that Toronto would get its "most magnificent" building in half a century. [7]

The prospect of committing $30 million and maybe as much as $40 million was enough to alarm Fred Gardiner thoroughly. He stalled at entering any agreement to rent space for Metro and in February 1960 revived his idea of a year earlier of simply duplicating the Neo-classical Registry Office (dating from 1917) with a similar structure at the northeast corner of the square to serve as a courthouse and linking the two together with an ordinary office block: "The type of building I have in mind is very similar to the Crown Life building at the corner of Bloor and Church Street. It is a very dignified structure of limestone and dark green Canadian granite. It is not as ornate or imposing as some might suggest for a city hall, but it is dignified and attractive and is economical from the point of view of the usable space provided." In other words, he envisioned a structure like that proposed by the consortium of three architectural firms (including the designers of Crown Life, Marani and Morris) which the voters had rejected in 1955.[8]

To counter this latest threat, Mayor Phillips called in the architects and told them that he believed the most he could persuade city council to accept was a project costing $25 million. He also managed to fight off an effort by the Parking Authority to have the city put up the $3 million needed to build a 1,100-space second stage of the garage under the northern part of the square.[9]

The architects quietly[10] got to work reviewing Revell's design in order to cut costs. The changes in the interest of economy and structural stability discussed in the previous chapter were developed. All this reworking meant that the architects could not promise the city that the Stage II drawings and specifications would be ready as planned by January 1961 to permit the calling of tenders. By early February, it was announced that designs had been reworked to make the building more compact and efficient while retaining all its essential features, but the completed documents were not ready for submission to the city until the end of April. When finally submitted near the end of the month, John B. Parkin was able to advise project coordinator Harry Rogers that he believed that costs might be around $24 million or perhaps less.[11]

This emboldened Mayor Phillips to seek the approval of city council to go ahead, and to approach Fred Gardiner once more about Metro renting space in the new building. The city solicitor and his Metro counterpart were directed to draft a thirty-year lease with the stream of rental payments to go towards servicing the debentures that the city was to issue to finance the project. By June, the executive committee of Metro council recommended the purchase of the old city hall for $4.5 million and the rental of 250,000 square feet in the new building.[12]

A defensible cost estimate and a firm agreement with Metro were necessary because the city had to receive the approval of the provincially appointed Ontario Municipal Board to borrow the required funds without the approval of the ratepayers. The board insisted on reviewing the city's entire capital works program for 1961 through 1965 and its plan for debt retirement, as well as getting an assurance that the provincial government would pass legislation at the next session of the legislature to permit the city to lease space to Metro. Fortunately, both Gardiner and Phillips were staunch Conservatives who could count upon the cooperation of their fellow party member Premier Leslie Frost. Before the OMB's scheduled hearing, the cabinet discussed the matter, and Frost promised to write to board chair J.A. Kennedy (another Conservative) to advise him that the government intended to act and even to make the legislation retroactive if necessary.[13]

At a short hearing on 5 October 1961, the OMB considered the city's request to make the capital expenditure. G. Allan Burton, head of Simpson's department store and chair of an advisory committee on downtown redevelopment, testified in favour of the application. Former mayor Allan Lamport and the Metro Property Owners' Association demanded that the ratepayers be polled once again. Kennedy observed that the voters had already been consulted twice about a new city hall and noted that, from the rentals paid by Metro, $780,000 would be earmarked annually to pay interest and retire the debentures. Within forty-eight hours, he delivered the board's decision allowing the city to borrow $20.8 million by issuing thirty-year debentures without a vote.[14]

Meanwhile, with plans and specifications at last in hand, the city could begin preparation of the tender documents, which were released in June 1963. Immediately, however, the Ontario General Contractors' Association protested strongly against a condition that gave Harry Rogers authority to decide about what methods of construction should be used, claiming that this was arbitrary and made bidders responsible for all errors and omissions. Rogers replied that the terms followed city practices in place for years and years. Any dispute would be fairly settled, and mistakes would not be corrected at the contractor's expense since changes would be treated as extras to be added to costs. Mayor Phillips telephoned the association and used strong language to try to convince the members that the city would not be held up in this way. With this backing, Rogers insisted that the conditions remain as specified.[15]

When four tenders were opened on 17 August, it was discovered that three firms[16] had followed the advice of their association and modified the terms of their offers. Only Anglin Norcross Ontario, subsidiary of a large Montreal-based company, had complied with the city's requirements. As a result, officials decided that this was the only valid bid. The aldermen were so delighted that

the Anglin Norcross bid had come in at only $23.58 million that they readily accepted Nathan Phillips's suggestion that an additional floor be added to each tower, which was predicted, without any real assessment, to cost an additional $600,000. When the cost of the $96,000 in architects' fees for the rejected 1955 design plus $110,600 for the international competition were included, the total expenditure was calculated at about $25.1 million. Council quickly approved the additional floors despite the lack of any serious analysis of the cost and decided unanimously to honour the mayor by naming the square after him.[17]

By the end of September, plans were afoot for a formal sod turning. Rather than simply wielding the traditional chrome-plated shovel, John B. Parkin suggested that it would be "more effective" to have Nathan Phillips depress a plunder which would trigger a small explosion somewhere near the southern edge of the square.[18] Sadly, nothing came of this fine idea. On 7 November 1961, Phillips's sixty-ninth birthday, he told a crowd that "some historians may be exact enough to set down the fact that although it took almost fifteen years to get to the starting line, none of us arrived out of breath." "All of the people ... have shared this dream." The international competition had turned out to be a tremendous success once Eric Arthur "locked the judges in the attic of the City Hall to sweat out their decision." Fred Gardiner and the Metro government had decided to "get married" and join in the project, perhaps a first step towards the amalgamation of the entire greater Toronto area into one unit. In cooperation with Parkin Associates, Viljo Revell had produced the plans for a building that embodied "a whole new concept of architecture." Alderman Horace Brown even penned a celebratory poem entitled "Soul of the City," promising that Torontonians would "see in these twin towers the hand of God" along with the wonders of peace and democracy.

The contract specified that the architects would "liaise" with the property commissioner about design, planning, and construction, and he would be in charge of the "conduct of the contract" so far as the city and Anglin Norcross were concerned, as well as acting as the contact and arbitrator between the contractors and Revell-Parkin. The Parking Authority retained John B. Parkin Associates to design the underground garage beneath the northerly part of the square, whose construction must be coordinated with the foundations of the west tower. The Registry Office would eventually be vacated and demolished at some point during construction, its staff relocated to the new building.[19]

Even before construction had been under way for a month, however, there were bad omens. The Anglin Norcross contract specified completion in thirty months, but the architects reported that the contractors had unilaterally extended that period to thirty-five and one-half. Meanwhile, city council added to the problems. In September 1961 several aldermen had requested a report on the inclusion of a restaurant or cafeteria in the building rather than simply providing employee lunchrooms on most floors of the towers. The architects reported that a four- or five-hundred seat cafeteria could be created in a space in the towers on top of the podium, with the food

arriving by dumbwaiter from kitchens in the basement. Or a single large cafeteria could be installed in the windowless basement underneath the public library beneath the east tower. If something fancier was envisaged, a restaurant seating up to two hundred might be created on the twenty-fifth floor of the taller east tower with an observation deck above. The restaurant might cost an additional $225,000, the cafeteria about $250,000, but in any event decisions needed to be taken quickly since the floor layouts were to be fixed early in 1962 and later changes would be costly.[20]

Viljo Revell told a local newspaper columnist that he was unhappy with the idea of hiding a cafeteria away in a windowless basement. A professor at the Osgoode Hall Law School run by the Law Society also protested to Controller Philip Givens against the idea: "The planned city hall is known around the world already. But somehow that old Hogtown[21] mentality has blocked the vision of our city fathers somewhat." Givens pointed out that a rooftop restaurant atop the east tower hardly seemed ideal. The top two floors (twenty-six and twenty-seven) would be filled with mechanical equipment so that a dining room would have to be on the twenty-fifth, which meant that the views westward over the smaller tower would be rather limited. Because of the curved floor plan with its narrow ends and the solid outside wall, only a few of the seats would have views south and west towards the downtown and Lake Ontario. This would be nothing like the "Top of the Mark" in San Francisco, and the city could hardly subsidize a small restaurant for its publicity value.[22]

In May 1962 Phillips was told that construction was only about three weeks behind schedule and the time could be made up. Yet, when the contractors finally produced a critical progress report in July 1962, it indicated that the building would not be completed until late 1964 or the spring of 1965, seven months late. When Phillips complained about the slowness of the work, Anglin Norcross's president, R.W. Johnstone, laid the blame squarely upon others. The contract had been signed in October 1961, but the architects had failed to deliver the necessary drawings to permit work to go ahead at full speed. The delay seemed to put paid to Phillips's plans to invite the queen to formally open the building in the summer of 1964.[23]

Further complaints produced a lengthy indictment of the architects from the contractor in September 1962 about the way the job was being managed. Revell-Parkin had not even established a site office until early July, leaving the Anglin Norcross foremen nothing much to do except hold a daily "prayer meeting." Ten months of work had been done without a "straightforward" up-to-date set of plans and specifications for the subcontractors. Mechanical and electrical work was more or less at a standstill. Now the architects were complaining about the quality of the concrete work in the basement because of the failure to use special formwork, but they had failed to approve the use of readily available Canadian products. City Hall Coordinator Rogers demanded that Revell-Parkin undertake a full review of the situation. By the end of October, the Board of Control was informed that the architects did not even believe that

the deadlines in the critical progress report could be met, and that the plan for completion by the spring of 1965 included no allowance for strikes, bad weather, further design changes, or other unanticipated events.[24]

Matters were not helped by continuing uncertainty about other critical issues. Revell's design called for the outside walls of the towers to be clad in precast concrete panels with 3/4-inch-wide vertical strips of yellowish Botticino marble set about 1 1/4 inches apart that would cause the building to sparkle when floodlit. The $2.5-million contract to do the job was won by the Toronto Cast Stone Company, which had to develop a special machine to turn out the four thousand curved panels, each containing a hundred marble strips, within the required eighteen months.[25]

The contractors also wanted to use the panels as the formwork for the eighteen-inch-thick reinforced concrete structural walls inside them that actually supported the towers, something never done before on such a large scale. Revell-Parkin had serious doubts about the scheme because they believed that gaps between the panels would have to be carefully sealed up. Anglin Norcross insisted that using separate formwork would add at least four months to the three years that the towers were expected to be under construction.[26] In the end the contractors got their way.

In October 1962 Harry Rogers advised that the project was already eight weeks behind the thirty-eight-month schedule though Anglin Norcross refused to alter its progress report, insisting that a margin of error of 10 per cent was quite normal. The contractor still claimed to believe that parts of the building could be occupied in October 1964 if the queen were invited to open it then.[27]

Anglin's R.W. Johnstone turned his guns upon the city, complaining that he had been protesting about delays and indecision since July 1962 but Rogers had persuaded him to be patient. Yet required information had not been delivered while the dithering about the cafeteria continued. As a result, by late 1962 only 2 per cent of the mechanical and electrical work had been completed; the east tower should have risen to the fifth floor and the west to the fourth but, owing to the lack of drawings, little had been achieved above grade.[28]

Calling these allegations "very serious," Rogers tried to deflect them by demanding a "full explanation" from the architects. They, of course, replied that they could not respond to general criticisms but that the concrete work did not meet specifications. The contractors had failed to erect the necessary formwork or reused it so frequently that the finishing on the exterior columns that would support the podium was not acceptable.

Anglin Norcross tried to bring the city to heel by threatening to stop all work until all the changes were properly compiled and submitted. If a cafeteria was to be included, a formal order was needed at once.[29] The contractors admitted that such a drastic step was bound to anger the architects and the city, but they insisted work could not continue without an agreement on outstanding payments, having wasted $250,000 on overhead which must be reimbursed.[30]

On 17 January 1963 Anglin Norcross addressed a letter to John B. Parkin and Viljo Revell announcing the intention to stop construction entirely. Work would resume only with the issuance of formal "Contemplated Change Orders," and henceforth Anglin Norcross would stick to the letter of the contract. No longer would the contractors accept alterations to shop drawings unless approved by the city, since the architects appeared merely to be assuming that some changes would cost more, some less, maintaining a rough balance. Most crucial was the decision on whether to include food services.[31]

On 21 January, city council finally voted in principle against a rooftop restaurant, endorsing the installation of the windowless basement cafeteria in the southeast corner of the building. Negotiations with the contractor ultimately fixed the cost of the cafeteria at $867,568 so that an additional $692,558 had to be provided. Still, the elimination of thirty-two lunchrooms in the tower would free up 10,660 square feet of space to be used in other ways. Council approved this plan in May 1963.[32]

By that time, Nathan Phillips had been defeated at the election in December 1962, depriving the project of its most prominent backer. A number of people attributed the victory of former controller Donald Summerville to growing discontent among the voters with the delays and the rising cost of the city hall. R.W. Johnstone laid out his complaints personally to the new mayor at the end of January. Over the sixteen months since the contract was signed, Anglin Norcross had been beset by constant demands for design changes. The contractors had told the architects and Harry Rogers back in September 1962 that concrete for the floor slab at the southeast corner could not be poured until a decision on the cafeteria was taken. The empty forms had been in place for two and a half months while the contractor awaited direction. In addition, there were no less than sixty other changes requiring similar approval. In late 1962 there had been 370 people employed on the site, a number that should by then have increased to over 500, but, owing to lack of approvals, this had now been reduced to 249 and would soon be cut in half again.

Johnstone said it was "ridiculous" that there should be enough work for only ninety-four carpenters and thirty-two mechanical tradesmen. Over the previous two months, Anglin Norcross had undertaken $120,000 worth of work without proper authorization, but, with overhead running at $57,800 per month, such a big job could not be efficiently carried out in "bits and pieces." To get the project "back on the rails," the firm required proper signed instructions. A "deep freeze" must be imposed on further changes to create a "green light" for Anglin Norcross to proceed on the work with no more adjustments ordered by the architects.[33]

In a letter to Rogers, Johnstone rejected demands to conform to the "concept" of the architects unless the city agreed to pay for remedying any errors or omissions. He should have put his foot down sooner and now intended to press his demands for $250,000 in overhead wasted since September 1962 and would "not take mañana for an answer." Rogers protested the tone of Johnstone's letter and insisted that he had sought only to see the work continue in a businesslike manner. Naturally, the press soon got wind of the dispute, and charges were heard that Phillips had concealed the fact that the delays were wasting thousands of city dollars.[34]

Donald Summerville had acted as city budget chief under Phillips but claimed not to have known anything about these problems. He summoned a private meeting of the four controllers, John B. Parkin, and Johnstone, along with Rogers and the city solicitor, to try and iron things out. Rogers insisted that he had always dealt with the project as "just another building" and never believed that there were any real problems. Why had Johnstone told Phillips that the building could be ready for "beneficial occupancy" by the autumn of 1964? The contractor replied that he had made clear that only a portion of the building would be usable then and that completion would require many more months. Rogers was told that in future he should place any such information confidentially before the Board of Control.[35]

Summerville meanwhile tried to stop the Toronto *Star*'s "inaccurate and misleading" criticisms of him. When the charges and counter-charges began floating about, he had not been mayor and did not know what was going on, so it was "completely erroneous" to blame him. As mayor, he had learned of the problems and now agreed to freeze the plans and to get on with the work at top speed. Rogers tried to defend himself privately by insisting that he had never consulted Summerville as budget chief because he did not consider the contractor's claims for additional payments valid. John B. Parkin sought to shift any blame by insisting that the architects had discovered a claim from the contractors for extra work involved in the demolition of Eaton's parking garage on the square hidden in the price of another task. Yet he urged that nothing more be said publicly about this since any controversy would only arouse the population. Rogers admitted that big changes had been made, but he argued that, since these would have to be undertaken by the contractor without being put out to tender, the original design should be adhered to as far as possible.[36]

In March 1963 council voted 14–9 to refuse any additional payments to the contractor, and the city imposed a "freeze" on all "design changes." By 1 May the architects estimated that the structural work was now five months behind schedule, mechanical work even more. The podium structure would not be completed until 1964, and at present Anglin Norcross seemed unable to produce a revised time line. Rogers now claimed that it was impossible even to predict an opening date.[37]

This admission seems to have sealed Rogers's fate. Eager to secure some cover from criticism that time and money were being wasted on the project, the Board of Control moved the very next day to dismiss Rogers as the coordinator of the city hall and square project. The choice of his replacement was George Bell, the city's commissioner of parks and recreation. In his new job he was given a raise of $2,000 in his salary to $19,000 per year.[38]

Bell immediately wrote to Viljo Revell at the offices of John B. Parkin Associates directing him to send all correspondence about the project to him and to advise him of any important meetings, though the way he addressed this letter showed how little he apparently knew about the project.[39] Bell soon found that he could not even provide a complete cost estimate because of additions and deletions to the contract and change orders whether approved by council or not. Within ten days he had prepared a report on a meeting he had convened with the architects and the contractor. The contract contained no specific completion date, but Anglin Norcross had now definitely confirmed that only very limited occupancy of the new building would be possible by December 1964. Even that risked exposing employees and the public to harm from construction accidents and might delay work to some extent. Therefore, city council must decide whether it would be wiser to leave the whole structure empty until really finished – barring strikes – in the early autumn of 1965. Bell's cautious recommendation was to announce no firm opening date at present.[40]

By now, it was clear that city council was not going to cease discussing time-consuming and expensive modifications to the building. In March 1963 Rogers had been directed to have the architects report on the cost of reviving the scheme to put a 144-seat restaurant atop the east tower with an observation deck on the twenty-seventh floor above. A serious problem was that, if the building were closed around 10 p.m. while the restaurant stayed open until 1 a.m., security would have to be provided to shepherd patrons on the ground floor to and from the elevators and to ensure that people did not disembark in the municipal offices above. Yet the idea proved hard to kill. That summer, some aldermen were still toying with the restaurant idea. Revell was not unsympathetic, especially if he could control the layout and the interiors, but he was determined not to do any design work without an amendment to the contract to ensure that the city should pay for this. He reminded John B. Parkin that they both knew "how easily the number of such planning variations can grow the more you make them, if a clear order is not received first."[41]

By mid-1963, popular enthusiasm for the new city hall had evidently begun to dwindle among Torontonians. On 9 July radio station CKEY broadcast an editorial warning against the rising cost of the project. Now there was talk that the total expenditure might balloon as high as $30 million owing to the number of changes being demanded. What had begun with "a burst of civic pride" was now being viewed "apathetically if not downright antagonistically" as indecision on the part of a city council that had created "one more big bureaucratic jumble." Mayor Summerville defended his conduct, insisting that he had been the first elected official to bring the project under firm control by fixing certain elements of the design and recruiting George Bell.[42]

Eric Arthur had mostly been absent from the public eye of late, but now he surfaced in an effort to rekindle support. In the introduction to a pamphlet published by the city, and rather archly titled *New City Hall and Nathan Phillips Square: A Sidewalk Superintendent's Report No. 1*,[43] he argued that despite "growing impatience" to see the building finished there was nothing to worry about. Arthur rehashed the history of the project from Nathan Phillips's visionary insistence upon holding an international competition. The original cost figure of $18 million had always been no more than "mythical." Despite a multitude of changes and the impact of inflation, "to the obvious joy of the multitude, including all

the daily newspapers, and the dismay of a rather vociferous uninformed minority, the lowest bid was well under the agreed maximum figure."

Arthur harked back to the creation of the old city hall. In 1899 Mayor John Shaw had faced a "hornet's nest" of criticism when he revealed that the building would cost half a million dollars more than the $2-million estimate. Yet the results had garnered well-deserved praise. Rising behind the hoardings at Queen and Bay streets was a new structure that would eventually dominate the city skyline like St Paul's in London or St Peter's in Rome. Arthur even repeated the (now privately abandoned) promise that Revell's building would be ready to open by the summer of 1964.

All the same, there were plain warnings that tight control over costs was needed. In the autumn of 1961 the Ontario Municipal Board had approved the city taking on $20 million in long-term debt to finance the $24.4-million project. But over the next eighteen months the city had made a succession of applications to the OMB for increases, pushing the total up to $25.7 million. The board was empowered to permit increases adding up to one-quarter of the total costs without ordering a further vote by the ratepayers, provided it was convinced of the city's fiscal capacity. Bell set out to arrive at a revised total and discovered that there were nearly $1.3 million in additional unaccounted expenditures, more than two-thirds of which would be needed for furnishing the new building.[44] And city council was still considering the conversion of the top of the east tower into a fancy restaurant for which no cost estimate existed.

J.A. Kennedy, the crusty chair of the OMB, called in Mayor Summerville and Controller Philip Givens along with Bell, the city treasurer, and the city solicitor to discuss the situation. Kennedy applauded the appointment of Bell, though he was particularly critical of council's casual decision in 1961 to add one floor to each tower at a notional cost of $600,000. That sum, he pointed out, had not been based on any kind of systematic analysis of the type needed in the management of a project of that size. While cost overruns were almost inevitable on such a large contract, care must be taken in spending public money. Kennedy agreed to grant the city's application to spend another $1.3 million since Bell was now monitoring costs as closely as possible and otherwise some work might have to stop altogether. But he made it clear that any future additions would have to be funded from current revenues, and that if the city came back to the OMB for any more sizable increases he would feel compelled to order a public hearing to listen to objections. Unless the case was extraordinarily strong, the OMB would almost certainly order a vote by the ratepayers. If the voters rejected such a proposal, the whole project might grind to a halt pending another costly and time-consuming revamp. CKEY welcomed the OMB decision, observing that Controller Allan Lamport, long a critic of the scheme, was entirely right to say, "It's about time."[45]

To placate Kennedy, Bell proposed to the mayor and the Board of Control that the city ought to drop the restaurant, which would save not only on construction costs but on the sizable fees to the architects for a redesign. In August 1963 Bell also persuaded the Board of Control that

it ought to avoid any expenditure on artwork and floodlighting for the building until it was completed. But the restaurant proposal stayed alive pending a cost estimate, now expected in October.[46]

How shaky were the promises to finish the project even by 1965 was dramatically demonstrated on 8 July 1963 when the carpenters went on strike. Throwing up picket lines, they caused a complete shutdown on the work for two days. Anglin Norcross warned that other strikes were quite possible, leading the architects to note succinctly, "Outlook grim." More walkouts did ensue and it was not until late August that all the trades were back at work and no further labour interruptions were anticipated. The contractors still had no revised schedule for the completion of construction. And it was only then that Bell received a complete up-to-date set of drawings after repeated requests to the architects. In an effort to exercise more control over the work, the coordinator created the new position of construction superintendent, which was handed to city employee Raymond Bremner for two years from 30 September at an annual salary of $15,000.[47]

In November 1963 the city was advised by the architects that just to rough-in the space for the restaurant would involve structural changes costing over $550,000. The politicians continued to dither about whether or not such a venture could ever be economically viable. The OMB's Kennedy had made it clear that, if there were any more major changes, he would order a public hearing which could well result in a requirement that the ratepayers vote on such an expenditure. Bell advised that

4.2
The new
construction
reaches ground
level, 1963.

the city was already committed to spending $3.9 million in fiscal 1963, $2.5 million in 1964, and another $2 million in 1965 out of current revenues. Finally, the Board of Control agreed that, if the funds for the restaurant were not appropriated by city council before 15 November, the idea would be dropped. When no action was taken, the scheme finally faded away.[48]

George Bell was also concerned about the separate contract for the northerly half of the underground parking garage beneath the square, which had to be completed by 1 July 1964 to avoid interfering with work on the new building. The architects thought that the garage could be ready if tenders were called by June 1963, though that would require speedy work.[49] On 1 August 1963 it was announced that Perini Ltd had made the winning bid of $3.3 million. The first step was to excavate around the 1917 Registry Office building. Fifty-seven hundred square feet of the northerly section of that building had already been demolished in 1962, when it was concluded that the work on the foundations of the podium had rendered it unsafe, but the rest was still in use; what remained standing was to be torn down starting in May 1964, just as soon as the Registry staff could be moved out into temporary quarters in the podium.

The excavation work proceeded slowly in the autumn of 1963. Perini failed to deliver on the promise of a firm schedule in September, and soon there were complaints from judges sitting in Osgoode Hall, just across the street, that noise from the jackhammers breaking up concrete was disrupting trials. The sheriff of York County warned Bell that, if this nuisance did not cease, a summons for

contempt of court would be issued. All that could be done was to suggest that Mayor Summerville consult with the judiciary to see if the work could not be planned so as to minimize any interference.[50]

By February 1964, Perini was four or five weeks behind schedule, a delay the company blamed on limitations on driving piles to times when the courts were not sitting and the city's rules about trucking away the excavated soil over the Christmas holiday season. Bell rejected these excuses as "sheer nonsense," a ridiculous effort to establish grounds for a damage claim against the city. He warned the Parking Authority that he believed Perini was deliberately stalling on the work because it had failed to price some modifications to the contract for the north wall of the garage near the city hall. Further problems would be created like a chain reaction if the Registry Office building was not demolished as promised, because Anglin Norcross would not be able to start work on that part of the podium. This news was "highly disturbing" to the mayor, who requested a meeting between Perini and the Board of Control. Perini officials insisted that the delay was no more than five days, which could easily be rectified, and promised that demolition would be complete by 1 October 1964.[51]

The Registry Office was vacated on 1 May, but then St Clair House Wrecking, retained by Anglin Norcross to remove the building, failed to get busy. Promises to have the job done by 15 June and then by 10 July were not fulfilled. An effort by the city to hold Anglin Norcross liable for any damages claimed by Perini for delays on the garage work sparked a revival of the ill-tempered

exchanges between the city and the contractor. Anglin Norcross insisted that it had been promised that it could start work in January 1963, and that any losses to other parties were "peanuts" compared to the costs it had suffered owing to eighteen months of indecision and delay on the project by the city. Anglin Norcross needed to take over the garage structure as soon as possible in order to lay the slab paving of the square and get to work on the southwest part of the podium. Yet now Perini was saying that it could not complete its work on the garage before Christmas 1964, which George Bell dismissed as a "weak attempt to cover their own deficiencies."[52]

In the meantime, an interminable wrangle was going on between Revell-Parkin and Anglin Norcross over the design of some electrical convection-heating units. After a meeting where J.G. Spence set out the complaints of the architects, H.W. Miles for the contractor replied scathingly that Spence's letter was so full of "misunderstandings and downright mistakes" it couldn't really have been signed by somebody who had actually attended the meeting. Miles said statements attributed to him were downright "false." When this missive was forwarded to Bell, he mounted his high horse, telling the architects that "I do not like letters of this tone and I require that you give me a full report on the background."[53]

Charges and counter-charges flew back and forth between Revell-Parkin and Anglin Norcross as to who was responsible for all the delays. For the contractors, R.W. Johnstone suggested that the project was at the "crossroads of design and construction" and that meetings with the architects at the site should cease since his "key men" were wasting too much time at them. When the weather improved in the spring of 1964, his staff needed to be on the job directing the subcontractors. If the architects and the city staff met fortnightly with the contractors, important decisions could be taken on the spot. Bell also chastised the architects: "I am none too happy with your current arrangements on the site and ask that you review, improve and strengthen the present method." Parkin's Jack Mar tried to calm the troubled waters by telling Anglin Norcross how much he appreciated their past efforts, but he pointed out that the thirty-month completion period specified in the contract had been arrived at after consultations with four leading firms of contractors including Anglin Norcross. He welcomed the news that a revised progress report would be ready in March 1964, while Bell offered to meet with both parties to see if the completion date could be further advanced.[54]

Despite these efforts at peacemaking, the dispute over the electric heating rumbled on, and on 1 April Anglin Norcross expressed regret that no "reasonable economical solution" could be found: "Being practical people we find it extremely difficult to cope with matters of 'intent.'" Since all efforts to reach agreement with the architects seemed "futile," the contractor would hand the matter over to a lawyer as part of a general claim for losses created by others. J.G. Spence of Revell-Parkin noted, "This letter indicates once again that we should be careful not to give any grounds for claims re errors & omissions or delays." He suggested that City Solicitor W.R. Callow should vet any reply. After a long delay, Callow approved a response stating that Anglin Norcross already had drawings that fully explained the "intent" of the architects and specifically denying that the contractor had any right to claim damages.[55]

While all this skirmishing was going on, the architects and the contractor got into more squabbles over the speed and quality of the work. Complaints from the architects focused first upon the podium roof. In October 1963 Anglin Norcross protested that this criticism was "totally unacceptable." The specifications had been followed to the letter, and if there were leaks or other defects it was a matter not for the roofers but for the architects and the city to solve. By April 1964, D.G. Ritchie of Revell-Parkin was protesting that problems identified months earlier remained uncorrected: "The disturbing element about this business is that procrastination on your part is definitely a disadvantage to all but the contractor in that as the work is finished off it becomes more and more difficult for possible remedial work, should the same be necessary."[56]

Poor supervision was permitting substandard work by subcontractors, said Ritchie. The architects had recently had to suspend work on the lathing and plastering of ceilings because the masonry and mechanical work had not been done properly. If Anglin Norcross had inspected the area before allowing the lathing to go ahead, problems could have been corrected beforehand. Constant supervision was required on such a complex job, and both architects and contractors needed to work closely to solve problems as soon as they appeared.[57]

4.4
Sidewalk
superintendent 1,
summer 1964.

4.5
Sidewalk
superintendent 2,
summer 1964.

The concrete panels designed to clad the exterior walls also created problems. In September 1963 Anglin Norcross complained about colour variation in several sections of the balustrade of the podium. Toronto Cast Stone admitted that the results looked terrible and ought to be replaced, but it declined to cover the additional cost since the architects had been warned uniformity could not be guaranteed. The contractor should pay. When Anglin Norcross tried to drag the city into the dispute, Bell gruffly observed, "They should resolve this themselves." When the panels were being attached to the tower walls, the architects complained that the contractors were using ones that had been damaged. Revell-Parkin rejected patching on the grounds that the patches might fall out, and threatened to withhold all payments for precast concrete work in future if Anglin Norcross did not rectify this at its own expense.[58]

Meanwhile, Viljo Revell remained absent from Toronto. So far as the city was concerned, Revell's last recorded stay had been at the Four Seasons Motor Hotel on Jarvis Street on 14 February 1963, while he was teaching at MIT.[59] In November 1963 John B. Parkin learned that Revell had suffered a stroke in Mexico and had returned to Finland. Later that month, Toronto Mayor Donald Summerville died suddenly and was replaced by Philip Givens. When the Finn wrote to express his sympathy upon receiving this news, Givens replied, "I am very anxious to discuss some matters with you. Can you give me some indication of when we may likely see you in Toronto, or anywhere else where I may be able to see you?" Revell's reply wished Givens luck as mayor but

added that as a result of his illness he required medical clearance before he would be able to travel again.[60]

In March 1964 Revell wrote to John B. Parkin to say that he had been back in hospital but was now home again. His doctors had told him that he could return to work but that he should avoid the risks and mental stress of a transatlantic flight at least until the autumn. He would not be coming to Toronto anytime soon. In April, Revell underwent another week of tests in hospital, and his doctors again warned against taking the risks of travelling overseas at least until the fall, news he asked Parkin to pass along to city officials.[61]

Nevertheless, in early 1964 construction picked up speed. One of Bell's regular progress reports noted that little had been achieved during the cold weather but that, as the spring arrived, things should speed up. The towers were already rising at a respectable pace. The east tower had been completed as high as the eleventh floor while the twelfth floor of the west tower was one-third finished. Even during the cold weather new tower floors would continue to be poured every three and a half weeks, which was excellent under the conditions. The complex domed roof of the council chamber had been formed and would be poured continuously whenever a couple of days of relatively mild weather would permit.[62]

Anglin Norcross reported that it had been hoping to start a new tower floor every three weeks and was constrained only by the speed with which the elevators could be installed. Otis Elevators was somewhat pessimistic but improvements seemed possible. The aim was to complete the framing of the towers by November 1964, at which point the glazing could be installed to permit the interior work over the next winter. Part of the podium was being finished so that the Registry Office staff could move in as scheduled on 1 May. The biggest obstacle remained the slow work on the garage, as well as the equally slow pace on the demolition of the Registry Office so that the southwest corner of the podium could be completed.[63]

The greatest danger was still meddling by the politicians. In April 1964 the Board of Control decided to enquire about the possibility of installing bridges between the two towers at every third or fourth floor. George Bell patiently explained that "the basic aesthetic design" was a two-tower structure so bridges would change the "whole concept." Revell would certainly have to be consulted. In order to sidetrack this hare-brained notion, Bell pointed out that the bridges were really unnecessary, since there wasn't a lot of pedestrian traffic between various municipal departments and what there was involved junior staff like mail-delivery people. Soothingly, he observed that the bridges could certainly be added later, but that it seemed a good idea to see how the completed building functioned before taking any such decision.[64] No more was heard of this idea.

By mid-1964, it seemed clear that the building would be mostly finished in the autumn of 1965. Philip Givens wrote to Governor General Georges Vanier to ask whether the queen could be invited to come for a formal opening in the spring of 1966. After a long delay, the Government Hospitality Committee in Ottawa, which was responsible for organizing royal visits, replied that the queen had recently been in Canada and was definitely

coming again in 1967 for the Centennial of Confederation, so a 1966 visit was not possible. Givens had to settle for an effort to interest the editors of the American magazines *Time* and *Life* in running stories on the city hall project. After all, the underground garage would be the largest in the world when finally completed.[65]

Viljo Revell did finally visit Toronto for the first time in eighteen months in the autumn of 1964. The *Star* noted that the Finn had last seen his building when only the foundation was in place and had never met personally with George Bell. City aldermen were keen to have Revell answer many questions during a visit expected to last up to a month.[66] Revell toured the site with George Bell and John B. Parkin. Though always somewhat nervous about his ability to express himself in English at a press conference, Revell pronounced himself generally pleased at what he had seen. Near the end of the month he took a *Star* reporter around the building. He did admit to seeing some mistakes in the way his design had been modified. The council chamber's streamlined rounded ceiling he pronounced "perhaps a bit overdone." As for the other noticeable changes to the sharp corners of the two towers, Revell said, "I still think the edges are quite powerful, and my disappointment at the modifications is less than I thought."[67] There appear to be no records of any discussions with George Bell or Mayor Givens; Revell departed after a couple of weeks and was not expected to return until the formal opening of the building in the autumn of 1965.

Within days he suffered a heart attack on 8 November 1964 and died at the age of only fifty-four. Back in

4.6
Revell's last visit.

Toronto, the politicians rushed to eulogize him in a letter of condolence to his widow. All of them claimed to have felt a "new excitement and pride" about his "jewel of modern architecture" that showed "a new dedication to his greatness." "This huge, shy, kindly shambling man" had left behind a "shafting [sic] monument whose twin fingers pointing to our destiny in the stars will forever mark his name against our skies." In his very modesty, he was a foreigner who nevertheless seemed one with Torontonians: "A self-effacing stranger, the future will say of him that he was our finest friend." Far into the future, pilgrims would come to stand in awe of his work, and "the flame of his genius that smouldered in his quiet eyes and gentle heart will be forever lit in the modern Athens he began in this 'place of meeting.'"[68] To assuage any lingering feelings of guilt at the way Revell had been treated by Toronto, the city agreed to pay the travel expenses of $3,157 for his final trip even though his contract had specified only $3,000 annually. After all, Mrs Revell had accompanied him on his trip on the advice of his doctor in case of a medical emergency.[69] A mere $157 seemed a small sum to atone for some guilty feelings.

Local architects marked Revell's visit by mounting a roundtable discussion about the project published in the December 1964 issue of *Canadian Architect*.[70] Jerome Markson confessed his feeling of astonishment every time he saw a building, like Revell's, which would stand as a future challenge to other architects. Jack Klein thought that the new city hall would have an important impact upon Toronto's downtown by breaking up its rectangularity, as did Ron Thom, who praised it both

as an oasis in the grid and as a good neighbour. Mandel Sprachman and C.F.T. Rounthwaite each remarked upon the building's importance as a symbol, although the former dismissed the council chamber design as something of a cliché. The latter remarked upon the public's acceptance of the novel design. Both Thom and Klein were inclined to criticize the way in which the towers now seemed to spring from the podium, and Thom raised a concern which often recurred, the way in which the colonnade around the square cut off the view of the base of the building from the surrounding streets.

A number of members of the public also raised the same complaint, to which Philip Givens responded by suggesting that it would be best to wait until construction was complete to consider if anything should be done.[71] But the issue refused to die. In March 1965 Yale professor Serge Chermayeff came to town and repeated his 1958 criticisms of Revell's building to an audience of architecture students at the University of Toronto: "It's going to be cold even though three queens come to open it. It's much too pretentious, and it's made of cardboard, and it lacks a sense of space ... The whole thing is ridiculous. The elevated walk around the square is ridiculous, and so is that thing [the pool with its three arches] in the middle. The walkway is like great heavy mullion put across the middle of a picture window. You have either to try to see over it or duck down to see under it."[72]

The citizenry proved more positive, at least about the pool. The city took formal possession of the southern part of the square on 24 November 1964, and new refrigeration equipment quickly turned the pool to ice that attracted enthusiastic crowds of skaters. By the autumn of 1964, the Registry Office had finally been demolished completely and the garage finished, permitting work to be completed on the southwest corner of the podium. The west tower was nearly finished structurally, and the taller east tower was up to the twenty-third floor. The contractors now promised that the podium would be finished by April 1965, the west tower by June, the northerly part of the square by July, and the east tower by the autumn.[73]

One controversial idea was that the hundred-year-old wrought-iron fence that surrounded the front lawn of Osgoode Hall ought to be removed to blend that space with the square. This provoked a personal protest to the mayor from Eric Arthur, who recounted the number of occasions on which he had had to defend the fence in the past and warned that such a plan would produce the strongest protests from the hundreds of members of the Architectural Conservancy of Ontario and the Committee on the Preservation of Historic Buildings in Canada. Givens hastened to reply that all that was being considered was a plan to move the fence back from a widened Queen Street.[74] The only other issue that thoroughly aroused some of the citizenry was the news that the city proposed to seek permission to allow the serving of alcohol in the building. Ferocious complaints against locating a "tavern" in the city hall led Givens to explain that the city council was seeking only legislation permitting private parties using the cafeteria after business hours to apply for a temporary liquor licence.[75] Nevertheless, the issue bubbled up from time to time,

with predictions that this was but the first step on the road to damnation.[76]

By now, George Bell had reached retirement age, which meant that he would have to step down as coordinator on 31 December 1964, but in view of his achievements council decided to re-engage him immediately to continue the job for $45 per day.[77] The biggest blot on the landscape remained the apparently endless wrangle between the contractor and the city over Anglin Norcross's claims for reimbursement for costs incurred owing to the number of changes in the original contract. In January 1965 R.W. Johnstone reiterated all his complaints: 60 changes had been requested in the first sixteen months and another 174 over the last twenty-four months. Eight alterations worth $40,000 were now under way while another fourteen costed at $288,000 still awaited approval. Surely this should never have happened on a job originally planned to take thirty months but now predicted to last forty-eight months. Anglin Norcross demanded that pricing such tasks under the original contract should cease, and that all such work in future be paid for at "regular" costs plus 10 per cent. Altogether Johnstone entered both a general and a specific claim for a least $940,000 more than the contract on account of overhead costs and the delay in demolishing the Registry Office. In addition, he protested that the city was holding back payments of $3.1 million (or more than 100 per cent of the contract fee if the bond were included). He wanted $1.78 million (including interest) for work completed or almost done. Why would George Bell and City Solicitor W.R. Callow not agree?[78]

Callow and Bell drafted a response which pointed out that the number of changes hardly seemed out of line for a project of this size, and that a good many of them were minor and inevitable, something Anglin Norcross must have taken into account when preparing its tender. Bell wrote to Johnstone saying, "I fail to see where you have any cause for complaint," and adding that he was "firmly of the opinion" that there were no grounds for any claim, general or specific. The contract contained no provision for the progressive release of the holdback. Moreover, the architects advised that many of the completion dates predicted by Anglin Norcross were unrealistic and would have to be pushed back a month or more, which the contractor was forced to concede.[79] That seemed to put an end to the controversy at least for the time being.

By the end of May 1965, George Bell was demanding a realistic schedule for the completion of each of the towers and the podium so that he could plan the move out of the old city hall and the Annex into the new building. At the same time, the city discovered that costs had risen again and requested that the Ontario Municipal Board approve an additional $577,400 worth of thirty-year debentures to raise the necessary money. The board quickly reminded the city solicitor that the city had been told quite clearly back in July 1963 that if more borrowing was requested a hearing would have to be held and likely a vote of the ratepayers. Chastened, the city asked instead for approval of short-term borrowing to be repaid out of current revenue in three equal instalments between 1966 and 1969.[80]

On 30 April 1965 contracts between Anglin Norcross and twenty-four trade-union locals expired, and by late June no agreements had been reached with the cement masons, carpenters, operating engineers, rodmen, bricklayers, and stonemasons who were all threatening to strike. The carpenters promptly went out for six weeks along with some other unions so that the entire moving schedule had to be revised near the end of July.[81] Anglin Norcross continued to demand that payment of its claims against the city receive "utmost priority" so as to be settled before the official opening, but Callow and Bell stalled, refusing even to consider this pressure on the grounds that the contractor had never provided any details about the $940,000 over the contract price that was being sought. It was feared that the strikes might have put back moving day by at least two months. When the disputes were finally settled, Bell called in the Anglin Norcross people and "told them bluntly that I wanted them to give me factual dates for completions." The contractors were instructed to get busy and use all hands to finish the podium and the council chamber so that the formal opening could take place even if this delayed completion of the towers.[82]

All these problems put everybody's nerves on edge. In late August, John Spence of Revell-Parkin requested a meeting with Bell; it resulted in a foolish argument in which the architect said that his firm was responsible to the city of Toronto, not to the coordinator. Spence even added that his colleague, Jack Mar, did not speak for the firm. Bell got himself into a tizzy, huffing and puffing about "certain personal abusive remarks which being personal are not dealt with here," and claiming that Spence did "not recognize my appointment by the city to act on their behalf." Mar had been almost "our only contact" since Bell was appointed, while he had met with Spence only about half a dozen times. John B. Parkin was dragged in, but he mollified Bell by saying he was recognized as the only city representative on the project, and that Mar had done much of the firm's work so he should continue to be the architect's point man.[83] With a final lunge the council chamber was put in shape so that the public could be admitted at least to parts of the building for the formal opening on 13 September. Two days later the architects gave their approval for the city to formally take over the chamber, the podium, and the square outside, though many tasks large and small still remained to be completed.[84] Against the odds, New City Hall was finished, and politicians and municipal officials could begin to take up residence there.

From the outset in 1959, there was uncertainty about whether the building would even be started. Fred Gardiner's suggestions that an ordinary office tower would suffice just as well for municipal offices, and his reluctance to commit Metro to lease a large amount of space from the city, cast doubt about whether the project would go forward. Only skilful manoeuvring by Nathan Phillips kept negotiations open until the Metro chair finally agreed to terms that allowed the city to borrow the necessary capital funds to finance construction. Phillips's

defeat in the election in 1962 deprived the scheme of its most persistent and powerful advocate. A few months later, George Bell was chosen as coordinator to establish a firm managerial grasp on the project.

Like others who sought to bring about change in Toronto, George Bell encountered numerous obstacles in driving the new city hall to completion. The most worrisome for Bell were the members of the city council who continued to dither about the inclusion of a restaurant atop the building until the notion finally expired in November 1963. He had less trouble in smothering the hare-brained notion that bridges be built between the two towers at every third or fourth level, which would have wrecked Viljo Revell's design. Still, there were always fears that the citizenry might become disillusioned with the amount being spent of the project, leading to demands from council for other drastic changes.

As he did his best to push the building to completion by the autumn of 1965, Bell also had to cope with constant complaints from the contractors, Anglin Norcross, about the number of alterations to the plans proposed by the architects. The result was an acrimonious row about whether the city should pay the contractors additional sums in compensation, demands that Bell and other city officials rejected. And the architects at Revell-Parkin were also quick to blame the builders or the city for failing to decide upon alterations in time to allow them to be incorporated relatively economically. Bell was probably right on occasion simply to tell the squabbling parties to settle their differences and get on with the job. If popular enthusiasm for the project seemed to flag in the face of apparently interminable delays and worries about cost overruns by 1963, Bell was able to keep progress going until the speed of construction finally picked up the following year. With the twin towers rising steadily at Queen and Bay streets, the enthusiasm of Torontonians for the undertaking seemed to revive.

Furnishings

PREVIOUS PAGE
5.1
The "main hall"
completed and at
work; the public
upper balcony
visible above at
left.

Nothing in his dealings with the city of Toronto frustrated Viljo Revell as much as the matter of the design of the furnishings and interiors of the new city hall. He was convinced that once he won the competition for the building he would be permitted to create a *gesamptkunstwerk*, a total program that included all the interiors and the furniture at least for the public spaces.[1] From the beginning he asked that the city agree at least in principle to include the design of the furnishings in its agreement with Revell-Parkin. The city refused on the ostensible grounds that it was uncertain whether or not the building could be built at all owing to the projected cost. However, City Hall Coordinator H.H. Rogers noted that it had been understood from the outset that Revell's wishes would be considered, and that a separate agreement covering the furnishings would be signed if the construction costs remained within the estimates prepared by Revell-Parkin.[2]

When the construction contract between the city and Revell-Parkin was finally signed, it did specify that the wall coverings and fixed furniture for the council chamber should be the responsibility of the architects as part of their 6 per cent fee on the total costs of the building. The construction tenders were received in August 1961, and Anglin Norcross's bid was less than the $25 million estimated by the architects. Council giddily agreed to add a floor to each of the towers without any real costing. Revell expected that the city would now offer a separate furnishing contract including a fee of 10 per cent of the costs. He made preparations to take on the furnishings by having somebody in his office prepare

an outline budget. This document predicted that public spaces and offices for senior city politicians and officials would cost $605,300 and for Metro staff $568,800. Other office areas would require another $121,600, making a total of $1,297,760. It was noted that no allowance had been made for transferring existing furnishings from the old city hall, but if the best of this stock was to be used in offices visited by the public it should be brought up to date. Meanwhile, surplus pieces could be sold off to create a fund to cover contingencies.[3]

Revell had made it clear from the outset that he intended to use certain Finnish designers to undertake part of the "furniture work." Since his firm would continue to operate even if he was absent in Toronto much of the time, he told John B. Parkin in January 1959, before their partnership agreement was finalized, that "it may be possible due to my other unfinished work I will be obliged to spend months in Helsinki, during which time I would like to develop some details and bring them to greater maturity here."[4] In September 1961 he again wrote to John B. Parkin to say that he had selected two people to work on the job in Helsinki; Ollii Berg and Antii Nurmesniemi had collaborated with him on the interiors for his Palace building and had since become well known for their work. Overall he proposed that the job would be shared by the Revell-Parkin partnership on the same basis as the construction work.[5]

John B. Parkin was not at all happy with the idea of having much of the furniture design done in Helsinki, coming as it did at a time when he was already having problems with the Finn over the need to redo many of the construction drawings at considerable expense. He rejected the proposal as "quite unacceptable." If it was pursued, he insisted that Revell would have to make an independent deal with the city: "We would, as a result[,] have nothing to do with this part of the project." He suggested instead that Revell take full responsibility for the design stage by bringing the Finnish designers to Toronto to work in the Don Mills offices but leaving Parkin Associates responsible for schematics, prototypes, working drawings, and specifications, along with the calling of tenders from suppliers. That might mean adjusting the profit split in Parkin Associates' favour as a recognition of their larger responsibilities. In order to persuade the city to agree to a contract with Revell-Parkin, the copyright on the designs in Canada would be granted to the manufacturers selected, though Revell could decide how to handle copyright in other countries. It was absolutely essential that the design work be done in Toronto in order to ensure maximum cooperation from potential suppliers. Parkin added, "I would again caution you that there is very little likelihood that this commission would be awarded by the city unless our firm is very definitely involved. As you are aware a very considerable selling job still had to be done." He would insist on proceeding this way, although he tried to mollify Revell somewhat by remarking, "I need hardly remind you that in all our dealings together I have always indicated that your design control of this project must be maintained throughout."[6]

Revell replied by repeating his assertion that the city hall project had been much less successful financially for him than expected (something that a change in the profit split on a furnishings contract would presumably exacerbate). He then declared that John B. Parkin had originally proposed that Revell could undertake the furnishings alone without damaging the relations between the partners but was now insisting on a joint venture. He supported that idea and recognized that Parkin could make a major contribution. If the design budget totalled about $80,000, only $30,000 of that would be spent in Helsinki.[7] The two men apparently resolved their differences.

The city, however, failed to proffer a contract for the furnishings. In October 1961, with construction finally getting under way, Alderman Horace Brown proposed that Revell be consulted about the way in which the building should be furnished, but suggested that he be asked if there ought to be another international competition. The city council passed a motion referring the idea to the architects.[8]

Revell responded with a memorandum arguing that it was vital to remember that the competition had sought not an "ordinary building" but a "trademark" for the city. Another international competition could not be "arranged sensibly." "Furnishing design should be handled as a direct extension of the building design," and he had always expected to design the interiors. Run-of-the-mill furniture would not be satisfactory owing to the unusual "circular and curved spaces." He sought to refute claims that specially designed furniture would be more expensive, because the size of the order and the prestige that could be secured by the chosen manufacturers would make it attractive. Since the existing contract already made the architects responsible for wall finishes, everything else should be covered. It was "self evident" that such an arrangement should cover "all furnishings" in the offices occupied by both city and Metro staff since any contrasts would be "ridiculous." Revell pointed out that spaces like the council chamber gallery and the members' lounge ought to harmonize with the rest of the desks and seating in the chamber, since wall fabrics and carpeting would affect both appearance and acoustics. In order to allow for the likely delays, orders ought to be placed as soon as possible. He did offer to supply a program of locations for murals and sculptures which might be the subject of another competition.[9]

In January 1962 Harry Rogers endorsed Revell's arguments and suggested that the Board of Control endorse a contract with the architects in principle, subject to later subsidiary agreements. John B. Parkin reported to Revell in Helsinki that Rogers had put the case very well. Parkin had also addressed the controllers and suggested that they visit his home along with the mayor and their wives to see the kind of furnishings the architects had in mind, adding, "I feel it is essential that you should be present."[10] In March, Revell-Parkin prepared a detailed timeline for the design of the furnishings. First would come consultations to see exactly what was required, followed by a presentation to the city of preliminary designs and budgets for various layouts. Then would come a final selection with approval to call for tenders, which could be analysed in preparation for an itemized contract for placing orders. The final designs would be

checked, production undertaken, and the furniture installed.[11]

Concerned that time was slipping away, Revell complained to John B. Parkin that as

the question of design is still unsettled I feel compelled to remind you of the following: We have, as you will remember, several times explained to our client the importance of the furnishings for the city hall and further why their significance for this city hall is more absolute than customary. However, since submitting the report of November 30th, 1961, no further progress has been made in dealing with this matter.

Personally I have come to the conclusion that our client REALLY DOES NOT UNDERSTAND (or believe) the situation, and DOES NOT APPRECIATE the functions or role that these furnishings must play – aside from the practical. Otherwise I cannot understand the delay and suspicion surrounding what is, in my opinion, a self-evident continuation [of the delay].

He believed that planning the furnishings was already six months behind time, and that if the architects were forced to wait any longer "we'll lose the base of what we are supposed to do." If the city did not make up its mind immediately, he thought officials should be informed of his "definite" view: "viz: the city hall will never become what the world-wide competition intended and what the citizens expect if the building and furnishings are not done simultaneously. The architect cannot take responsibility for the integrity of the entire result. I have earlier said that the small-minded dealing of this question is out of proportion with regard to the whole and actually is an expense of relatively small size." If the city decided it did not like the proposed designs, it would lose only the 10 per cent fee and could always purchase standard furnishings, "but an integration of the building and the furnishings cannot be done later … I am also of the opinion that a complete design of the building furnished is not an unreasonable requirement of the architect, even though all of it would not be used."[12]

In April 1962 Revell-Parkin sent the city an outline of furnishings that would be prepared for a fee equalling 10 per cent of the net cost of both specialized and standard designs. Revell insisted upon a quick decision to guarantee the "integrity" of the building. It was "not unreasonable" for an architect to exercise such control, a practice common for public buildings in Scandinavia.

Harry Rogers supported that proposal but there were already some bad omens. Metro was reportedly considering its own furnishing program based upon advice from local architect Hans Elte, and the city's chief librarian pointed out that the lease for a branch left him free to choose his own designs though he expressed a willingness to try and harmonize with the rest of the building. The Library Board agreed to seek agreement with Revell-Parkin but reserved the right to choose its own designs.

Rogers did some investigating and discovered that the interiors of some Scandinavian public buildings had required up to twenty years of costly work to complete. Revell was forced to concede that point and to admit that in Copenhagen the furnishings had consumed almost a quarter of the total budget for the city hall while Toronto was considering allocating only 8 per cent. Nevertheless, Rogers remained supportive, and, after hearing from both Revell and from John B. Parkin, the Board of Control concurred. The architects pointed out that the 10 per cent fee was quite reasonable – the Ontario Association of Architects allowed charges of 10 per cent for design and 15 per cent on the cost of furnishings – though a quick decision was needed or total costs would surely rise.[13] In June 1962 the Board of Control approved in principle a contract for the furnishings with a 10 per cent fee for the architects but nothing more was done.

The ill-feeling between the city and the contractor boiled over in January 1963, with Anglin Norcross threatening to stop work altogether unless a final set of construction plans was developed. A few days later, Parkin staff member Jack Mar was chosen as executive architect for the furnishings, with Graham Tudor to head up the designers, but the very same day came formal instructions from Tudor that all work on the furniture contract was to cease pending further instructions.[14] To expedite the whole project, George Bell was appointed as coordinator in May 1963.

In June, J.M. Houghton of the furniture supply firm of Mitchell Houghton began complaining to Controller Allan Lamport about the proposed 10 per cent fee: the money was simply going to be wasted on selecting products readily available in Canada. Lamport agreed that it was an "insult" that local firms had been "left out in the cold" and made such a fuss that in July Bell was ordered to prepare a report on the whole situation. At the same time, Metro council's executive committee decided that it would furnish the public spaces in the new building in harmony with the city's plans but seek its own sources for other offices. Taken together with the library's reservations, this meant that more than half of the building's interiors would be left to whims of tenants.[15]

In September 1963 Bell reported that the city solicitor had advised that in the absence of any formal agreement the architects were owed nothing for their work to date on the furnishings. The coordinator declared that he felt it was still of "utmost importance" that the city should use specially designed furnishings in the public areas, even if the office towers were at least partly filled with existing stock from the old building. But he revived the idea of a design competition to be supervised by a new committee though all its decisions would be subject to his approval. Bell did have the good grace to add that the controllers might feel a "moral responsibility" to pay the architects for work already done.[16]

In November Mayor Donald Summerville, who had defeated Nathan Phillips, died and was replaced by Philip Givens. The architects continued to press the city to sign a contract, but Givens was not keen on the idea. He questioned the wisdom of paying the architects a 10 per cent fee for designs that would then be put out to tender. He advised a local newspaperman that he felt a competition would give Canadian manufacturers a better chance of obtaining the commission.[17]

By the end of November 1963, George Bell showed his customary determination to get things moving. He proposed that he, along with the commissioners of property and purchasing, should make a complete inventory of furniture like filing cabinets and desks that could be transferred to the new offices excluding all curtains and carpets. Then department heads could be asked to enumerate their additional needs, and Carl J. Lochnan, director of the federal Department of Industry's Nation Design Branch, should be asked to nominate an expert "specifier" who could decide exactly what new items were required. Afterwards the city would announce a furnishings competition. This would be judged by a new Furnishing Design Committee headed by Eric Arthur and including Viljo Revell, architect Howard Chapman, interior designer Robin Bush, and Lochnan. They could select up to five suppliers who would be summoned to a meeting and told the amount of the "total budget" which "must not be exceeded." Each competitor would receive $5,000 to cover the cost of preparing designs along with any samples or prototypes.[18]

Since the city had been warned by the Ontario Municipal Board that no additional borrowing would be approved without a hearing and a likely vote of the ratepayers, the question arose of how to pay for the furnishings, estimated to cost somewhere in the vicinity of $1 million. The city treasurer devised a solution. In recent years money from the sale of the city's capital assets had been placed in a special fund used for new purchases, and the treasurer had been building this up to provide at least $750,000 for the new furniture. He asked that the OMB be asked to issue an order specifically designating these funds for that purpose.[19]

Philip Givens warned John B. Parkin that the architects should not make "any real fuss, but in the best interests of the [city hall] project we should not cause any stir at this time. This is probably correct as the project is running quite smoothly at the moment." By this time, Revell had suffered a stroke on a trip to Mexico and was making his way back to Finland to commence a long recuperation.[20]

Every effort was made to obscure the fact that the city was reneging on its commitment to allow Viljo Revell to have the final say on the design of the furnishings. In January 1964 Bell wrote formally to the proposed members of the Furnishing Design Committee to ask if they would serve. Robin Bush and Howard Chapman agreed, though the latter specified he would do so only if Revell was a member.[21] Revell, however, had already written to the Parkin office to say that "my first impression is that a furniture competition is the wrong way, as I have already stated both officially and unofficially to our client, and it presently seems to me that I am not going to be a member in such committee and cannot be obliged to do it."[22]

Revell explained to John B. Parkin that he had told Eric Arthur, "My proposal regarding the City Hall furnishings is now the following: design, selection and supervision of furnishing to Revell-Parkin, provided that the Parkins will agree. In case the Parkins don't agree I cannot (at this stage) do that commitment. If a competition will be arranged I think that my duty is to declare that I cannot participate, because I don't believe in it, and I cannot see how the practical questions could be arranged in favour of the entirety [sic] and the client." He also informed Parkin that his doctor had advised him that the earliest he could even consider travelling to Toronto was April 1964, and even that was only a guess.[23]

A few days later, Revell told Parkin that Eric Arthur had wired him about serving on the committee but "I have been forced to answer that I cannot handle this question by wires because I am confused and have the feeling that I don't know what actually happened."[24] George Bell even telephoned Revell in Helsinki but failed to persuade him to change his mind; the architect also told him of his recent stroke and advised that he would not even be able to visit Toronto until later in the spring. Eric Arthur tried his hand again, wiring Revell that his absence from the committee "creates a bad impression" unless it was clear that it arose only because of his illness; all the other committee members were keen for him to serve.[25]

Revell refused to bend. He explained his objections plainly in a letter to Bell. He had told Arthur that he was "surprised and disappointed" at the decision to hold a competition which was not likely to produce good results and so he did not think it "right" to join the committee. When he had asked for an explanation of the city's "change of attitude" leading to the abandonment of the architects' contract, he had received no answer. Revell-Parkin had already done a considerable amount of design and layout work so he could hardly be a disinterested committee member. Nor would he consider participating in the affairs of any committee from Helsinki. He wrote to Bell, "I hope that you understand my attitude, because I have always considered the furniture question to be one of the most important for the entirety of the city hall, and misunderstandings are great when [ex]changing cables and letters." Revell had considered the claim that it would be cheaper to have a competition but had always believed that "it would lead to a worse entirety." Nothing could change his mind.[26]

Arthur asked Revell whether John Andrews, a finalist in the city hall competition and now a Parkin employee, would be an acceptable substitute on the committee. Revell, however, suggested that John C. Parkin would be his choice, a man who would undoubtedly have wielded considerable influence. In the end a more junior Parkin staffer, Jack Mar, took the position, having already worked closely with Bell on the city hall project. Howard Chapman apparently decided that he would not insist on Revell's participation as a condition of his membership. As chair, Arthur was granted a retainer of $400 per month to serve until the city hall was complete. George Bell sought to conceal the true situation regarding Revell by reporting to the Board of Control that it was his illness that had made it impossible for him to agree to join the committee, but that he might be available in the not-too-distant future or at least designate one of his Finnish colleagues as a substitute.[27]

Now the question arose as to who would occupy the important position of "specifier" for the competition to determine the precise number of pieces of furniture that would be required. Carl Lochnan suggested a short list of three names including Allison Bain. Bell discovered

that she was a Toronto interior decorator who had established her own firm about six years previously. She had already secured some plum commissions such as Marani and Morris's Bank of Canada building in Toronto, Peter Dickinson's local headquarters for the Royal Bank, and Trinity College at the University of Toronto as well as big jobs in both Montreal and Winnipeg. It was quickly decided that she would be given the position, but she was not to be a member of the committee so interior decorator Budd Sugarman was asked to join.[28]

Work began immediately on organizing the furniture competition. Bell's staff drafted an advertisement inviting applications from established firms with the ability to secure a 100 per cent performance bond for a contract valued at about $1 million, the deadline to be 30 April 1964. In preparation, Bell sent Allison Bain a "colour schedule" for the new building and arranged for the committee to visit the site and talk to the mayor. There should also be discussion of what action was to be taken in view of the fact that Revell had now advised him that his health would not permit him to return to Toronto until the autumn. The committee promised a decision on the five eligible bidders by the end of May.[29]

In order to try and forestall any controversy, Howard Chapman wrote to Bell on the committee's behalf to explain that it believed itself autonomous and responsible for all aspects of design not covered by the architects' contract.[30] By the entry deadline, the city had received about a dozen applications. Eric Arthur was formally chosen as chair of the Furnishing Design Committee. The choice of a winner would be based upon "design capability," with the understanding that an entry need not simply be accepted in toto but that changes could be requested. Five applicants were judged acceptable: the three department stores of Henry Morgan and Company, the Robert Simpson Company, and the T. Eaton Company, along with two suppliers, Mitchell Houghton and Knoll International Canada.[31]

The FDC also agreed upon a series of firm directives: the finalists should immediately visit the building, since "they must endeavour to capture the spirit of the building as conceived by its designer … This is an outstanding piece of architecture to which labels like modern or contemporary are inadequate. It is contemporary but in its own way, and the successful competitor will be the one who, in the opinion of the Furnishings Committee, comes most nearly to their interpretation of the quality of the building. So important, in our view, is this attitude that several visits to all of the important areas is [sic] thought essential for the competitors." A high degree of creativity and sympathy with the building would be essential, and anything foreign to the basic concept must be avoided. The actual designers, their education, and their qualifications must be clearly identified in the bids.

Arthur persuaded the committee to endorse his repeated claim that the new city hall would dominate Toronto just as cathedrals had done in other cities during the eighteenth century. This was not just another city hall, rigidly planned and difficult to alter, but a symbolic centre of governance. The furnishings should express spiritual qualities (though not through extravagance), and creativity should be visible in fabrics, drap-

eries, upholstery, wall coverings, and desks. Only chairs would be exempt from the demand for originality since Canadian industry already displayed excellence here. Murals and sculpture were the purview of a separate art committee, though some wall and floor finishes had been mandated by the architect. Final entries were due by 30 September 1964, the winner to be announced on 15 October.[32]

Meanwhile, the committee's files were leaked to the press, which got busy criticizing the conduct of the competition. The *Globe and Mail* reported (correctly) that Revell had "refused" to serve on the FDC. Eric Arthur considered these "irresponsible charges" damaging not only to his "eccentric" Finnish friend but to the committee; he claimed that Revell had been preparing to come to Toronto in April 1964 and join the FDC but had been warned by his doctors that his health would not permit him to travel. George Bell was asked to issue a (misleading) statement that it was only Revell's little-known illness that had prevented his participation. Arthur advised that the mayor be given the same information, adding to Bell that "I hope you don't think I am deserting a sinking ship. I trust that when this blows over we are all still afloat."[33]

Alderman George Ben proved a particular thorn in the flesh of the members of the FDC. On the basis of complaints from several unsuccessful competitors, Ben insisted on reviewing the committee's choices. When he raised the matter with the Board of Control, he was told to put his complaints in writing so that the committee could address them. Eric Arthur tried to refute various objections but enough fuss was created that the drafting of the specifications was suspended, which meant that the deadline for a final decision had to be pushed forward.[34]

Arthur demanded to have Ben's complaints, in writing, within a week so that the committee could respond quickly. He then went off to his cottage on Georgian Bay but returned to find that no deadline had been set for Ben to lay out his complaints. Philip Givens did his best to avoid antagonizing the erratic alderman by wishing him the best for a family holiday in New York City and advising him to stay away from Harlem.[35] Ben circulated his objections to every member of city council and by the end of July was ready to lay his case before the mayor and Board of Control. He insisted that the committee had been wrong even to consider a "manufacturer" like Knoll International; Mitchell Houghton and two other firms had formed a syndicate for the competition which had never existed previously. Henry Morgan and Company was not of sufficient status even to secure the required performance bond.[36]

Arthur called the FDC to meet on 21 August 1964 to produce a response. The committee argued that, if the entrants had been strictly confined to suppliers, the matter of design would have been ignored completely. To do so would have eliminated all the five finalists. Ben's other complaints were dismissed as mere quibbles. Arthur agreed to appear before the Board of Control on 4 September, though he afterwards expressed deep dissatisfaction at "the kind of cross-examination" he was subjected to by Ben. The FDC was a group of unpaid citizens who

had volunteered their expertise to the city and should not be required to debate the merits of particular entries with the politicians. If city council refused to accept the committee's decision, they would resign in a body. This threat succeeded in putting an end to George Ben's quixotic campaign, and the five recommended finalists were approved (though Henry Morgan and Company subsequently withdrew).[37]

The members of the FDC were disturbed to learn that, while they were fending off criticism, Allison Bain seemed to be making little progress in developing the precise specifications. The deadline for releasing the competition conditions to the finalists had to be postponed until late October.[38] After much redrafting, this document's general outline bore a close relationship to statements that Eric Arthur had previously authored: city halls were often "obsolete and inconvenient," but the public required access to these buildings for various reasons and so they should express democratic traditions. Revell's design was "outstanding" and required "sensitive and highly imaginative" furnishings to capture the same spirit. Opportunities for creativity lay in a wide range of choices, including fabrics, desks, and work stations. (Unsaid was that Allison Bain had clearly failed to complete work on either a schedule of requirements or a budget.) The building was to be occupied beginning in the spring of 1965. Each application was to contain six hundred words on the names of the designers, the manufacturers, and unit prices. Metro had now agreed to furnish its public areas in the same way. A general meeting for entrants would be held early in November 1964, with the final submissions due on 4 February 1965.[39]

Viljo Revell finally visited Toronto in late October 1964 after an absence of about nineteen months. At a press conference he reiterated that "I have always felt the architect should create the entire environment from the landscaping to the furnishings." Asked by a *Star* reporter about the furnishing competition, he replied, "Why didn't they (the city council) pick a committee to design the building?"[40] Within a few days he was dead.

On 2 November, George Bell introduced the Furnishing Design Committee to the four competitors. Any questions should be submitted in writing to Arthur. Were the presentations to carry the names of their developers? The answer was yes. The architects would supply a selection of wall and floor colours for the building. Plans and sections of the tower floors were handed over, and layouts and a budget were promised directly from Allison Bain.[41]

More concern about her role was evident a fortnight later when the committee expressed "some alarm" at the oval marble tables Bain had specified along with "quite unworkable chair and table arrangements." At that point she seems to have been unceremoniously bundled out of sight, presumably in the hope that nobody would even remember the existence of the "specifier."[42]

Competitors were told that they should cost each item of furnishings that they were proposing separately but not to assume that any particular design would be adopted. At the same time, Eric Arthur asked Revell-Parkin to supply the committee with certain design ideas already developed. He admitted that this might

be troublesome, but the whole process had been held up at least ten weeks through no fault of the committee, and he wanted to placate the entrants by replying as promptly as possible to any queries. There was no need to provide a complete set of drawings to each of the four, but Bell would have the necessary documents and John C. Parkin and Jack Mar were left to decide which (if any) would be handed over though in the end it appears none were.[43]

No sooner was the competition finally launched than it proved a fruitful source for complaints from civic bureaucrats. The acknowledged master of these arts proved to be City Treasurer and Finance Commissioner W.M. Campbell. At the end of November 1964 he advised George Bell that he had told the architects three years earlier about exactly what was required in the way of filing space for dossiers under each of the counters in the city hall lobby: "By the merest chance yesterday I became aware that some boondoggling nincompoop, without consultation or notice to us, had so altered the heighth [sic] of the counters and their file storage capacity as to seriously impair the very purpose of their existence." Each wicket must accommodate a three-drawer filing cabinet, which dictated that the counter must be forty-five inches high. Now the "furniture consultants" had gone and made changes without any notice. Revell-Parkin was asked to look into the problem but could find no such request from the Finance people: the forty-inch counters had simply been designed to accommodate only two file drawers.[44]

Bell promised to have any future complaints taken up directly with department heads, but Campbell could not let the matter drop: "I am not pleased with kibolicksing [sic] that occurred over what should have been a simple design matter." The proposed solution would require much more counter space and leave each file sticking out eleven inches into the workspace. This wrangling dragged on and on. By June 1965, Finance officials were appealing to Controller William Dennison to interfere in this "grave situation." Campbell tried to recruit allies from the Fire Department and the city clerk's office who faced similar problems but had been loath to make a fuss in the hope of getting things sorted out, now a "forlorn hope." With opening day looming, he even threatened to tell the Board of Control that he would refuse to move his staff out of the old city hall until the offending counters were torn out and replaced.[45]

Now it was Bell's turn to explode: "At this time I am advising you in no uncertain terms that I am in charge of this project, and I do not intend to have you or any of your staff attempting to circumvent my authority. I am quite ready to go before the Board of Control in this matter ... I also take exception to any member of your staff meddling with relations between myself and other departments ... This is none of your business nor is it the business of any member of your staff and I would thank you to see there is no repetition of this." Here was just the fuel Campbell needed: "Dear Mr Coordinator," he wrote, "Your ridiculous charge of meddling is ignored." Half a million citizens visited the Finance Department each year to make payments, and if they were told that it was staying on in its old offices that would create "an extremely poor public image." "Your truly remarkable

outburst would appear to indicate that you have a different view."[46]

The politicians could hardly avoid being drawn in, and Controller William Dennison warned the mayor that "sweeping this problem under the rug is not the answer." Eventually Bell had to give in and order the architects to redesign the counters at top speed and new ones were installed so that the Finance Department could move on schedule in mid-September 1965.[47]

While the competitors in the furnishing design competition were in the midst of their efforts to meet the deadline of 30 March 1965, George Bell suddenly dropped a bombshell. No firm budget had ever been fixed though the sum of $1 million had been tossed around since early on. In his typical get-on-with-the-job spirit, Bell made a serious blunder. On 19 January 1965 he suddenly issued a document entitled "Bulletin No. 3" unilaterally fixing the maximum cost for furnishing the building at $850,000. He advised city budget chief William Dennison that "the figure of $850,000 for the competitor [sic] is definitely a maximum figure. It is quite possible and in fact probable that when the submissions are made they will total far less than this amount."[48] Facing the deadline of 30 March, the competitors were left on their own to decide how to handle the issue of costs (which were to be submitted separately). Some of them sought to revamp their bids to comply with the maximum while others did not.

With the entries in hand, the Furnishing Design Committee met intensively from 1 through 6 April and unanimously concluded that Knoll International had "caught the spirit of the building and maintained it consistently in major as well as minor areas." The view was that the late Viljo Revell would not have been displeased by the results, and indeed that his doubts about a competition might have been allayed. Top-quality materials had been used to create praiseworthy furniture with very highly rated colours and textures. Since the prices for items had been submitted by the competitors in separate unopened envelopes, the committee gave no consideration to whether the sum fixed by Bell had been followed or not. Knoll, it turned out, had simply decided what furnishings were required, paying no attention to the maximum specified in Bell's "Bulletin."[49]

The committee report was delivered on 8 April to the Board of Control, which ordered the cost estimates to be opened. Eaton's came in at $1,049,084, Knoll International at $1,015,030, Mitchell Houghton at $849,491, and Simpson's at $848,310. In light of the cost, the controllers decided to treat Knoll's bid as "informal," and Bell was directed to telephone Eric Arthur and ask the committee to reconsider the other three proposals. At a meeting with the Board of Control in the mayor's office the following day, Givens "confronted" Arthur by asking if the committee would be prepared to indicate a second choice. Arthur replied that it would not do so. He did offer to negotiate with Knoll to see if its total bid could be reduced without substantially altering the designs submitted. The company agreed to consider certain changes like replacing oak desk drawers and shelves with birch and changing some chair coverings from fabric to vinyl, but these alterations reduced the price by only $52,568.[50]

Meantime, Knoll quickly fired off a letter of thanks to Mayor Givens for the honour received from winning the competition. Regret was expressed that it had not been able to cut costs further, but the company felt it must maintain its design standards in Canada as well as the other twenty-two countries in which it operated. Eero Saarinen, a member of the jury for the Toronto city hall competition, was one of Knoll's original designers, and attached to the letter was a list of other prestigious Canadian contracts such as the BC Electric building in Vancouver designed by C.E. Pratt, another of the jury members.[51]

George Bell's ham-fistedness in fixing the total allowable cost at $850,000 in the very midst of the design process left the politicians in a complete quandary. Squirming to escape, the controllers decided to ask the Furnishing Design Committee to choose between the two lowest bidders and if it refused to recommend acceptance of the lowest bid from Simpson's. To help the politicians make up their minds before the decisive city council meeting on 15 April 1965, Bell set up an exhibition of samples next to his office on the second floor of the podium in the new building.[52]

In a letter to Mayor Givens, Arthur strongly defended the choice of Knoll on three grounds. Critics of the FDC had complained that it had paid attention only to aesthetics, but this was erroneous since materials, layout, and durability had also been taken into account and Knoll judged superior in each. The other competitors might have made stronger entries if they had increased costs, but that was no guarantee that their designs would have matched the spirit of Revell's building. Plans were afoot to include a memorial to the architect, and it would be "paradoxical" if not "dishonest" to recommend furnishings "inimical" to his basic philosophy: surely city council would not wish to commit such an "offence" to a "noble building."[53]

Before the council meeting on 15 April, Knoll's lawyers also took care to remind the city that the competition conditions of November 1964 had made no reference to the total cost of the furnishings but only to the quality of design and the unit cost of each piece. The company had never been told that the figure of $850,000 in Bell's January "Bulletin" could not be exceeded, that being only Bell's conception of what the city should pay for furnishings. Knoll would be significantly handicapped by that limit since eliminating some items was "virtually impossible" and there was little leeway to cut quality or cost. Profit margins had been very carefully calculated, leaving little scope for reductions particularly when a five-year guarantee was demanded. Moreover, it was pointed out that Knoll had later been told that an additional 1,840 square yards of carpeting would be required, a hint that this seemed to make a mockery of any cost estimates. Knoll therefore announced that it regarded itself as the winner of the design competition rather than as a tenderer. As a result, the company had established a "right" to be awarded the contract.[54] Clearly, this was an intimation that a lawsuit might be in the offing if another competitor was substituted.

The low bidders were equally unhappy. Mitchell Houghton wrote to Controller Herbert Orliffe to protest that it had played by the rules. If other competitors had exceeded the $850,000 budget by as much as Eaton's and Knoll, they could have made much more elaborate proposals. How could the city disregard its own tendering rules?[55]

Eric Arthur also rallied his troops on the Furnishing Design Committee: they must never agree to choose between the two lowest bids. Even telling the politicians that the plans from Eaton's, the highest bidder, showed some areas of excellence which matched the building had only backfired: there remained a "gap" between the offering from Eaton's and that from Knoll. The other competitors had suggested designs which might be worthy of a modern office building but which were not compatible with Revell's work. To take the sting out its position, the committee could tell the Board of Control that it understood that the willingness to accept the lowest bidder "was based more on ethics than on saving money," but the city council had to be reminded once again of Mayor John Shaw's words in 1899 about the continuing virtues of the old city hall because a building and its furnishings were "complementary and indivisible." Not to secure the best designs available was to reduce the new building to the run-of-the-mill: "It was that just such a concept would emerge from a furnishing competition that haunted Viljo Revell. It is the danger that we now face." With the committee's endorsement, Arthur forwarded a memorandum to the controllers before the council meeting.[56]

At their 15 April meeting, city aldermen showed their confusion. Were the four entries really tenders or not?

After discussions with George Bell, City Solicitor W.R. Callow had accepted Knoll's claim that they were not. Bell was forced to climb down and admit that the competitors had never been formally told that they were tendering. Yet he insisted that council had authorized him on 9 December 1963 to develop a budget for furnishings and that this budget, which he had announced in January 1965, totalled $850,000. Some council members expressed distaste for the modernistic designs despite Mayor Givens's strong endorsement. His motion to give the contract to Knoll was lost on a 10–10 tie vote in committee. But, when the issue came up again before the full council, one alderman had left the meeting in the belief that all the important matters had been settled, and Givens was able to obtain approval in principle for Knoll by a vote of 10 to 9.[57] Francess Halpenny of the University of Toronto Press was moved to write to Eric Arthur about the departing alderman, florist Charles Tidy, observing that the debate about the furniture had been "an overawing exhibition" and that "our florist alderman will perhaps live in memory … as an inadvertent man of the hour."[58]

When news of all this fumbling became public, a large group of the most prominent young local architects, "deeply interested in the total success" of the city hall project, decided to apply pressure to the politicians. This was not a normal tendering process where the lowest bid must win. After all, two highly reputable competitors had exceeded the $850,000 limit so that their ethical standards ought not to be questioned. Rather, they had interpreted the rules of the contest differently, which

was perfectly reasonable in the circumstances. All parties had acted in good faith. As instructed, the committee had chosen the best design, and the city was entitled to ignore any arbitrary cost limit and accept its recommendation. Otherwise the success of the whole project might be endangered. Holding the international architectural competition had generated controversy but delivered a great boost to Toronto's prestige around the world, and the present council should show the same imagination and leadership in approving the best possible interiors.[59]

It was left to the mayor to try and calm the waters by asking Eric Arthur to approach Knoll again to see if reductions could be made to reduce the cost of their designs to $850,000 without compromising quality. On 26 April he reported to the Furnishing Design Committee that he had persuaded the company to make the necessary cuts. The committee approved, but not everybody was happy. Howard Chapman expressed "complete disgust" at having to go before the Board of Control, which had created the "continuing schmozzle" by not having a budget announced until the designers had already been at work for three months, a delay that gave them no time to rework costs. Then some politicians had ignored aesthetic considerations and tried to adopt the lowest bid. The volunteers on the committee had done their best but these efforts seemed useless if council chopped and changed everything, so he threatened to resign; the Knoll designs should be installed throughout to complete a splendid undertaking.[60] As always in Toronto, protectionism reared its head over the choice. The Canadian Home Furnishings Institute wrote to Bell insisting that all the furnishings should be Canadian-designed. If that wasn't possible, at least two-thirds of them should be manufactured in Canada. After all, it was the 120 locally based furniture firms that would be paying the bill for the city hall. The Upholsterers' International Union also insisted that domestically produced furniture should have been required.[61]

Mitchell Houghton called for a formal investigation of why Knoll had been permitted to renegotiate its proposal when it was not even a qualified bidder. Questioning the "ethics and qualifications" of the Design Committee, Houghton demanded that his firm and Simpson's be allowed to make presentations to the Board of Control. The embarrassed politicians agreed to allow this though insisting that they could not discuss design philosophy.[62]

The Furnishing Design Committee met with controllers Margaret Campbell and Herbert Orliffe to explain its position and set forth "suggestions to break the furniture impasse." Arthur argued that it was quite unfair to allow all the competitors to resubmit their designs, since the fact that Knoll's proposals were already common knowledge would work specially to its disadvantage. To divide the job among the four would create only "a tangle that no one could unravel" and make clear that the decision was merely a "political" compromise. What about the idea of giving the public spaces in the podium to Knoll and allowing the lowest bidder, Simpson's, to do the towers? The whole point of choosing Knoll, said Arthur, was that its proposals suited the philosophy of the building and integrated all its elements. He was asked if the other

competitors could be permitted to make new submissions using Knoll's specifications. The chairs were the company's exclusive designs and allowing the others to acquire them would only raise prices, while many other pieces were stock items that could come from Canadian manufacturers.

While appearing to cooperate in seeking a solution, the committee refused to violate the original competition conditions. Only Knoll could produce furniture of suitable quality for $850,000. And there were practical considerations: with the formal opening only four months away, nobody else could finish the job on time. Committee members were on the verge of resigning en masse because their character had been impugned, though nobody had demonstrated that they had done anything beyond what they were asked to despite charges of "mess, confusion and outside 'business ethics.'" Arthur had even received anonymous letters suggesting he was going to get a cut of the money from Knoll. The committee reluctantly agreed to stay on but in future would discuss only the design qualities of the Knoll entry, which had been adjudged outstanding.[63]

Telegram columnist Harry Malcolmson suggested that his editors were seriously exaggerating in saying that the city council had created the worst mess in its entire 131-year history, and he rejected the call for Simpson's low bid to be accepted. But he insisted that the Tely along with both the *Globe and Mail* and the *Star* were right to say that the matter had been handled badly, and that Givens and his aldermen deserved severe criticism (though Bell escaped blame for the debacle). Malcolmson pointed out that simply trying to save money was to ignore Arthur's point that the other designs would reduce the interior of Revell's building to nothing more than an ordinary office tower. People should pay attention to the letter from the large group of prominent architects endorsing the choice of Knoll.[64]

After hearing the complaints from Mitchell Houghton, the Board of Control directed that a contract with low-bidder Simpson's be prepared for their consideration. George Bell advised his staff to get busy on this task and to prepare samples from both Simpson's and Knoll for display. On 4 June the controllers discussed a final contract with Knoll but took no action. Arthur again put the committee's case to the mayor and the council and announced that the members would resign if Knoll was not selected. Howard Chapman tried to stiffen Mayor Givens's spine by writing privately to commend him for his support for Knoll; it was heartening to find a politician who appreciated good design. As for the others, "Is Toronto's reputation as a civilized city a matter of indifference to them or can it be that they simply do not believe that there is actually anything such as art which distinguishes men from the 'brute beasts'?" The *Globe and Mail* was wrongly reporting that the committee had already resigned, but the members were prepared to stay on and fight for the Knoll designs only in order to avert a "dreary disaster." Givens wrote rather sourly to another correspondant that "we are still not out of the woods on the furniture as the matter has been reopened, and the editorial writers of our three daily newspapers have taken upon themselves the self-righteous mission

of instructing the members of council as to their public duty."[65]

By the end of May 1965, some politicians realized that if they continued to back and fill much longer the building could not be furnished in time for the opening. Knoll promised that the podium could still be 90 per cent equipped by mid-September, but over a fortnight later the Board of Control formally asked the company to consider sharing the contract with the other three competitors. Both Eaton's and Mitchell Houghton had made overtures to Knoll but it was not clear exactly what was being proposed. All Knoll's patented chairs must be provided by the company, and any commitments made to subcontractors over recent months to reserve production capacity would have to be honoured and transferred to others only if they reimbursed any costs. To date, Knoll had simply said publicly that it wished any successful competitor well and would make no further comments, but the Furnishing Design Committee must be kept in existence to demonstrate continuing confidence in their judgment concerning Knoll's reputation.[66]

Nevertheless, on 23 June the Board of Control directed George Bell to continue to try to persuade Knoll to agree to furnish only the podium and allow Simpson's to handle the office towers. Knoll immediately rejected this proposal as entailing a sizable loss if the current prices were maintained. And Simpson's also started wriggling and demanded that it be given the contract for all the general office furniture in the building, leaving Knoll with only the special pieces for the public spaces and executive offices. At a meeting on 28 June, city council compounded the confusion by first ordering that a deal with Simpson's for $751,038 be prepared and then granting the contract to Knoll for $859,719. The company quickly promised to have all the furnishings for the public spaces and the offices of the mayor and the controllers and a large proportion of the rest of the podium ready in time for the opening; the tower furniture would be delivered as soon as possible thereafter.[67]

The controversy refused to die down. Complaints were heard that council members who disagreed with the choice of Knoll had not even been invited to a champagne party at city hall to celebrate the deal. Writing to Howard Chapman, the mayor was forced to concede that the furnishings debate had been allowed to descend into "utter confusion." He could only express the hope that, now that Knoll had finally been chosen, the Furnishing Design Committee would stay on to give the whole process some credibility. What was largely concealed from public view was that the sum of $859,719 to be paid to Knoll had been arrived at only by the city quietly lopping off $100,000 into a separate contract for carpeting to be supplied by Eaton's (which presumably mollified that company enough to avoid more protests). In the end, city council set aside a maximum of $925,000 for the furnishings to allow for contingencies.[68]

As the dust began to settle, Mayor Givens wrote to Eric Arthur to praise his work: "I wish to thank you for your constant support and encouragement during the entire period of trial and tribulation. I would like you to convey to the other members of your Furnishing Design Committee my gratitude for their forbearance."[69]

With the decision finally taken, the periodical *Canadian Interiors* convened a panel to assess the quality of the entries; the members included interior decorators Jack Dixon (of Dixon Designs) and Alison Hymas (who worked for the architects Webb Zerafa Menkes) along with architects Alan Moody, Ron Thom, and Jack Mar (who had represented Revell-Parkin on the city's Furnishing Design Committee). The results were published in the magazine's July 1965 edition.[70] Moody largely excluded himself from the discussion by contending that Eaton's and Knoll, which had exceeded the $850,000 limit set by George Bell, should never have been considered at all. Editor David Piper asked Mar to explain the background to the competition and the committee's decision, which hinged upon the conviction that the Knoll designs best captured the spirit of Revell's building. Mar conceded that Eaton's entry had some fine elements but did not seem entirely coherent.

Ron Thom dismissed the quality of the designs from Mitchell Houghton and Simpson's as "just so much stuff," adding that Simpson's standards were "appalling." Eaton's had done a fine job, in particular with a "marvellous" members' lounge, but Knoll seemed to occupy a "curious halfway house" between architecture and furniture. Jack Dixon, however, thought Knoll had shown skill by integrating the two, though he expressed disappointment that the company had specified its Brno chairs rather than Mies van der Rohe's more famous Barcelona design. Alison Hymas agreed in dismissing the two low bidders for presenting no more than a "surface job."

In retrospect, all the panellists agreed that too little time had been allowed for the finest designs to emerge, and that allocating only half of 1 per cent of the total budget for the designs was not sufficient to get the best results. Thom said that the interiors should match the marvellous exterior, and that price should be no object in creating a "public icon." Hymas added that letting the politicians make the final decision had been a mistake: "I think we're electing the wrong kind of people, those who are not bright and astute. They've insulted the professional people." But, all in all, there seemed to be agreement that the Knoll designs provided pretty good solutions to the problems created by an unusual structure with its curved floor-plates in the towers.

What did the city get for its money? The furniture in the east tower, whose windows captured more afternoon sun, was to be upholstered in cool shades of green and blue, while the west tower had warmer shades of gold, orange, and yellow. The Knoll chairs were, of course, classics. Perhaps the most notable display of recognition of Viljo Revell's fondness for concrete was reflected in three-piece desks topped by broad wooden slabs resting upon massive precast rectangles. Unfortunately, the installation of these striking objects coincided almost exactly with the adoption of the miniskirt so that the women who sat behind them soon demanded the installation of "modesty panels" under the front of the tops to prevent "lascivious knee-watching."[71]

Furnishings **139**

With only forty days from the award of the contract to the opening date, Eric Arthur had to keep a very close eye upon the production of the furnishings.[72] The public spaces were rendered presentable in time for the mid-September opening of the building, and the office towers were completed during the following months.[73]

As with almost every other aspect of the furnishing of Toronto's New City Hall, however, there were several comic interludes before the saga ended. At a meeting of the Metro Executive Committee on 14 October 1965, Edwin Pivnick, the reeve of suburban Forest Hill, reportedly had a chair collapse underneath him. Knoll International was immediately called in to investigate. Meanwhile, the news emerged that rotund alderman Joe Piccininni had been filmed with several other aldermen looking on, bouncing on one end of a sofa in the members' lounge to see if he could lift the other end off the floor. Knoll's David Finch wrote confidentially to Raymond Bremner to complain about the "deliberate misuse" of the furniture. Further investigation by Finch could not uncover anybody who had actually witnessed Pivnick's fall, and Finch reported that he had taken the chair, a model that had been sold for several years without complaints, to a meeting of the Furnishing Design Committee to show them that it could be sat upon and even rocked from side to side quite safely.

More detective work by Knoll uncovered the remains of another chair that had been smashed beyond repair in one of the committee rooms after a weekend when the building was closed. Examination revealed several indentations like those from the head of a hammer just below the point where the arm joined the leg. Finch observed diplomatically that it appeared that the committee-room seating was being put to more "demanding" use than anticipated, but he promised some modifications to make the furniture sturdier.[74]

The secretaries at city hall complained that their new desks, however fine aesthetically, wobbled under their typewriters despite their massive concrete bases. Controller Herbert Orliffe complained because nobody had thought to test the design. The Furnishing Design Committee was summoned to consider the matter, but the Knoll people argued that, among the thousands of desks ordered by the city, there were bound to be a few defective ones. George Bell leapt to the company's defence, saying that he thought it had done a wonderful job in the face of all the chopping and changing by the city. In the end, nothing was done.[75]

In October, Finance Commissioner W.M. Campbell fired one last salvo in his war over the equipment for his department, asking for chairs that were two inches higher for the data processors. George Bell replied wearily that he would change the seating. Still, the venom seemed to have gone out of the relationship for Campbell, who even went so far as to reply to Bell, "Were I in your shoes I should be sick and tired of receiving complaints."[76]

Other people were even more laudatory about the city hall coordinator when it became clear that he would retire completely at end of October 1965. Fred Matthews wrote, "Congratulations on a job well done. To take over a job that has come to a standstill and move it forward on schedule as you did at city hall is quite a feat." (He added that his company, Servicemaster, would be happy to take on the carpet-cleaning contract in the building.) Mayor Givens was equally praiseful: "At a time when the city hall project was floundering in a rolling sea of non-direction, city council, recognizing your administrative background and executive ability, called upon you to rescue the project." He applauded Bell's advice and loyalty and wished him a happy retirement. City council quickly confirmed the promotion of Bell's second-in-command, Raymond Bremner, to finish off the project and granted him a $2,000 raise in salary.[77]

By early December 1965, Bremner was reporting to the Board of Control that Knoll had done a good job, especially in view of the shortness of time allowed, and that the furnishings would soon be complete. Now it was the company's turn to grumble in mid-January 1966 that it had so far not received a penny in payment though it could have demanded a supplement for rushing to finish on time. David Finch asked for up to $300,000, which would cover only about half the cost of the furniture already delivered. Bremner acknowledged this request for "two or three thousand dollars" [sic] and agreed to endorse a payment on account. In early February 1966 Knoll's work was adjudged to be over 70 per cent complete at a cost of $500,000 and the city promised $303,534 in mid-March. By December 1966, the city was prepared to certify that the contract was fully completed at a cost of $778,290.[78] When all the sums were totted up, it turned out that Knoll International was owed $953,314.83 while Eaton's had billed $64,606.75 for carpeting, bringing the

total to just over $1 million, just as Viljo Revell and Harry Rogers had predicted way back in 1961.[79]

At his own request, Eric Arthur's honorarium as chair of the Furnishing Design Committee was terminated at the end of February 1966.[80] At long last the great furnishings debate appeared to be over. Not quite, as it turned out, for Mitchell Houghton entered suit against the city claiming thousands in damages because its low "tender" had not been accepted, but this action seems to have faded away without going to trial.[81]

The debate about the furnishings of the new city hall revealed the limitations of the willingness of Toronto politicians to accept avant-garde notions. While an international architectural competition for the building had been accepted, there was much more resistance to the idea that the entire interior design be provided by Viljo Revell. After all, a chair was a chair, and Canada could produce perfectly adequate furniture to sit upon. The architect's demand that he be permitted to create a complete ensemble was met first with procrastination, then concern about the expense, and finally an insistence that there be another competition in which only Canadians were likely to participate. Revell's refusal to countenance this or to sit in judgment was obscured by misleading claims that only his serious illness had disqualified him.

The Furniture Design Committee chose the designs proposed by the well-known firm of Knoll International, but a row then blew up because George Bell had unilaterally announced a maximum budget. Some city aldermen used this as an excuse to insist that the lowest-cost designs be accepted. Despite resistance from local architects and the committee's refusal to reconsider, the aldermen found themselves deadlocked in a tie vote, resolved only because one of their number then left the meeting. Knoll's proposal was accepted by the narrowest of margins. In a great rush the public spaces were furnished in time for the formal opening in September 1965. The forces of traditionalism and conservatism were overcome one more time.

Opening

How was the formal opening of New City Hall to be celebrated in the autumn of 1965? A committee was created including Mayor Philip Givens, Metro Chair William Allen, City Clerk Edgar Norris, project Coordinator George Bell, and his deputy, Raymond Bremner. The kick-off would be a formal affair involving speeches and military pageantry, but Givens also wanted to attract a wider public through an extended series of events stretching over five days, featuring ethnic groups, sports stars, and popular entertainers, and concluding with fireworks each evening. Since the queen would not be opening the building, the mayor approached Governor General Georges Vanier, who eventually agreed to come along with Prime Minister Lester Pearson, Ontario Premier John Robarts, and Viljo Revell's widow. City council voted $50,550 to pay the bills.[1]

Givens also hoped that the Post Office could be induced to issue a commemorative stamp, but, despite his strong Liberal connections, he could not persuade the postmaster general, who was convinced that every other city would be wanting something similar. Givens could only grumble that "this is the kind of progressive attitude that keeps our stamps as dull as ditchwater."[2] He had better luck with minister Paul Hellyer at the Department of National Defence, who agreed to arrange a fly past of RCAF jet fighters and supply the customary honour guard from the regular army's Governor General's Horse Guards. This latter news produced a wave of protest from Toronto's local militia units at being excluded; the 48th Highlanders were "stunned" by the "grievous oversight"; Givens handed this "stunning" letter over to the city clerk to deal with "as I have no intention of getting involved in military warfare." In the end, it was agreed that the honour guard should be composed of elements from each of the local militias in "full ceremonial dress" with music provided by a military band.[3]

The trickiest assignment was to persuade the governing benchers of the Law Society of Upper Canada to allow the city to use the lawn of Osgoode Hall to set off fireworks. Permission was given only reluctantly owing to concerns about possible damage to the historic building, but eventually the property commissioner reported that enough land had been acquired for the planned redevelopment on the south side of Queen Street to use that space instead for the pyrotechnics. Givens, himself a lawyer, wrote to the treasurer (chief executive) of the Law Society that he was very thankful about this change "in view of threat to personally come over and throttle me if anything were to go wrong with the Law Society property." The other problem was arranging floodlighting for the exterior of the two towers each night since a permanent system had not yet been acquired. In the end, the city-owned Canadian National Exhibition agreed to set up temporary illumination for the towers, the council chamber, and the podium.[4]

Naturally, there were some people who did not feel they had been offered a sufficiently prominent role in the celebrations. One woman wrote to Givens from suburban Willowdale:

You do not have very long to decide whether I open the New City Hall – Or not? If you think that any

6.2
Nathan Philips
accepts his award
of merit, in front
of the ceremonial
ribbon, with
Maire Revell
(accompanied
by the Finnish
ambassador),
George Vanier,
Philip Givens and
Lester Pearson
listening, 13
September.

fact that I have written about is a *delusion*, believe me I learned it from someone else. The psychoanalysts would like to have a lot of questions answered including what would make Jews believe that they should own an Israel as big as the Earth? I only want to own a little bit under *True Democracy*. This leaves no room for political lies and deception. I cannot find any person who can interpret your version of ancient history as it is portrayed in the English bible. My opinion is that you, Mayor Givens, are a Canadian – loyal to the taxpayers – then old history is obsolete. Only the law of Right or Wrong remains.[5]

The Jewish mayor did not reply.

On 13 September 1965 the impressive ceremony unfolded. Just after two o'clock, city and Metro politicians and invited guests proceeded across Bay Street from the old city hall and took their seats on the podium outside the council chamber. The governor general was driven up the ramp and inspected the guard of honour. Mayor Givens and Metro Chair William Allen addressed a crowd estimated at 10,000-strong before Vanier presented a civic award of merit to Nathan Phillips and declared the building formally open with a salvo of fireworks. After a choral work performed by the Toronto Finnish Male Choir, Givens introduced Mrs Revell, and the event concluded with a prayer and "O Canada."

The dignitaries then retreated to a reception over tea in the mayor's office. The only real hitch was that a guard refused to let Premier Robarts in to join his wife until fortunately he was recognized and they were allowed to reunite. Meanwhile, about one thousand people flocked into the ground floor of the building. Despite the presence of uniformed guides, a number of visitors found themselves confused by the building's circular design,

6.3
"A city celebrates":
the week of
opening events.

"A City Celebrates"

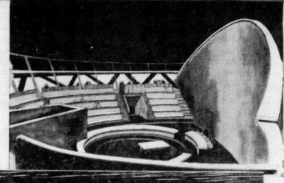

The New City Hall and Nathan Phillips Square will be formally opened by His Excellency The Rt. Hon. Georges P. Vanier, P.C., D.S.O., M.C., C.D., Governor General of Canada, at a ceremony to be held in the Square on Monday, September 13th, at 2.00 p.m.

To celebrate this historic occasion and to mark the inauguration of the City's 1967 Centennial celebrations, the following events will be presented in the Square throughout the ceremonial week.

Monday, September 13th
2.00 pm. — Formal Opening Ceremony.
8.30 p.m. — Tri-Service military pageant — an historical presentation with military bands, pipe bands; presented by units of the Canadian Navy, Army and Air Force.
Fireworks 10.00 p.m.

Tuesday, September 14th
8.30 p.m. — 1½ hour programme featuring the Toronto Symphony Orchestra, Canadian Opera Company and the National Ballet of Canada.
Fireworks 10.00 p.m.

Wednesday, September 15th
8.30 p.m. — Square Dancing — exhibition and audience participation programme.
Fireworks 10.00 p.m.

Thursday, September 16th
8.30 p.m. — Education Night — presentation by the Board of Education.
Fireworks 10.00 p.m.

Friday, September 17th
8.30 p.m. — "Nationbuilders" — a presentation by the Community Folk Art Council.
Fireworks 10.00 p.m.

Saturday, September 18th
8.30 p.m. — "Toronto A-Go-Go" — fun and entertainment with audience participation in dancing. Fireworks 11.05 p.m.

The New City Hall will be open to the public each day during the ceremonial week from 10.00 a.m. to 10.00 p.m., except from 12.00 noon to 6.00 p.m. on Monday, September 13th, during the official opening period.

I have much pleasure, on behalf of City Council, in extending to the citizens generally an invitation to visit their New City Hall and enjoy the fun and entertainment planned to be held from Sept. 13th to 18th.

Philip G. Givens
Mayor

INDUSTRY INTELLIGENCE INTEGRITY

City of Toronto

SQUABBLE!

THE NEW City Hall has been Big Brother to Toronto politicians for the last 10 years: they learned to love it or they perished.

Almost without exception the politicians who opposed its construction have been voted out.

The notable exception: former Mayor Nathan Phillips who was voted out even though he was the building's greatest champion.

Mayor Phillips was the one man with the vision and persistence to make a dazzling reality out of the voters' dimly-felt need for a new city hall.

In 1947 the voters had approved $2,000,000 for a civic square, but then things just stewed for a while.

In 1955 three local architectural firms drew up plans for a conventional 20-storey building with a three-storey section in front for the council chamber.

Professor Richard H. Groom described the plans as "at least 20 to 30 years behind the times."

But one of the architects, Alvin S. Mathers, replied that they were 15 to 20 years ahead of anything built in Toronto at that time, which perhaps said something about Toronto.

During a stormy meeting at which there were cries of "farce" and "insane asylum" the plans were approved, but in December of that year the voters turned down the $18,000,000 cost.

Prof. Eric Arthur commented at the time, "You can't get a fine design out of a committee," and by September of 1956 Mayor Phillips had his suggestion for an international competition adopted.

In December the voters, after hearing a better presentation of the new city hall plans, approved the $18,000,000 by a vote of 32,000 to 27,000.

NATE'S OYSTER — But Mayor Nathan Phillips could withstand such barbs with dignity. Indeed he, perhaps, was the first to recognize them as signs of acceptance, and somewhere he found the courage, the tenacity, the vision to make a dream come true.

In 1957 then-controller, now Metro Chairman William Allen tried to get the competition limited to Canadians, and Con. Ford Brand suggested that instead of a new hall, an extension should be built to the present one which would stand on stilts in the courtyard.

Even famed architect Frank Lloyd Wright was against the competition, and said it should be limited to a few men of proven ability.

But the rules were established in 1957, and by September, 1958 the Revell design had been chosen out of 532 entries from 42 countries.

Then the critics had their day.

Con. Roy Belyea called it "a monument to one of the dizziest times in civic history."

Metro Chairman Fred Gardiner called it a Taj Mahal, and an extravagant attempt to build a stairway to the stars. But he later changed his mind and called it "a unique and outstanding building."

Ald. Frank Nash said the taxpayers had been hoodwinked, and when booze was proposed Ald. George Ben said the two towers should be named Sodom and Gomorrah.

The most persistent critic was Alan Lamport, who promised to scrap the plans in his 1960 bid for mayor, but he lost to Mayor Phillips.

That didn't stop Mr. Lamport proposing later that there should be a statue of a hockey player out front, and enclosed cat-walks linking the towers for efficiency's sake.

Despite it all, the contract was signed with Anglin-Norcross in October, 1961. The company's first reward was expulsion from the Ontario General Contractors' Association, which was quibbling with the city at the time about contract requirements.

Nathan Phillips turned the first sod on his 69th birthday, and the crowd sang "Happy Birthday to You."

Right down to opening day the new building has been the subject of political wrangles, with the price being cited as anything up to $84,000,000 (present estimate: about $25,000,000).

And a last-minute controversy over furniture for the building produced more bitterness than the original decision to build.

All would have been well if the four firms competing for the contract had kept within the $850,000 ceiling suggested by the city. But two exceeded it, and one of them, Knoll International, was judged to have the best designs by the selection committee.

Council was deadlocked until rookie alderman Ken Dear left the meeting early by mistake, and in the ensuing vote Knoll was chosen.

BUT THAT didn't end it. A majority of the Board of Control, which awards contracts, was in favor of the low bidder, Simpson's.

For most of the summer the thorny problem went back and forth with Mayor Givens trying to sway the determined board members over to Knoll.

Finally the board sent down a contract for Simpson's. The vote was another deadlock.

Then, tired out with the endless argument, Ald. Fred Beavis switched his vote to Knoll, and one by one others followed until there was the necessary two-thirds majority to reverse the Board of Control decision. Knoll, which meantime had brought its prices down to the city ceiling, got the contract.

There will be other controversies in the necessary push and pull of the move but, like the hero of Orwell's book, 1984, many politicians attending the opening will shed tears for the departed critics and avow they have come to love Big Brother.

LAMPY — Ex-champion of the little guy lost a good deal of his support when he tried to shoot the whole project down.

ALSO RANS

6.4
"Squabble": reprising seven years.

6.5
The council chamber on
opening day.

6.6
The Hall of Memory on
opening day.

were waits of up to two hours for the other two, a problem compounded when one of the cars broke down on its second trip, leaving the passengers to pry open the doors and clamber up a couple of feet to the floor above. The elevators refused to budge whenever more than about fifteen people crowded aboard, but the citizenry seemed to take it all in good spirit. An unsigned letter to the mayor read, "I used to criticize your New City Hall but yesterday as I went through it I changed my mind. It's something out of this world. There is nothing to compare it [to] so far. [The] Eiffel Tower will have to take second place."[6]

The first evening there was a military pageant in the square with band music until it was time for the nightly fireworks at ten o'clock. Tuesday was reserved for high culture with the Toronto Symphony Orchestra, the Canadian Opera Company, and the National Ballet of Canada performing snippets, and the next evening for square and round dancing by the public. Thursday featured various activities by Toronto high school students, while Friday was reserved for performances by groups from the city's ethnic communities. The grand finale on Saturday was a concert entitled "Toronto A Go-Go," emceed by Bobby Curtola with acts like David Clayton-Thomas and J.B. and the Playboys, capped off by closing remarks at 11 p.m. by the mayor and the customary fireworks display.

During the first week hundreds of curious Torontonians continued to troop through the new building, leading the elevators to break down periodically from overloading. The council chamber was used for the

and some who went seeking coffee in the basement cafeteria ended up in the chauffeurs' garage. One woman predicted that people were likely to be found wandering around for a week or more, especially in search of the washrooms.

Those who sought to get a look at the council chamber found that the stairs from the ground floor were blocked off because of fears that high heels would punch holes in the newly asphalted surface. With one of the three elevators reserved for the governor general's party, there

6.7
The opening-day crowds viewed from the public observation deck atop the east tower, with the colour guard at the upper left.

6.8
... what the observers down below were seeing.

first time. Eric Arthur set down this description of the interior:[7]

On entering the hall off the square through some very handsome teak doors … the visitor is struck by the lowness of the ceiling. This is a design device not unknown to the ancients & fully exploited by contemporary architects like Frank Lloyd Wright. The visitor is in a space with a ceiling height of exactly his own suburban home, 8'0", and except for exciting vistas beyond he feels he is in a place that is vaguely familiar- at any rate in terms of scale. In this mood he approaches the central space which contains the Hall of Memory, and here he receives the pleasant shock of great scale, a huge central column, & exciting views above, and beyond the exposed levels of the second & third floor. The surprise is all the greater because of the walk through the area with the familiar ceiling height …

Looking over the parapet at the second floor one gets an even more exciting view of the central column & the Hall of Memory, & the view from the third floor is, if anything, more dramatic. It is the sort of view that Piranesi, the great Italian etcher loved to draw …

On this [second] floor are the offices of the Mayor and the Metropolitan Chairman … Both of the senior officials have fine offices that look south over the square …

The council chamber takes the form of a Greek theatre in which the encircling seats are done in

gold broadloom with black leather cushions …

The gold broadloom of the council chamber sweeps up the rows of seats until it reach an ambulatory against the outside glass wall, but even the ambulatory is in the same gold broadloom which flows without interruption into the Members' Lounge. This room is of heroic scale with a view of Nathan Phillips Square, the old City Hall & the commercial and financial towers to the south

ABOVE
6.9
Ethnic dance.
6.10
"Toronto A Go Go."

RIGHT
6.11
The quieter side of
the reflecting pool.
6.12
The fireworks, as
seen by the crowd
on the podium.

unsurpassed in the building ... The lounge & the view are a suitable climax to such magnificence.

Just as the building opened came the big news that Eaton's department store was planning to buy the old city hall from Metro and raze the entire area north of Queen between Bay and Yonge streets as far as Dundas in order create an Eaton Centre including a sixty-storey tower. Immediately city politicians were plunged into a debate about the redevelopment of downtown as a means to keep up with Montreal, which was seen to be outpacing Toronto with Expo '67 in the offing. Eric Arthur and the Architectural Conservancy of Ontario launched a furious campaign to block the scheme to destroy E.J. Lennox's "irreplaceable" 1899 building while other architects endorsed the idea of getting rid of this "obsolete" structure.[8] A heated debate ensued over the months ahead. At the same time, city council was considering the expropriation of several properties on the south side of Queen Street opposite the civic square in order to allow a unified development to complement it, another element in the hoped-for renaissance of Toronto's downtown.

With Viljo Revell's building finally open for inspection, Toronto architects began to scrutinize the design closely. In the *Journal* of the Royal Architectural Institute of Canada, John B. Parkin Associates supplied "The Architects' Statement on the Competition and Construction and the Structural Solution." A panel discussion on "The Civic Design Aspects of the City Hall" provided a platform where unsuccessful finalist John Andrews could once more parade his criticisms: the building was

too close to the north edge of the square because of the unwise location for the underground parking garage. Unlike Lennox's castle at the head of Bay Street, the towers did not close off a vista. Irving Grossman defended the attempt to build a structure with heavy symbolic meaning, but Andrews unsubtly denounced the results of architectural competitions as being no better than their jury members.[9]

Canadian Architect solicited more opinions. James A. Murray wondered if Revell's layout was the rational way to make a contrast with the skyscrapers beginning to grow to the south like Mies van der Rohe's austere Toronto-Dominion Centre. Was it really necessary to adopt such a radical solution for the city hall or had the pursuit of symbolism produced an "uninhabitable" structure? He concluded that the design was successful because it did try to meet the conditions fully laid out in the competition documents and showed the value of architectural competitions.[10]

Ron Thom praised the square as a public gathering place, summer and winter, and the well-defined council chamber with its seating for an audience of up to three hundred. Revell's unique design had avoided eclecticism and would become a symbol of Toronto.

The Finn had met the known needs of the city while detecting unknown ones. Thom was, however, less

6.13
Among the new developments that followed New City Hall's completion, hoping to benefit from its public space, the south side of Queen Street didn't live up to the inspiration provided by Revell.

enthusiastic about the podium, which masked the bases of the towers both externally and internally. Like others, he was also cool towards the surrounding colonnade, which obscured the view of the council chamber and the lower part of the towers from the surrounding streets. He praised the chamber itself although regretting the awkward division of the upstairs lounge and the public seating. Yet such problems seemed rather minor, and the immediate popular enthusiasm for the square and the building was something to be celebrated.[11]

In the spring of 1966 the RAIC *Journal* presented a lengthy and detailed critique of the entire project by Douglas Shadbolt, another unsuccessful entrant in the 1958 design competition. He had analysed Revell's original sketches up through the final plans and particularly regretted the elimination of the council chamber supported on three legs with a sky-lit entrance hall below, now replaced by the central trunk. To Shadbolt, that alteration seemed a fundamental error in spatial composition created by changing horses in mid-stream without a complete rethinking of the original concept. He was also critical of some of the interior finishes which did not always feature exposed concrete but were plastered over.[12]

This assessment was followed by one from Guy Desbarats, who concurred with Ron Thom's view in *Canadian Architect* the previous October in admiring the boldness of the concept. Desbarats was, however, concerned about the way in which the towers seemed to squash the podium. Inside, the rectilinear ceilings seemed to blend poorly with the curved corridors. He admitted that these changes had been made in the interests of economy but lamented that the details like the staircases and internal surfaces had not been more carefully handled by the Parkin firm.[13]

These criticisms provoked a response from jury member Gordon Stephenson, who had by then moved from Toronto to the University of Western Australia. Revell's winning entry had been presented as a beautiful model with minimal drawings, but it had subsequently become clear that the original project could not have been executed at a cost the city was willing to pay. As one of the two jurors who did not support Revell as winner, Stephenson had argued that there were other entries that were equally good and more economical to build, but he had accepted that the three people in the majority should have the final say. At 3 a.m., when the decision was finally taken, the main desire of all the jurors was that the project should go ahead. The jury did not tell Revell how to modify his proposal, nor which Ontario architectural firm he should ally with, leaving that to Eric Arthur. Stephenson noted that both Shadbolt and Desbarats had made favourable references to the bold design of the Sydney Opera House, but from his vantage point in Australia he was able to point out that anything resembling the eightfold rise in the estimated cost of that building would have imperilled the entire scheme since the Toronto city hall was not financed by lottery profits but by taxes.[14]

Those people who had to work in the new building had their own more mundane complaints. In the interests of economy, the podium roof had never been landscaped

6.14
New City Hall,
complete.

so as to attract the public to walk there as Revell had intended, and the architects needed to come up with a plan to finish it off. Also in the interests of economy, solar curtains to cut the heat and glare of the sun had been provided only for the towers and the executive offices on the second floor of the podium, but without them elsewhere the air-conditioning would not work properly. The occupants of the other offices felt they were working in a goldfish bowl and wanted some privacy. City council agreed to set aside up to $28,000 to curtain the ground and third floors of the podium.[15]

The council chamber and the podium offices felt like "ovens" owing to a lack of humidity. The wife of one city employee claimed that her husband was so dehydrated that the skin was peeling off his tongue. The architects were ordered to adjust the air-conditioning. Mayor Givens then complained that the blast from the vent right over his desk was causing "great inconvenience" and needed attention "before I get pneumonia." A particular bugbear for the mayor was that when staff left their offices in the evening, they failed to draw the curtains, so that the lighted towers looked "like a man or a woman who have had some of their teeth knocked out." The inner solar curtains were not supposed to be drawn back at all, but repeated reminders failed to rectify this gap-toothed look. Eventually Property Commissioner Harry Rogers decided to see if he could fix the inner ones in place to cure this problem.[16]

Yet public opinion remained highly enthusiastic about the new building and the almost thirteen acres of square around it. Just to enumerate the physical components of the structure seemed to demonstrate the achievement: 91,000 cubic yards of concrete, 9,000 tons of reinforcing steel, 94,000 square feet of glass, and 4,200 four-foot-by-eleven-foot precast panels covering 170,000 square feet and weighing 6,000 tons.[17] Truly a marvel.

Coda

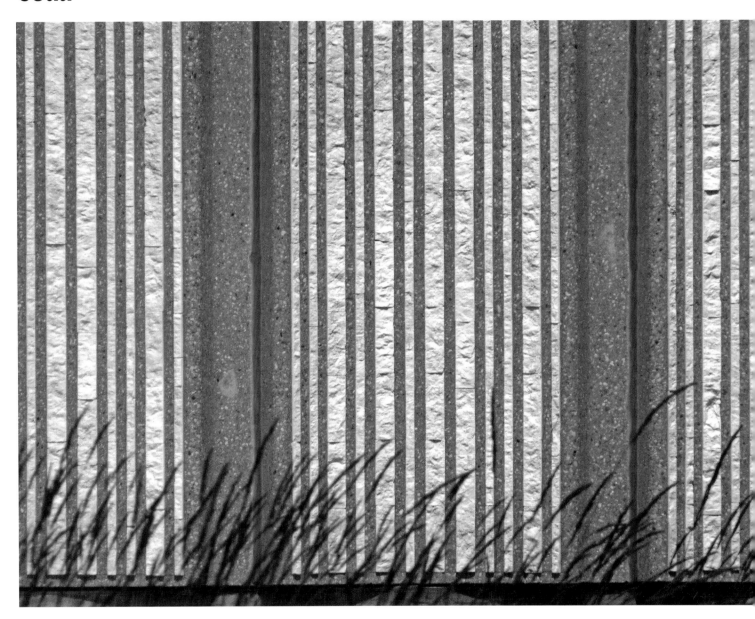

"Coda: *Mus.*, A passage added after the natural
completion of a movement, so as to form a
more definite and satisfactory conclusion."
— *Oxford English Dictionary*

PREVIOUS PAGE
7.1
Detail: the marble-
inlaid concrete
panels that encase
the towers.

Like the coda to a silly symphony, the months after
New City Hall finally opened in September 1965 featured
a forceful reprise of certain aspects of the city's political
culture as though they sprang from some inner chords in
the life of Toronto. First of all, municipal penny-pinching
led to a seemingly endless dispute with the building
contractors which dragged on for years before reaching
an inglorious conclusion. And local politicians continued
to show their boundless enthusiasm for interfering in
matters well beyond their depth, which threatened
to block the full execution of the aesthetic ensemble
envisaged by the late Viljo Revell. Private citizens who
valued up-to-date aesthetic ideas had to contribute funds
to realize the project fully. Nevertheless, in the end the
building and the square were satisfactorily completed
and became the hub of municipal political life.

Almost from the moment that the contract was signed
with Anglin Norcross in October 1961, there had arisen a
series of disputes between the company, city officials, and
the supervising architects which at times descended into
personal abuse and the threat of lawsuits. Even after the

formal takeover of the building by the city in December
1965, work remained to be done and the wrangling
continued.

With an estimated $500,000 in progress payments still
due Anglin Norcross, the city announced that it intended
to hold back $150,000 on the grounds that the contractors
had damaged the roof membrane of the southern part
of the garage, causing it to leak. The contractors denied
any responsibility, insisting that the roof had always
leaked despite their efforts to remedy the problem at
considerable expense. The city announced its intention
to retain another $150,000 from future progress pay-
ments to pay for the repair work. In addition, the city
kept back $3,139,719 for work on the building itself, 36 per
cent ($868,230) of which was due to the contractor and the
remainder to its various subcontractors.[1]

Early in 1966, City Hall Coordinator Raymond Bremner reported that he expected Anglin Norcross to present
a list of claims for $1 million in losses suffered under the
contract, mainly due to the many changes in the plans
made by the city and its architects. He did not expect
the company to file a lawsuit but admitted that holding back more than $3 million seemed unduly severe;
instead, he suggested that the city take the calculated
risk of releasing $2.6 million to the contractors in a show
of good faith while still holding back about $500,000 plus
another $180,000 in progress payments until the repair
of the garage roof was settled.[2]

As with all new buildings, unexpected problems
continued to arise. In August 1966 something was discovered growing below the ceiling of the ground floor.

The Botany Department at the University of Toronto reported that this proved to be oyster mushrooms; Bremner wondered what to do though he told architect Jack Mar of Revell-Parkin that "we are at least growing edible mushrooms."[3]

By November, the city was prepared to release the $500,000 provided that the contractors agreed to remedy the remaining deficiencies, but it would not accept the work on the podium roof, which was leaking at its expansion joints despite a five-year warranty. Reluctantly, Anglin Norcross agreed, but the city refused to pay extra for a second roofing job. Meanwhile, Bremner drafted a counter-claim against the company to be used if necessary, totalling $712,000 for extra rentals paid by the city owing to the delay in finishing the new building as promised. In May 1967 city council approved payment of $450,000 to the contractors with $50,000 being retained to pay for fixing the leaks in the garage roof.[4]

In September 1967, with the garage roof still unrepaired, Anglin Norcross Ontario entered voluntary bankruptcy. Worried that they might not be fully paid for services on the roofing job, Revell-Parkin began agitating for an outstanding fee of $750 from the city. This was finally paid.[5] The bankruptcy receiver argued that the $50,000 holdback from Anglin Norcross should be handed over on the grounds that it was the fault of the architects for not ordering a complete reroofing of the garage. Finally, in the summer of 1968, the city ordered the job done at a cost of $38,700.[6]

That left the leaking podium roof. Efforts were made to correct the problem but by November 1968 a "grave situation" had developed as moisture poured through. A year later, the city was continuing to hold back $50,000 until the matter was addressed. But when a pool designed as part of the landscaping plan for the roof was refilled in the summer of 1970, the leaks recurred there and elsewhere. Raymond Bremner concluded that the pool would have to be completely rebuilt to be used.[7] Ultimately, Viljo Revell's vision of a landscaped open space atop the podium was abandoned, leaving a concrete emptiness rarely visited by anyone.

Another part of Revell's vision involved the provision of an artistic focal point on the surrounding square. In 1960 the architect became friendly with the English sculptor Henry Moore, one of whose works he decided would be the perfect choice. Peter Didrichsen, for whom Revell had designed a house in Finland that included such a sculpture in the garden, remembered him saying, "None of my buildings is ready until there's a Henry Moore sculpture in front of it." Revell began discussing the acquisition of Moore's two-piece work *Reclining Figure No. 2* for Toronto.[8]

In the autumn of 1961 Revell and Moore also began talking about another possible work to be called *Flame in Stone*, which would form a cenotaph on the square to commemorate Toronto's war dead. The two men agreed to meet in England at the end of the year, but by the following spring the sculptor reported that he had not made much progress on the project.[9]

Once work began on the building, Mayor Nathan Phillips decided upon the creation of a Fine Arts Committee to select works to complement it both inside and out. After discussions, Eric Arthur suggested the names of a small group of people with connections in the arts community who agreed to serve.[10] Perhaps because of fears of criticism about spending more money on artwork at a time when the project was in danger of going over budget and falling behind schedule, nothing was done. In the summer of 1962 city council did approve the cost of a stopover in London for Revell en route from Helsinki to Toronto so that he might meet with Moore.

Early in 1963 Moore and Revell met again, but Revell reported to John B. Parkin that he had not got a firm commitment from the sculptor for *Flame in Stone* along the lines that the architect had conceived of. Moore now talked of a symbolic flame, a sharp-edged plate of white marble which he claimed was inspired by the building's design. But this would merely be attached to a two-piece sculpture complete in itself, presumably *Reclining Figure No. 2*. Revell had by then spotted another piece by Moore that he considered more powerful, to which the flame might be attached as a war memorial; he asked the sculptor not to show this work to others but to keep it reserved for Toronto until the proposed art committee could approve it.[11] Parkin replied that he expected to be in London in mid-April and would see if he could arrange a meeting with Moore.[12]

The idea of a committee was not raised again until early 1963, by which time Phillips had been defeated in the elections and replaced by Donald Summerville. City

Hall Coordinator Harry Rogers again brought up the idea of a committee with the suggestion that the Board of Control might discuss it in private session, but no action was taken.[13]

In June 1963 Revell told Eric Arthur that he had planned to be in Toronto in September but had not received a formal invitation to consult about the city hall furnishings on which he had been working and so was changing his plans. He also said that either of the two Moore sculptures would be suitable for Toronto, though such a work would cost at least $100,000. As for other artwork in the building, Revell stated that he would have taken care to acquaint himself with Canadian art and artists, but in his absence those choices would have to be made in Toronto. He suggested that, if Moore's work were included, that should form the first charge upon the artwork budget, with the rest of the money set aside for Canadian designs.[14]

After Philip Givens became mayor following Summerville's death in the autumn of 1963, Eric Arthur approached him with the idea of finally creating an art committee. Arthur prepared a memorandum pointing out that in Europe works were routinely created for new public buildings. He had prepared a study for the Massey Commission on the arts in Canada showing it was common to set aside a sum between 1 and 10 per cent of the total budget to embellish such structures. The federal Department of Transport had adopted this practice for its new airports, setting aside half of 1 per cent, or $160,000, to be used at the new Toronto terminal. Artwork and sculpture had gone hand in hand in with grand architecture for centuries, and Arthur was keen to see works, particularly by Canadians, commissioned for the new city hall.[15] ꞏ

Back in Helsinki in January 1964, recovering from the stroke he had suffered in Mexico, Revell sent John B. Parkin a picture of Henry Moore's *Knife Edge*, which the sculptor claimed had been inspired by the building design, though Revell pointed out that this work was thirteen or fourteen feet high while he had been thinking of something only eight or nine feet tall.[16]

Though Revell's doctors had warned him that he should not travel to Toronto until the spring, he did promise Arthur advice on the number and location of works of art and endorsed the idea of a committee to select them. Asked who might represent his views on such a body, Revell suggested John C. Parkin. Arthur proposed to the mayor that one half of 1 per cent of the project's budget should be set aside to purchase works by Canadians, these works to be chosen by a group of volunteers having broad connections within the artistic community who could examine proposals and commission sculptures and paintings.[17]

Eric Arthur realized from the first that the choice of artwork was bound to create problems. In March 1964 he met privately with the mayor and Board of Control, who made it clear that they were not willing to give any committee the power to commission works of art or even to approve sketches or maquettes without a vote by city council. Arthur told his son that he had pointed out that the city had handed over the final choice of the building design to a jury with splendid results, but that the poli-

ticians were dreaming of sculptures of hockey players carved out of granite ten feet high or refugee women in white marble. The committee should have final authority: "Of course, I won't give way an inch. I fear a big-scale Hamilton fiasco," he wrote, referring to the great public controversy that had arisen when the local council in the nearby Ontario city had insisted upon imposing its own choices for art in its newly built city hall.[18] In the end, however, the matter remained unresolved when the city council finally approved the creation of an Art Selection Committee in April 1964.[19]

That the choice of art was certain to be controversial was evident from letters like one to Givens from a local journalist who began with a denunciation of the Art Gallery of Toronto's recent acquisition of Pablo Picasso's Sitting Woman at a cost of $125,000. No doubt the seller had been delighted to find a sucker to take the picture off his hands. Givens was told that an "Ontario Institute of Painters" had recently been founded specifically to "fight Modern Art" and promote "young artists (traditionalists)." Rumours were already circulating of a plan to buy a Henry Moore, "a grotesque chunk of marble with a few holes in it – for a huge sum"; one of Moore's works had recently been placed outside the Bank of Commerce's new building in Montreal, a "monstrosity" acquired by the bank's president on his own initiative to the dismay of his board of directors. The only good thing was that city council had reserved the right of final approval for the acquisition of any works since the judgment of Toronto's "Committee of Experts" was not to be trusted: "They are nihilists in art."[20]

Eric Arthur was hopeful that he could count upon Philip Givens to support progressive recommendations from the committee. In February 1965 Arthur suggested to his son that he should be sure to send the mayor the most recent issue of the magazine *Canadian Art*: "His wife paints & he seems very interested in art, & unlike others does not condemn what he does not understand."[21]

The art committee's first task was to familiarize itself with the interior and exterior of the building and decide where artwork should be placed in "one of the great buildings of the world" (as Arthur put it). Once that was done, consideration could be given as to whether a sum equal to one half of 1 per cent of the budget was adequate, and city council could be asked to appropriate the money.[22]

Ultimately, however, council decided that such spending should not even be considered until the building was completed and opened. In the rush to finish by September 1965, the matter of artwork was pushed into the background. Nevertheless, opponents of modern art were still occasionally heard from. At the time of the opening, a member of the editorial committee of the magazine *Canadian Art* wrote to the mayor to warn that any such controversy "must embarrass anyone who is concerned with Toronto's reputation as a leading Canadian cultural centre. The vulgar spectacle that resulted from Hamilton's city fathers' excursion into modern art must not be repeated here ... To accept anything less than the very best in contemporary expression would be catastrophe." The advice of the "expert professionals or cultivated collectors" on Arthur's committee should be adopted by council. The mayor replied, "I totally

share your sentiments," adding that the pressure should be applied to the four members of the Board of Control "who are in basic disagreement with these views."[23]

In February 1966 the Art Committee announced that Henry Moore had approached them with the offer of his monumental work entitled *Three-Way Piece No. 2* (*The Archer*), which he claimed he had created specially with Revell's Toronto building in mind. This was not a commission but a tribute to his late friend. Moore asked to be paid $150,000. Eric Arthur cautiously opined that it was "no doubt worth it," but the news produced immediate controversy. Committee member Alderman Horace Brown said, "I figure it's going to be scuttled by the city council or Board of Control. And if it is, it will be an eternal disgrace ... The committee is in despair that council or Board of Control will say no to us. It's tragic."[24]

The public response was immediate. A petition from about a dozen people was sent to Arthur declaring, "How Dare You Compare This Ghastly Object With the Works of Michelangelo." The "hideous" piece might have "snob appeal," but it would be much better to beautify the square by planting shrubs and trees. Letters began to pour into the mayor's office. Dozens of employees on a single floor of a local insurance company added their names to a petition that voiced their "overwhelming opinion" against the purchase. Another man predicted that, even without any formal training in art, he or the mayor could have put together a lump of metal that was just as good as Moore's work. A rival sculptor said that it might be "futile" to oppose the experts on the Art Committee but that public art must please the public;

to that end, he offered a sample his own work, a bad sort of Moore-ish knock-off. Sensing an opportunity, one art dealer proposed that, if the Moore was too expensive, his "brilliant" client, Sorel Etrog, could easily produce something suitable.[25]

Some people praised the Moore. One woman urged Givens to keep up the fight against the "barbarians" for a work produced specifically for New City Hall. An eleven-year-old told him that a modern sculpture was just what the square needed since the building would look "silly" with an old-fashioned statue out front.[26]

The Art Committee's recommendation to acquire the Moore came before the Board of Control on 10 March 1966. Somewhat surprisingly, the controllers supported Mayor Givens by a vote of 4 to 1, only William Dennison dissenting: "I feel the people of Toronto don't appreciate this type of sculpture." By this time, Henry Moore had reduced his asking price to $120,000 (plus $3,410 in taxes). Interviewed in England by the CBC, the sculptor was asked if he would not prefer to place his work before a "more sophisticated" European audience; he replied diplomatically that "in some ways an audience that isn't absolutely sure of what it wants may be better. A work of art or a piece of sculpture should not be immediately obvious to everyone."

Philip Givens tried to rally support. To a woman who said it was "idiotic" to spend this kind of money on such a "monstrosity" (a favourite derogatory term) at a time when taxes were rising continually, he replied it was a sound investment since Henry Moore was recognized as the world's greatest contemporary sculptor. The piece

was well worth the price and likely to be valued at nearly $1 million within a decade: "It was designed specifically with the New City Hall in mind, and at this price [of $120,000] will cost the taxpayers of Metropolitan Toronto about six cents apiece. It will unquestionably draw tens of thousands of people from all over the world who will come to see it as well as the New City Hall. This means that these thousands of people will be spending money in downtown Toronto at hotels, restaurants, stores and theatres, and other places. This brings many thousands of dollars of revenue into the city and therefore the burden of the small taxpayers like yourself will be lessened and not made greater." Not only was it good business but it would make a wonderful aesthetic complement to Revell's design. Publicly, Givens said, "We've got to have the guts to go through with it. I know this will make money for us by drawing tourists by the thousands. If they won't go for it I am not going to put my tail between my legs."

On the eve of the 16 March city council meeting to take up the recommendation, the press predicted that only five members would support the purchase while twelve were opposed and five undecided. Opponents did not hold back. Controller Dennison said "I wouldn't want it in my front yard or in my back yard." Alderman Ben Grys revealed that his wife had told him that she didn't like it and not to bother coming home if he supported the purchase (though in the end he did so anyway). Alderwoman Alice Summerville said that the telephone calls to her office were unanimously hostile. Aldermen Oscar Sigsworth and Fred Beavis took the populist line, saying, "There's only so much of this stuff the mayor can stuff down the taxpayer's throat," and "We've got cul-ture coming out of our ears and this is the last straw." When the vote came, the purchase was defeated by 13 to 10, leading the *Star*'s editorialists to remark upon "what a cornpone bunch we've elected to city council."[27]

The editors at *Canadian Architect* could not pass up the chance to note the comedy being played out in Toronto by the city council turning down the purchase of the Moore sculpture. Not only were the hostile aldermen ignoring the fact that such a work had been produced specifically for the site in consultation with Viljo Rev-ell, but they justified their decision on the grounds that they knew what they liked when it came to art. Special note was taken of the eighty office workers who had signed the petition calling *Three-Way Piece No. 2* "lurid, grotesque and ludicrous," to whom the editors offered a statue of a Coca-Cola bottle recently pictured in their magazine that might be paid for with one million Coke bottlecaps.[28]

To a person who lamented the decision, the mayor wrote that "it is most unfortunate that certain mem-bers of council did not measure up to the challenge." Eric Arthur declared that the rejection of the Art Selection Committee's recommendation indicated that it did not have the confidence of the city council, and he asked for a private meeting with the Board of Control to consider whether the committee could serve a useful purpose or ought to have its terms of reference revised.[29]

To a man from nearby Cooksville who complained of the city's extravagance, Givens replied that his mail was running two to one in favour of buying the Moore statue. He delivered a civics lesson, pointing out that, as well as its own spending, Toronto had to raise tax money to pay for the Board of Education (which made its own budget) and to cover 40 per cent of the cost of Metro (also beyond the city's control). He concluded cheekily, "How are things in Cooksville?"[30]

Even before the dust had settled, the idea was put for-ward of raising all the purchase money from voluntary donors. John C. Parkin claimed that he had been the first to suggest the idea to Mayor Givens right after the vote. Within a few days, a prominent local businessman wrote to pledge a gift of $500 towards a fund to buy the work privately and instal it on the civic square.[31] By the end of April 1966, Givens had received verbal pledges totalling $70,000. At that point he initiated his first direct contact with Henry Moore.

An important go-between was Joseph Hirshhorn, the multimillionaire American mining promoter who had amassed his fortune largely from the development of uranium deposits at Blind River, Ontario.[32] Hirshhorn was a great enthusiast for Moore, having secured over forty of his works for his huge collection, and had his eye upon *Three-Way Piece No. 2*. He offered to telephone Moore and lay the groundwork by telling the sculptor that he would relinquish any claim to it to make sure that Toronto got it. After talking to Moore, Hirshhorn advised Mayor Givens to get on the telephone and talk to the Englishman directly. When he did so, Moore agreed to accept the $120,000 in four annual instalments to ease the strain upon the city's budget. Money, said Moore, was not "the most important thing."

Moore agreed to wait until September for any payment to allow Givens time to get firm commitments for the additional $50,000 required to reach $120,000. The bronze was due to be cast in about two weeks to go to an exhibition near Arnhem in Holland whence it could be shipped to Toronto at the end of September. The only condition that Moore imposed was that he be allowed to order a second cast before the mould was broken, the second copy to be sold to the new National Gallery in West Berlin being designed by Mies van der Rohe. Givens readily accepted these conditions.[33]

Nevertheless, back in Toronto the debate over the virtues of the Moore sculpture rumbled on. One woman complained that Givens would be "letting down" the vast majority of Torontonians if it purchased this "monstrosity, and I doubt you or anyone else honestly think it beautiful." The bronze was like the "beaded lamps" or "horsehair furniture" with which women had filled their homes after the Second World War; to burden the "sensational" New City Hall with something so faddy was just as much of a nightmare.[34]

Rhetorical thunder boomed from a man who insisted that Moore was popular only owing to the "universal acclaim of the academic community": "It is a sad commentary on contemporary culture that the intellectuals have severed their once fruitful relationship with trained artists. This unfortunate schism between thinker and intellectual may derive from the former's tendency to verbalize knowledge and thus remove it from practice. Misdirected attempts to bridge the gulf have favoured the emergence of pseudo-messiahs in the visual arts. Such figures may be identified by the taint of commercial promotion invariably clinging to the whipped-up adulation wherein the professor has supplied idealogical amminication [sic] to the press agent." Maybe Givens felt an interest in the arts, but as a "trained administer [sic]" the man advised that advice should be sought from somebody "seasoned in practicing practical politics."[35]

The mayor tried to present reasoned responses to such diatribes. To the woman he wrote, "I do not 'profess' to like the Moore sculpture, I do like it, and as for adopting one of the latest fashions just to be 'in,' it may interest you to know that Moore's works have been 'in' for about forty years." Forty-three municipalities and countless institutions owned pieces by him. Anyone might admire realist art, "but the ability to understand and appreciate that which is purely symbolic must be acquired, and you cannot acquire it if you do not keep an open mind about all forms of art." To those who condemned him for arguing that the purchase was a sound investment, he admitted that he had tried to sway the city council with this argument, "but that is not now nor never [sic] has been my sole reason for acquiring it. I want this masterpiece on the square for the cultural enjoyment of this and future generations."[36]

He told the angry man that the decision to purchase was not a whim of his alone. The Art Selection Committee had enthusiastically responded to the chance of a lifetime by seeking to acquire a statue specifically designed for the square after consultations between Revell and Moore. Each age had its own way of life, art, and architecture, and the present one ought to be commemorated in this way.[37]

To those who registered the "beef" that a Torontonian or at least a Canadian had not been given the commission, Givens responded that "artistic greatness is international and knows no national boundaries." Canadians would have "this great standard of perfection" from the foremost sculptor of the age. The mayor promised that next year there would be an exhibition of sculpture in the square organized by Canada's National Gallery, and at that time it was quite likely that the city would decide to purchase a home-grown work.[38]

Those who wrote in praise of his views got an enthusiastic response from Givens. To the claim that people like William Dennison showed a "tragic" lack of "spiritual awareness," the mayor responded that "it is not easy to convince all the members of the council that objects of cultural significance are a boon to the city – some of them would be happy to see the city regress to the cobblestone days, although others have a little more imagination."[39]

Meanwhile, the scheme to raise the money to buy the sculpture from private donations gained momentum though getting firm commitments for the final thousands proved challenging. Ontario's former lieutenant governor, Keiller Mackay, agreed to head up the campaign. Working through the noted photographer Roloff Beny, Givens arranged the final details. Beny reported from London that Moore was "deeply touched" by efforts to find the proper home for his work. Over a scotch-and-soda at the Atheneum Club, the sculptor agreed to reduce his asking price to $100,000 out of esteem for Revell, pro-

vided that no publicity was given to this concession. On a practical level, Givens telephoned the federal minister of national revenue and secured his consent that, if the city issued receipts to people labelled "Donations for the Henry Moore Sculpture Fund," the amounts subscribed by individuals and corporations would be tax-deductible.[40]

By the beginning of June, Keiller Mackay was reporting that the purchase fund was within easy reach of the target of $100,000 (or £33,033) so that the final details could be ironed out. Givens wrote directly to Moore to advise him that Toronto art dealer Blair Laing would be coming to give him a banker's draft for £5,000 pounds as a deposit. Givens promised the balance in four instalments of £7,000 (plus £33 extra at the end) in 1967, 1968, 1969, and 1970 (with no interest payable), though he was sufficiently embarrassed by Moore's generosity that he even offered to pay the full cost upon delivery. When the sculptor agreed to the instalment purchase, Givens professed himself "thrilled and delighted" at the prospect of completing Revell's ensemble.[41]

Within three weeks Moore replied that he was very happy with the offer but that he would take no payment until the work was actually installed in Toronto. Only the two copies had been made and he would not authorize any miniature replicas to be produced. Givens requested that it should be shipped to Toronto as soon as possible, since it had become something of a "cause celebre," and he wished to organize a public unveiling while the weather was still fine. Because the work was almost eleven feet high, over eleven feet long, and seven feet wide, weighing 1,800 kilos with a base of 800 kilos, it seemed impossible to send it by air so that it would have to come by sea to Toronto harbour. The mayor also consulted the sculptor about the proper placement of the work on the square, noting that there were some limitations on exactly where it could go owing to the structure of the underground garage beneath the paving. The best place seemed to be just south of the west tower where it would be visible not only from the square but from the west along the vista through the new courthouse that Metro was building on University Avenue north of Osgoode Hall.[42]

With the funds to purchase the sculpture in hand, there now arose the question of how to pay for a proper base and lighting to display it to best advantage. Eric Arthur reported that he had been offered a contribution of $5,000 that he believed could be used for this purpose. The mayor asked if John B. Parkin Associates would be prepared to design the base, and John C. Parkin agreed. He telephoned Henry Moore in England and consulted him about the shape and materials that would be most suitable. The sculptor pointed out a location where he and Revell had talked of placing the work, roughly where the mayor had suggested; the base ought to be elliptical with discreet lights shining upward. Moore promised a final recommendation in early July but failed to deliver, so the Parkin firm got to work on its own designing something suitable.[43]

The Art Selection Committee also wanted to have its say and suggested that for safety reasons the sculpture should be mounted at ground level but with a base and embedded lighting surrounded by large pebbles that might discourage people from trying to climb onto the bronze. In mid-August, Keiller Mackay appeared before the Board of Control along with the committee members to advise them that the work had been purchased and would be presented to the city. He promised that the plinth would also be paid for out of contributions, and once the plans were set the city could begin issuing the tax receipts for the donors to the fund.[44]

By that time, City Hall Coordinator Raymond Bremner was becoming concerned that decisions must be taken so work on the base could start as soon as possible to be completed in time for an unveiling ceremony in October. City employee Nicholas Vardin, who had been placed in charge of preparing the final drawings, complained to Bremner that passing all the paper back and forth between the committee and the Parkin offices was taking up a great deal of time, "but in matters of art it appears that everybody and his uncle wants to get into the act. You know from past experience that once you have a committee dealing with a thing like this we are likely to end up with no base at all, therefore I should appreciate if you would give this matter your personal attention." Construction had to begin by the third week of September at the latest. Tony Pellegrino, the man responsible for the actual work, was going to be "hopping mad" about the rush. Claiming to be to frightened to do so himself, Vardin asked Bremner to break the news to Pellegrino and wished him "the best of luck."

Anything that the city of Toronto did was bound to become enmeshed in endless debate. As late as 22 June

1966, council members Alice Summerville and Fred Beavis stood alone in voting against the placement of the sculpture on the square. The Board of Control and city council had to approve the exact location, and there were fears that William Dennison, always the squeaky wheel, would demand last-minute changes.[45] In the end, various companies contributed a total of $1,555 for materials to build the base, and the city charged the private purchase fund $3,464 for construction and lighting of the plinth.[46]

Meanwhile, Henry Moore had gone travelling and did not respond to requests for his views on the siting of the sculpture and the design of the base. The architects delivered their final plans on 31 August without his advice and shipped them off to England.[47]

Eric Arthur became highly irritated because at the same time John C. Parkin sent him a confidential letter setting out his views on exactly where the statue ought to be placed but simultaneously copied his letter to the mayor. Never before, said Arthur, had he received a confidential message that had also been sent at the same time to somebody else. He was particularly annoyed because Parkin seemed to be misinformed about several matters: he had rarely attended any meetings of the Art Selection Committee and his delegate, Peter Warren, had remained silent. Why did Parkin want the committee reconstructed and its membership broadened so that it could deal with the entire fabric of the new city hall and the square, since that was precisely what it was already doing with the approval of the Board of Control? That was why the committee had recommended the Parkin

firm do the overall landscape plan for the podium and asked for advice on locating the Moore as well as many other tasks.

Arthur said that the committee was unhappy with the overall landscaping plan (particularly the deplorable bandshell). There had been improvements to the square since it opened but there was still a lack of professional control. The parks commissioner was keen to discuss the landscaping of the podium, but this was a good time to deal with the whole ensemble. The committee had been asked to give its opinion on a multitude of matters (like uniform signage) and had authority from the Board of Control to commission designs inside or out of city hall and even pay fees for these services, so there existed no lack of support from the politicians. Recently, the committee had been asked about Christmas decorations for the square in order to prevent a repetition of a hackneyed design endorsed the previous year by the property commissioner that involved a low-cost artificial tree with a result "equally suitable (or not, as you please) for a house across the Humber or the most ordinary office building."

Parkin was reproved for arousing unnecessary alarm; better to have kept such views for the committee alone. Why create the impression for the mayor that the committee could not make decisions in the spirit of Revell's design, particularly since Givens seemed to want to give it more and more responsibility? "May I add, finally, that we cannot for all occasions think of the City Hall in terms of purity and light": some occasions like Christmas were for the citizenry to enjoy as even Westminster

Abbey showed on occasion. Arthur said he believed that he and John C. Parkin shared a kind of trusteeship over Revell's legacy and that he would feel obliged to resign if he thought he had let other trustees down.[48]

Since Parkin had sent his views to the mayor, this dust-up could not be entirely hushed up, and Arthur passed on his response to the Board of Control, which discussed the matter. On 12 September 1966 the Art Selection Committee decided that the city should award a five-year contract to prepare and oversee the embellishment of the podium, and, in order to mollify Parkin, it proposed retaining his firm to prepare a detailed plan. On 14 September the Board of Control formally recommended that the city accept the gift of the Moore statue on a plinth in the recommended location, and that a suitable unveiling ceremony be planned.[49]

Givens continued to defend the new city hall and the square against complaints of municipal excess. He repeated the argument that careless spending and extravagance were not the cause of much of the rise in municipal taxes, which were equally driven by the funding of the Board of Education and the Metro government. Still, "it is not easy to convince every citizen that objects of cultural significance are a boon to the city – some would be happy to see the city regress to the horse-and-buggy days although others have a little more imagination." And the Moore sculpture would cost the taxpayers nothing since it was being funded by civic-minded folk who appreciated that there existed more than just the "physical aspects of living." To a woman who applauded his determination to secure the bronze,

Givens wrote, "I hope that what you call my courage does not cost me the next election."[50]

On 7 October 1966 came the news that the Moore sculpture had been loaded aboard ship in Rotterdam to arrive in Toronto in a fortnight. The Hendrie Cartage Company donated its services to move the large object from the docks to Nathan Phillips Square.[51] With the unveiling set for 27 October, Givens tried to persuade art collector Joseph Hirshhorn to attend in honour of his role in the negotiations with Moore, but he declined to appear. On the eve of the ceremony, Roloff Beny wired that he had drunk a toast to the event with Moore at his home in Much Hadham in England.[52]

Philip Givens organized a suitable celebration with a band concert beginning at 7:30 in the evening and the unveiling at 8:30. The mayor informed Moore that the affair had been a "smashing success" with a "fantastic" public response, attended by ten thousand people (though some of them were undoubtedly attracted by the fact that the city hall rink was being opened for its third season of skating at 9:20 by Otto and Maria Jelenek, stars of the Ice Capades and local celebrities).[53]

Mayor Givens began the proceedings by proclaiming that "the Philistines have retreated in disorder." The only discordant note was struck by a group of about fifteen architecture students from the University of Toronto, who marched through the crowd with their own creation, a piece of "junk sculpture" labelled the "Archer Tester," consisting of a coffee pot nailed to an old spinning wheel to which was also attached a rusty can and some other bits and pieces. A sign was raised announc-

ing, "8 out of 10 pigeons prefer Archer Tester." A dozen police promptly stepped in to remove the protesters, whereupon their "sculpture" disintegrated. The students shouted "Take it off" about the shrouded "Archer," as though attending the now-demolished burlesque house on the south side of Queen Street. The reporter from the New York *Times* recorded, "Thus did instant culture come last night to Toronto, a city known more for its hockey than its art."[54]

Showing that talent for humourless indignation that was a Toronto staple, student leader Maldwyn G. Williams and his associates immediately protested to the mayor that their sculpture had been "tragically destroyed" by the militaristic actions of the guardians of law and order. This "forceful dismemberment" was typical of current attitudes towards sculptors and artists. Givens's restrained answer observed that if city officials

had been told in advance about this piece of public theatre, it would have been welcomed with "open arms," but that it smacked more of "serious discourtesy" to interrupt speeches by eminent Canadians like Keiller Mackay and Eric Arthur. Not knowing what was happening, the police had acted swiftly to quell the disturbance. The mayor added that young and broadminded students surely ought to appreciate the celebration of a piece of sculpture by an Englishman adorning a wonderful building designed by a Finn.[55]

As the covering fell away from Moore's bronze, a baby cried out and one woman muttered, "Oh my god," but most people cheered. The man from the New York *Times* took the avuncular view that "it was a night to cheer those who hope that gloomy old Toronto has acquired a new image." Givens also thought that things had come off pretty well: on a formal letter of congratulations to City Hall Coordinator Raymond Bremner, "Phil" scrawled, "You're the greatest – till next time."[56] But just to show that the old demons that plagued the city had not entirely been exorcised, Philip Givens was defeated in the next mayoralty election. The victory of William Dennison was widely attributed to Givens's over-enthusiastic promotion of Viljo Revell's building and Henry Moore's sculpture.

There was no Torontonian who had devoted more time and energy to creating New City Hall than Eric Arthur. For his efforts Arthur was roundly attacked by one city

7.3
The tourist view of the Archer and the square.

7.4
The tourist view of a civic symbol sunset.

alderman in the spring of 1968 for the large sums that he and his son were receiving for overseeing the renovation of the historic St Lawrence Hall as the city's Centennial celebration project.[57] A detailed accounting for the years 1957 to 1968 revealed that Eric Arthur had been paid the princely sum of $32,685.14 in civic funds for his work on the new city hall competition and later on the Art Selection and Furnishing Design committees.[58]

The professor was so offended by the attack that he instructed his lawyer to write to Mayor Dennison to protest that a "distinguished career" "should not be blemished much less destroyed in the discussions which involve the expenditure of public funds." This was especially true, said the lawyer, for "a quiet, gentle, scholarly architect of Professor Arthur's age and standing." The lawyer carefully enumerated the various tasks that Arthur had been asked to undertake, all approved by city council, and conveyed to the mayor Arthur's wish to resign from all such activities. Chastened by the counter-attack, Dennison had a confidential discussion with the Board of Control, though the end result seems to have been the dissolution of the Art Selection Committee and the creation of a formal policy concerning the display of artwork in New City Hall.[59]

The entire drama of the creation of New City Hall revealed, as Charles Porteus, a bemused Montrealer, had observed in the 1890s over the debate on whether or not electric trolleys should be allowed to run on Sundays, that "the spirit of mischief" was "Toronto's curse."[60]

7.5
New City Hall site,
view from the
south, 1957.

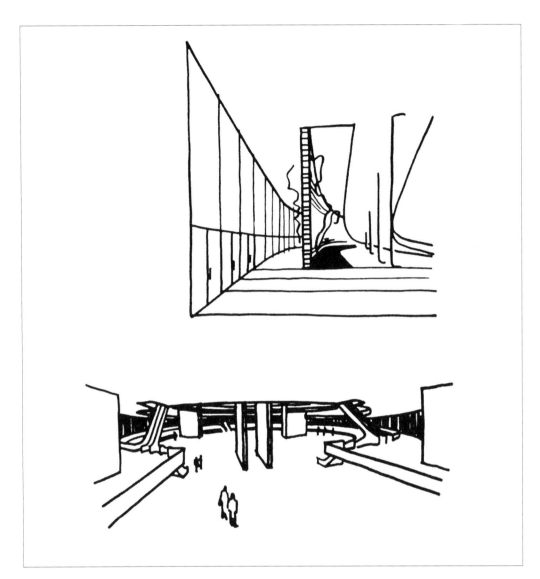

7.6
Revell's winning
sketches,
September 1957:
"Main entrance"
(outside the front
doors, looking
east, beneath
the ramp to the
podium), and
"Public access
area" (a double-
height space inside
the front doors,
not built).

7·7
Revell's winning sketches, September 1957: "The council chamber" (less theatrical than the ultimate version), and "View from gallery level" (the interior promenade around the council chamber, with views of the public square to the south).

7.8
New City Hall,
view from the
south, 1965.

Appendix

International Competition, 1957–1958

It was essential that the competitors were not known to the judges by name. The number assigned to each corresponded to the date of their initial expression of interest. Viljo Rewell (or Revell) from Helsinki, Finland, was number 401. There were 513 enquiries for competition instructions. Almost 500 entries were ultimately submitted.

The full list of entrants has never been published until now.

The order here is by geography, that is, alphabetically by nation and by city. Architectural practices may be individuals, groups or firms, and the almost 500 submissions reflected the work of thousands of individuals worldwide. "Extra" names that appeared in entrants' information have been included here. The names of the eight finalists are signalled as well.

Some errors may persist from the period; the locales and addresses are spelled as they were submitted by the entrants and transcribed in 1958. Personal, company, municipal, and even national names may have changed since, though street names often endure.

The original typescript of entrants, by number from 1 to 513, is contained in City of Toronto Archives, Series 843 (New City Hall Competition), Box 147081, File 43.

ARGENTINA

BUENOS AIRES
A.J. Dubourg, San Martin 662

BUENOS AIRES
J.C. Ferro, Cervino 3931, Cap. Federal

BUENOS AIRES
A. Vilmanis, Gallardo 3250, San Miguel

BUENOS AIRES
M. Szabo, Juncal 2842

BUENOS AIRES
A. Baccara, Parana 1038

MENDOZA
Ernesto Tedeschi, Casilla de Correo 73 (with C.E. Vallhonrat)

TIGRE
Jacobo Saal, Los Andes 624

AUSTRALIA

BLAXLAND, NSW
Craig, Hall, Webber, Wooley, Catalpa Ave.

BOX HILL, VICTORIA
S. Mackintosh, 24 Arnott St.

CANBERRA
R.G. Warren, Capitol Chambers, Civic Centre

CANBERRA
R. Purkis, 14 McGregor St. Deakin

CANBERRA
O.A. Balogh, Australian National University, Architect's Office

CANBERRA
D.W. Ryan, 12 Yapanyah St. O'Connor

EAGLEMONT, IVANHOE N21, VICTORIA
W.A.J.P. Holgar, 22 Ormond Rd.

EAST MELBOURNE
D. Mirams, 121 Grey St.

KEW E4, VICTORIA
Peter Burns, 20 Edgecombe St.

PYMBLE, NSW
Dr. H. Epstein, 67 Telegraph Rd.

SEAFORTH NSW
L.P. Kollar, 6 Battle Bldg.

SYDNEY, NSW
M.J. Barnes, 110 Phillip St.

SYDNEY, NSW
E.M. Nicholls, Caltex House, 167 Kent St.

YERONGA, S. BRISBANE
R.F. Gibson, 104 Rome St. (with D. Winson)

AUSTRIA

WIEN 17
O. Erhartt, Promenadeg 31 (with P. Detre)

BELGIUM

ANTWERP
V. Maermans, 18 Rue des Juifs

BRUSSELS
Groupe Forum, 12 Rue des Deux Eglisses (with Rene Aerto)

EVERE-BRUSSELS 14
H. Vijfeyken, 931 Chaussé de Louvain

BOLIVIA

LA PAZ
L.&A. Iturralde, Edificio de la Compania Boliviana de Seguros, Calle Colon No. 152, Oficina 502, Casilla Postale No. 229

BRAZIL

BOTAFOGO, RIO DE JANEIRO
J.H. Rocha, Rua Visconde de Ouro Preto No. 64, Apt. 20 (with N. Fontes Goncalves)

BROOKLYN PAULISTA, SAO PAULO
J.M. Ruchti, Rua Barao de Jaceguai No. 28

RIO DE JANEIRO
R. Galvao Jr. , Av. Rio Branco 128, Sala 15

RIO DE JANEIRO
F.M. Regio Paixao, Eigueiredo Magalhaes 823, Apt. 612

SAO PAULO
Prof. G.R. Caron, Rua Joao Bricola 67-4 Andar

SAO PAULO
F.A. Pestalozzi, Avenida Ipiranga 1123, 11°

SAO PAULO
F.M. Penteado, Rua Bento Freitas 305 R. 61

SAO PAULO
A. Rubio Morales, Rua Bento Freitas 306

SAO PAULO
R. Carneiro Vianna, Bento Freitas 306-Sala 53 (with R. Sievers)

SAO PAULO 10
L. Marsicano Guedes & Assoc. Rua Barao de Itopetininga 124, Sala 1002

CANADA

CALGARY, ALBERTA
J.K. English, 1531 Centre St. N.E.

DON MILLS, ONTARIO
M. Ruchlewicz, 19 Donway West

DON MILLS, ONTARIO
R.M. Legge, 24 Mocassin Trail

DON MILLS, ONTARIO
J.H. Andrews, (c/o Graduate School of Design, Harvard University), J.B. Parkin & Associates, 1500 Don Mills Rd.
(FINALIST #7)

DON MILLS, ONTARIO
A.B. Leman, 17 Bradgate Rd.

DON MILLS, ONTARIO
Maxwell Miller, 1 Birchbank Lane (with G. Robinson)

DOWNSVIEW, ONTARIO
R.W. Anderson, R.R.1

EDMONTON, ALBERTA
J.D. Annett, 11316 109A Ave.

ELLIOTT LAKE, ONTARIO
D. Perry Short, MacFarlane Rd.

FORT WILLIAM, ONTARIO
R.I. Ferguson, c/o McIntosh Assoc. 308 Victoria Ave.

GRANBY, QUEBEC
E. Hansen, 38 Ottawa St.

HAMILTON, ONTARIO
A.F. Taylor, 228 Bay St. S. Apt. 7

HAMILTON, ONTARIO
M.W.A. Jones, 175 Park St. S.

LONDON, ONTARIO
Philip C. Johnson, 362 Queens Ave.

MONTREAL, QUEBEC
I.W. Campbell, 161 5th St. Pont Viau (with I.D. Elliott)

MONTREAL, QUEBEC
Dobush & Stewart, 4635 Sherbrooke St. W.

MONTREAL, QUEBEC
H.A. Nottidge, 3300 Ridgewood Ave. Apt. 11

MONTREAL, QUEBEC
Mayerovitch & Bernstein, 1500 St. Catherine St. West

MONTREAL, QUEBEC
Victor Prus, 4693 Sherbrooke St. W.

MONTREAL, QUEBEC
Dimitri Dimakopoulos, Room 410, Dominion Square Bldg.

MONTREAL, QUEBEC
Oscar G. Vagi, 5735 Cote des Neiges, Apt. 20

MONTREAL, QUEBEC
J. Kolenda, 3850 Cote St. Catherine

MONTREAL, QUEBEC
Rother/Bland/Trudeau, 1552 St. Matthew St. W.

MONTREAL, QUEBEC
A. Meyer, 456 Pine Ave. W. Apt. 19

MONTREAL, QUEBEC
André Blouin, 420 Cote St. Antoine

MONTREAL, QUEBEC
unnamed (possibly a second entry from André Blouin)

MONTREAL 26, QUEBEC
Aza Avramovitz, 5485 Lavoie Ave

MORRISBURG, ONTARIO
C.C. Wilkie, P.O. Box 155

OTTAWA, ONTARIO
A. Birkhans, 9 Elmdale Ave.

OTTAWA, ONTARIO
P.R. Moy, 677 Maclaren St. Apt. 2

OTTAWA, ONTARIO
H.V. Massey, Commonwealth Bldg.

OTTAWA, ONTARIO
C.L. Morris, 36 Melgund Ave.

OTTAWA, ONTARIO
J.N. Way, c/o D.L. Turnbull, 34 Belmont Ave.

PETERBOROUGH, ONTARIO
Craig & Zeidler, 147 Hunter St. W.

QUEBEC CITY, QUEBEC
A.F. Gilbert, 915 St. Cyrille St.

REXDALE, ONTARIO
S. Sheldon, 60 Porterfield Rd.

ST. LAURENT, QUEBEC
L.D. Warshaw, 440 Bertrand St.

SUDBURY, ONTARIO
L. Rebanks, c/o Messrs. Fabbro & Townend, 251 Lorne St. (with J. Fielding)

TORONTO, ONTARIO
J.H. Scheel, 620 Avenue Rd.

TORONTO, ONTARIO
Sieghard Schmidt, 98 Lyndhurst Ave.

TORONTO, ONTARIO
Vladan Milic, Ing. Arch., 347 Bayview Ave.

TORONTO, ONTARIO
Bregmann & Hamann, 7 Adelaide St. E.

TORONTO, ONTARIO
David Horne, 556 Huron St. (FINALIST #2)

TORONTO, ONTARIO
Alan Graham, 24 Cottingham Rd.

TORONTO, ONTARIO
Pentland & Baker, 490 Jarvis St.

TORONTO, ONTARIO
Wilson & Newton, 696 Yonge St.

TORONTO, ONTARIO
A. Crossley (*no address listed*)

TORONTO, ONTARIO
Walter Agius, 15 Charles St. E. Apt. 806

TORONTO, ONTARIO
Govan, Ferguson, Lindsay et al., 10 Price St.

TORONTO, ONTARIO
Eugene Janiss, 745 Mt. Pleasant Rd.

TORONTO, ONTARIO
Michael Bach, 31 Kirkbradden Rd. W.

TORONTO, ONTARIO
Leslie Forster, 77 York St.

TORONTO, ONTARIO
J.L. Blatherwick, Associated Arch. 119 Davenport Rd.

TORONTO, ONTARIO
Sharp, Webb & Gillespie, Apt. 1105, Falcon Tower, 111 Lawton Blvd.

TORONTO 5, ONTARIO
Brian Shawcroft, 40 Park Rd.

TORONTO 5, ONTARIO
Wiles, Wasteneys & Wilkes, 62 Charles St. E.

TORONTO 5, ONTARIO
J. Pring, 40 Park Road

TORONTO 6, ONTARIO
J.C. Parkins [sic], 1500 Don Mills Rd. Postal Station J

TORONTO 7, ONTARIO
Gordon S. Adamson & Assoc., 52 St. Clair Ave. E.

TORONTO 7, ONTARIO
H. Fliess, 224 Merton St., (with J.A. Murray)

TORONTO 12, ONTARIO
Keith C. Spratley, 133 Broadway Ave.

TORONTO 12, ONTARIO
C.M. Bakker, 122 Ridley Blvd.

TORONTO 12, ONTARIO
D.M.A. Shewan, 3054A Yonge St.

TORONTO 13, ONTARIO
Carter, Colemand & Rankin, 2201 Kingston Rd.

TORONTO 17, ONTARIO
Servos & Cauley, 619 Bayview Ave.

TORONTO 17, ONTARIO
L. Marinoff, 970 Eglinton Ave. E.

VANCOUVER, BRITISH COLUMBIA
E.L. Phelps, Grosvenor Hotel

VANCOUVER, BRITISH COLUMBIA
R.B. Ritchie, c/o Townley & Matheson, 1376 Hornby St.

VANCOUVER, BRITISH COLUMBIA
Chris Owtram, 1684 Harwood St.

VANCOUVER, BRITISH COLUMBIA
W.R. Ussner, 709 W. Georgia St.

VANCOUVER, BRITISH COLUMBIA
A.D. Geach, 2222 Allison Rd.

VANCOUVER, BRITISH COLUMBIA
C.B.K. Van Norman, 1030 West Georgia St.

VANCOUVER 9, BRITISH COLUMBIA
P. Mees, Hale & Harrison, 2594 West Broadway

VICTORIA, BRITISH COLUMBIA
P. Cotton, 975 Fairfield Rd.

WEST VANCOUVER, BRITISH COLUMBIA
A. Webber, 5055 Bear Lane

WESTMOUNT, QUEBEC
W. Lukasik, 364 Oliver Ave.

WESTMOUNT, QUEBEC
C. Frey, 439 Grosvenor Ave. Apt. 18

WESTMOUNT, QUEBEC
D.K. Linden, 310 Victoria Ave.

WESTMOUNT, QUEBEC
A. Schrier, 4139 Sherbrooke St. W.

WESTMOUNT, QUEBEC
H.T. Langston, 1375 Greene Ave.

WESTON, ONTARIO
J.H. Albarda, 5 Lawrence Ave. W.

WESTON, TORONTO 15, ONTARIO
R. Brown, 39 Walsh Ave.

WINNIPEG, MANITOBA
W. Holzbauer, University of Manitoba

CUBA

LA HABANA
G. Moreno Lopez, Av. de las Misones 29

CZECHOSLOVAKIA

AUGUSTA 12
Dedecek, Minovsky, Stolicny, Spu-Bratislava U129

BRATISLAVA
J. Chovanec, Jasenova U1.c.13

BRATISLAVA
M. Chorvat, Ul. Csl. armady 37/c

BRATISLAVA
J. Rajchjl, Malinovskeho Blok 38

BRNO
Ivan Ruller, Hroznova 24

BRNO
Prof. B. Fuchs, Hvezdarenska 2

E. BRNO
V. Radimski, Lesnicka 46 (with E. Steflicek)

PRAGUE 6
Dr. J. Otruba, Kijevska 6

PRAGUE 6
J. Vaculik, Na. Piskach 5

PRAGUE 7
Jiri Kaderabek, Kostelni 44

PRAHA 12
J. Bradac, V Horni Stromce 6

PRAHA 6
J. Stursa, Zikova 4 (with S. Snadjr)

PRAHA XIX
K. Filsak, Zukovova 41

PRAHA XIX
M. Stoklasa, Zelena 7 (with J. Myslbek)

PRAHA-BUBENEC
J. Havlicek, Smeralove 21

DENMARK

COPENHAGEN
Ib Rasmussen, Badsteestraede 11 C

COPENHAGEN
Gunnlogson & Nielsen (*no address listed*)
(FINALIST #4)

ODENSE
Kai Boergen, Vestergade 17

VIBY J
J.K. Schmidt, Balagervej 7

ENGLAND

AYLESBURY, BUCKINGHAMSHIRE
T.P. Bolton, Doveleat, Ellesborough Rd. Wendover

BLACKPOOL
John Farrar, 257 Church St.

BRENTWOOD, ESSEX
D.J. Appleby, Strawberry Fair, Tennyson Rd., Hutton

BRISTOL
K.W. Smithers, 7 Percival Rd., Clifton

BRISTOL 9
P.N. Taylor, Avon Lodge, The Avenue, Sneyd Park

BUSHEY, HERTFORDSHIRE
J.F. Metcalfe, 6 Bournehall Lane

CANTERBURY, KENT
R. Paine & Partners, The White House, St. Peter's Lane

CASTELTOWN
K.H. Murta, (Hutchinson), School House, Sunderland

CHISLEHURST, KENT
A. Ball, Elmside, St. Nicholas Lane

DERBY
H.O.J. Hogg, 124 Stenson RD.

EASTBOURNE
D.R. Evans, 35 Albion Rd. Sussex

FOLKESTONE
K. Waite, 127 Sandgate Rd. Kent (with D.A. Stewart)

GREAT MISSENDON, BUCKINGHAMSHIRE
W. Leslie Jones, 59 High St.

HAM, SURREY
J.A. Strubbe, Beaufort Studio, Ham St.

HARLOW, ESSEX
E. Jones, 158 Halling Hill (with Harding & Gorgoloewski)

HATCH END, MIDDLESEX
H.G. Herbert, 252 Uxbridge Rd.

HERTFORD
R.Y. MacDonald, 29 Byde St.

HORNCHURCH, ESSEX
F.G. James, 31 Burnway

KENILWORTH, WARWICKSHIRE
J.M. McLellan, 24 Southbank Rd.

KINGSTON-ON-THAMES
J.S. Collins, 63 Gibbon Rd.

LEICESTER
T.R. Hancock, 113 Spencefield Lane, Evington

LEIGH-ON-SEA, ESSEX
R.J. Turner, 34 Tudor Gdns.

LONDON E11
R. Hardy, 27 Wanstead Pl. Wanstead

LONDON E15
H.C. Pratt, 399-401 High St. Stratford

LONDON N2
D. Cole, 79 Fortis Green

LONDON NW1
R.H. Rosner, 2 Clarence Terrace, Regents Park

LONDON NW1
J. Dartford, 59 Gloucester Cres.

LONDON NW3
M. Hillman (Lehrman), 61 Hampstead High St.

LONDON NW6
P.P. Krasucki, 16 Narcissus Rd.

LONDON SW 15
F.S. Hodge, 2 Ponsonby Rd. Roehampton

LONDON SW1
Sir J. Brown, Henson & Part., 117 Sloane St.

LONDON SW1
R. Stout, 93 St. George's Square

LONDON SW11
R.G. Smith, 18 St. John's Hill

LONDON SW3
D. Bristow, 1 Whiteheads Grove, Chelsea

LONDON SW5
P. Hamilton, 44 Earls Court Square (with J. Bicknell)

LONDON SW7
Challen & Floyd, 7 Cromwell Rd.

LONDON SW7
A.F. Bennett, 35 Queens Gate Mews, Kensington

LONDON SW7
K.R. Saillard, 57 Onslow Gardens, South Kensington

LONDON SW 20
R.V.P. Mawson, 119 Aylward Rd., Merton Park

LONDON W1
A. Park, C/43 Portland Place (with D. Duck)

LONDON W1
G. Subiotta, 71 Blandford St.

LONDON W1
R.C. Arnold, Hanover Court, Hanover Square

LONDON W1
Douglas Stephen & Partner, 306 Wimpole St.

LONDON W1
Architects' Co-Partnership, 44 Charlotte St.

LONDON W11
M. Brawne & Assoc., 46 Chepstow Villas

LONDON W14
Gordon Redfern, 28 Glyn Mansions, Addison Bridge

LONDON W2
M.G. LePelley, 2 Maida Ave.

LONDON W8
K. Scott & Assoc., 177 Kensington High St.

LONDON WC1
Boissevain & Osmond, 2 Field Court, Gray's Inn

LONDON WC1
J.B. Wride, 67 Gordon Mansions, Torrington Pl.

LONDON WC1
Arthur W. Kenyon & Part., 15 Adeline Place, Bedford Square

LONDON WC1
Howes & Jackman, 1 Verulam Bldgs. Gray's Inn

LONDON WC1
D.DuR. Aberdeen & Partners, 19 Southampton Pl.

MAIDENHEAD
A.W. Snowdon Robertson, 27 High St.

MANCHESTER 15
G.R. Lovell, C.B.Pearson & Son, 24 Loxford St, All Saints

MANCHESTER 20
R.C. Stones, 300 Burton Rd. West Didsbury

NEWCASTLE-UPON-TYNE
F. Fielden, The Design Partnership, 27 Ridley Place

PRESTON, LANCASHIRE
Grenfell, Baines & Hargreaves, 12-24 Guildhall St.

PUTNEY, LONDON SW15
D. Marshall, 62 Belvedere Court (with B. Adams)

REDHILL, SURREY
A. Clark, The White Cottage, Somerset Rd. (with P. Hudson, A. Low, S. Smith)

RICHMOND, SURREY
T. Bliss, 6A Chilton Rd.

SUNDERLAND
S.W. Milburn & Partners, 9 The Esplanade

TEWIN, HERTFORDSHIRE
V.H. Lee, Whitespar, Queen Hoo Lane

UXBRIDGE, MIDDLESEX
D. Lanham, 27 The Greenway (with E. Barber)

WALLACEY, CHESHIRE
D.P. Reay, 20 The Oval

ETHIOPIA

ADDIS ABABA
E. Perret, P.O. Box 1409

FINLAND

HELSINKI
M. & R. Ypya, Johanneksentie 6

HELSINKI
V. Rewell (*alternate spelling, V. Revell; no address listed*) (FINALIST #6)

FRANCE

PARIS 6
A. Bourbonnais, 45 Rue Jacob

PARIS 6
Hoy Tse Nang, 9 Rue Monsieur le Prince

PARIS 7
E. Albert, 46 Rue de l'université

PARIS 8
M.P. Rainaut, 83 Rue la Boetie

PARIS 8
A. Remondet (Menkes), 79 Rue des Champs Elysées

PARIS VIII
P. Dufau, 28 Rue Bayard

PARIS 9
Jean Fayeton, 23 Rue Taitbout

PARIS 9
J. Semichon, 39 Rue de Treuse

PARIS 9
J. Bosson, 3 Rue Lafitte

PARIS 14
Casefont Franc, 97 Rue Champagne

PARIS 16
P. Branche, 16 Avenue de Versailles

PARIS 16
M. Galloy, 5 Rue du General Langlois (with A. Karney)

PARIS 16
P.E.G. Vaugelaude, 13 Rue du General Delestrain

PARIS 17
P. Van Waeyenberghe, 21 Cité des Fleurs

PARIS 17
D. Zavaroni, 201 Blvd. Pereire

SEINE-MARNE
J. Warnery, Palais de Fontainebleau

ADAM LA VARENNE
E. Dubroux, 12 Avenue Josephine, Seine (with C. Mabileau)

GERMAN DEMOCRATIC REPUBLIC

DRESDEN A20
W. Rauda, Heinrich-Zille-Strasse 14

GERMANY (WEST)

BERLIN LICHTERFELDE 11
K.H. Gassman, Schillerstrasse 17 (with J. Vogel, J. Assmann)

BERLIN-DAHLEM
Wassili Luckhardt, Fabeckstrasse 48

BOCHUM
F. Schulz, Ewaldstrasse 18

BREMEN
H. Reischel, Thos. Mann Strasse 50

DARMSTADT
T. Pabst, Dieburgerstrasse 146

DUSSELDORF
Bruno Lambard, Baden-Wurttemberg

ESSEN/RUHR
A. Schwelm, Hindenburgstrasse 21

FRANKFURT/MAIN
F. Kramer, Senckenberganlage 34

HAMBURG 26
H.W. Prell, Hammerlandstrasse 26, (with H. Beckmand)

HAMELIN
Werner Wunshmann, Ohsenerstrasse 6

HANNOVER
Fritz Eggeling, Saarstrasse 6

HANNOVER–ISERHAGEN
F. Wienker, Grosse Heide

KASSEL–WILHELMSHOHE
W. Haeseler, Landgraf-Karl-Strasse 11

MUNSTER/WEST F.
P. Eling (or Eggeling), Lonsstrasse 9

OBERHAUSEN-RHINELAND
Herbert W. List, Bebelstrasse 102

WIESBADEN
Rainer Schell, Nerotal 29

GREECE

ATHENS
Costa DeCavalla, 14 Karnun St.

HAITI

PORT-AU-PRINCE
S. Godefroy, P.O. Box 1294

PORT-AU-PRINCE
P. Baussan, c/o Batir Etage Pierre Coles, Rue Pavée

HOLLAND

AMSTERDAM
C.J.B. Nierstrasz, Van Breestraat 33

DELFT
Corney W. Manger, Soendastraat 12

HAARLEM
W.P. van Harreveld, Spaarnelaan 27

KATWIJKAANZEE
A. Botenbal, Risnonond 31

ROTTERDAM
G.L. Molenbroek, Pijnackersplein 21

ROTTERDAM
H.V. Andersen, Statenweg 66d

THE HAGUE
A.H. Tielman, Wagenstraat 135 (with N.J. Habraken)

HONG KONG

HONG KONG
Stanley Kwok, 14 Embassy Court

HONG KONG
H.E. Basto, Prince's Bldg.

HUNGARY
BUDAPEST
Benjamin, Boross, Preisich, VIII
Shahzy-Ul
BUDAPEST
Erwin Schomer, XII Ormodi V. 12

INDIA
AHMEDABAD
B.V. Doshi, Vasu/Shipla Town
Planning Architecture Industrial
Design, Balentine's Haveli, near
Three Gates
AHMEDABAD
D.M. Asarpota, 28 Adarsh Society
BOMBAY
J. Narwekar, Crescent Chambers,
Tamarind Lane, Fort
BOMBAY NO. 28
V.H. Karandikar, 129 Shivaji Park
LUCKNOW
B.D. Kshirsagar, c/o Chief Engineer
Eastern Command
MADRAS
P.M. Thacker, 31/1 Pantheon Rd.
Egmore
NEW DELHI
Dr. V.J. Mistry, "L" Bl. Room 113-A,
Central P.W.D.
NEW DELHI
A.P. Kanvinde, 14-F Central Ring,
Connaught Place

IRELAND
DUBLIN
D. O'Toole, 2 Lower Hatch St.
LIMERICK
C.J. Quinn, 86 O'Connell St.

ISRAEL
TEL AVIV
S.H. Nadler, 16-Bar-Kochbah St. (with
M. Nadler)
TEL AVIV
D. Karmi, 5 Ben-Zion Blvd.

ITALY
BOLOGNA
G. Marzuttini, Via Lame 31
BRESCIA
D. Gorlani Veronica, Gambera Str.
No. 2
FIRENZE
B. Luigi Dr. Arch., Via Masaccio 58
MILAN
Tekne, Via Durini 29/1
MILAN
Clerici, Faglia, Terzaghi, Magnaghi,
Via San Spirito 24
MILAN
Carlo Bassi, Via Borromei 11
MILAN
Dr. Prof. G. Bernasconi, Via Dell'Orso
16
MILAN
G. Simonetti, Via C. Battisti 1, (with P.
Ranzani)
ROME
G. Roisecco, Via Della Farnesina-
Camilluccia
ROME
C.H. Kahn, c/o American
Commission for Cultural Exchange
with Italy, Via Barberini 86
ROME
Dr. R. Severino, Via Giacinta Pezzana
27
ROME
Roberto Regala Jr., Via Prisciano 72
ROME
M. Nicoletti, Via F. Pinelli 7
ROME
P. Barucci, Dr. Arch. Via Salaria 346
ROME
F. Palpacelli, Piazza Galeria 1
TRIESTE
G. Beer, Piazza Liberta 3 (with Aldo
Cervi)

JAPAN
CHIYODA-KU, TOKYO
Y. Ohsuga, 6, 2-Chome, Kudan
CHIYODA-KU, TOKYO
Y. Nosu, Nosu Kentiku Sekkei
Zimusyo, 2-18 Uchisaiwai-cho

CHIYODA-KU, TOKYO
S. Hirata, Matsuda & Hirata, 1-2
Chome, Uchiwaiwai-cho
CHIYODA-KU, TOKYO
Takayoshi Yoda, 7 1-Chome,
Kojimachi
CHIYODA-KU, TOKYO
K. Ichiura, No. 18, 2-Chome,
Uchisaiwaicho
CHIYODA-KU, TOKYO
B. Yamaguchi, Maranouchi Bldg. #6
Naka-Yonga-Kan, Maranouchi
(with Y. Ishimura)
CHUO-KU, TOKYO
Denji Nakamura, c/o Yokogawa-
Komusho, No. 1-3 Chome, Ginza-
Nishi
CHUO-KU, TOKYO
S. Yoshikawa, c/o Sukiyabshiki Bldg.
No. 3 4-Chome, Ginza
CHUO-KU, TOKYO
Dr. G.M. Kume, New Ginza Dai-ichi
Bldg. No. 5, 7-Chome, Ginza
HIGASHI-KU, OSAKA
K. Oszaki, c/o Nikken Sekkei Kom V
Co. Ltd, 135-Chome, Kitahama
HIROSHIMA-SHI
Shigeo Sato, Engineering Faculty,
Hiroshima University, 3-Chome,
Senda-Machi
MINATO-KU, TOKYO
S. Aratani, 17 Fukide-cho, Shiba
MINATOKU, TOKYO
N. Hozumi, 16 3-Chome, Azabu-1,
Guramachi
NISHIKU, OSAKA
F. Nishizawa, 2-12 Kyomachibori-Dori
SETAGAYA-KU, TOKYO
Nag. Tsuchihaschi, c/o Mitomi, 1-381
Daita
SHINJUKU-TO, TOKYO
K. Mayekawa, No. 8, Honshio-cho
SHOWA-KU, NAGOYA
M. Kurokawa, 4-2, Kobaricho
SUGINAMIKU, TOKYO
H. Kosaka, 263 Eifukucho
TOKYO
K. Kawashima, No. 229, Jiyogaoka
Meguro-Ku

TOKYO
Fukunaga Mitsuya, 1 Akasaka-
Tameike, Minato-ku

TOKYO
Kyosuke Mori, 299 Honancho,
Suginami-ku

TOKYO
J. Sakakura, 6 Akasaka-Hinoki-cho,
Minato-ku

TOKYO
Kenzo Tange, 689 Seijo Setagaya

UCHIDE
K. Tanimoto, 63 Nishijura-cho

URAWA-CITY
Taneo Oki, 47 Shirahata

MORIGUCHI CITY
S. Nakazawa, 3-27 Takii-Motomachi,
Osaka Prefecture

KENYA

NAIROBI
Imre Rosza, P.O. Box 2309

LEBANON

BEIRUT
F. Willy Lups, P.O.B. 3708

MEXICO

MEXICO CITY
A.C. Asenjo, Casa Grandes 93-103,
Zona 12, Esq. Av. de la Morena

MEXICO CITY
O.G. Cotta, 2P181, Galveston 53

MEXICO CITY
A.A. Alvarez, Campos Eliseos 432,
Colonia Polanco

MEXICO CITY
A. Prieto Damas, 118 S. Jose
Insurgentes

MEXICO CITY
J.A. Pina, Palmas y Fresnos 71, San
Angelinn (with Whittemore &
Gomez)

MEXICO CITY
Ramon Marcos, Av. Edgar A. Poe, No.
30

MEXICO CITY
E. Castaneda Tamborel, Nuevo Leon
185

MEXICO CITY
E. Asunsolo, Liverpool #10-401

MEXICO CITY
J.C. Cevallos, Reformar & Lieja 8-602

MEXICO CITY 10
Antonio Peyri Macia, Presa Solis 35

MEXICO CITY 12
J. Konigsberg (Thomas), Nuevo Leon
No. 112-101

NEW ZEALAND

AUCKLAND
P.N. Morgan, Flat 2, 41 Shelley Beach
Rd., Herne Bay

WANGANUI
D.A. Wilson, E.E. Belchambers, 28
Victoria Ave.

PERU

LIMA
J.G. Lecca H., Chiclayo 353, Miraflores

POLAND

(CITY UNKNOWN)
J. Keernsienki (with A. Fajans) *(no
address listed)*

BY ZAKOPANE
Jan. Friedel, Ul Zatompem 32, Poronin

KRAKOW
Z. Gadek, Ul.Bohaterow, Stalingradu
84 m 7

KRAKOW
F. Dabowski, Odrowaza 10/5

POZNAN
Zenon Stepniowski, U1 Cybulskiego 7

SOPOT
Prof. W.S. Rembiszewski, Ul
Zeromskiego 15

TYCHY
G. Okolowicz, OsBl. 102 M.30

WARSAW
S. Jaszczewska, Karlowicza 1/1m 45

WARSAW
A. & M. Markiewicz, Walecznych
38M4

WARSAW
Czyz, Freta 28 (with A. Geppert, W.
Geppert, Skopinski)

WARSAW
S. Bienkunski, 19a Gosjezynskiego

WARSAW
J. Zbigniew Polak, U1 Kozia 3 m 11

WARSAW
M. Gintowt, Gosjecka 18/20 m 75

WARSAW
E. Bakowski, Ul. Chmielna 73/56

WARSZAWA-WLOCHY
Jan. Miserski, Cietrzewia 14

WROCLAW
Miron Sikorski, Ul. Nowoinejska
62/10

PUERTO RICO

SAN JUAN
H.F. Pinto, 204 San Juan Darlington
Bldg. (with R. Perez-Marchand)

RUMANIA

BUCHAREST
H. Bernard, Strasse Moise Nicoara 16

BUCHAREST
I. Serban, Str. Maria Rosetti 19 (with
W.D. Hardt, A. Ghelber)

BUCHAREST
Mihai Enescu, Arch., Calea Dorobant
232, Rion Stalin

BUCHAREST
I.M. Enescu, 5 Str. Belgrad

SCOTLAND

EDINBURGH 8
P. Nuttgens, Department of
Architecture, 16 George Square

SOUTH AFRICA

CAPE TOWN
J.M. Miszewski, School of
Architecture, University of Cape
Town (with R. Soltynski)

CAPE TOWN
F.L. Sturrock, 417 African Homes
Trust Bldg. 38 Wale St. (with J.
Barnett)

JOHANNESBURG
K.E.F. Gardiner & McFadyen, 22 Beresford House, Main St.

JOHANNESBURG
G.T. Gibson Henry, c/o Barclays Bank DCO, Commissioner St. Central

SCOTTBURG
J.J. Van Voorst, P.O. Box 78

STELLENBOSCH
Leroux & Malan, Senper Bldg. No. 3, Plein St.

SOUTHERN RHODESIA
SALISBURY
Don Fraser, P.O. Box 272

SPAIN
BARCELONA
Dennis Ball, Paseo de Gracia 47, 1°, 2°

BARCELONA
F.J. Barba Corsini, Aribau No. 195, 3°

MADRID
Jose M. Bustinduy Rodriguez, Castello St. 38

MADRID
R. De Aburto, Cea Bermudez 34

MADRID
Miguel Fisac, Villanueva 5

SEVILLE
P.M. Benjumea, Paseo de Colon No. 10

SWEDEN
STOCKHOLM
Hans Akerblad, Grevmagnigatan 4

STOCKHOLM
Jan Lunding, Norvagen 22

STOCKHOLM
S.Y. Alva, Farkisvagen 2, Lidingo

STOCKHOLM
L. Kurpatow, Vastmannagatan 14

STOCKHOLM
S. Backstrom, Blasieholmstorg 11 C

SWITZERLAND
GENEVA
R. Frei, 32 Chemin Naville, Conches (with K. Campbell)

GENEVA
A. Gaillard, 11 Rue Chantepoulet

LAUSANNE
Marice Bovey, Passage Saint-Francois 12

SIA ZURICH 6
C. Zuppiger, Stussistrasse 15

ST. GALLEN
P. Haas, Vadianstrasse 31

ST. GALLEN
F. Staheli, Tigersbergstrasse Nr 9

KIRCHBERG
D. Dietrich, Kanalweg 4, BE

SYRIA
ALEPPO
Z.K. Kaplan, Faculté des Ingenieurs

TRINIDAD
ST. CLAIR
Alfie Franco, 14 Cotton Hill

URUGUAY
MONTEVIDEO
Romeu, Requena, Careri, Stratta, Bacacay No. 1325

MONTEVIDEO
C. Baranano, Paysandu 1305

MONTEVIDEO
R. Fresnedo Siri, Av. Suarez 3281

USA
ALGIERS, LOUISIANA
M.I. Rubin, 3601 Pittari Pl.

ANN ARBOR, MICHIGAN
S.A. Sherman, 1117 Granger Ave.

AUSTIN 5, TEXAS
C.M. Pendley, 2410 San Antonio St.

BALTIMORE 18, MARYLAND
J. Elbridge Moxley & Son, 12 East 24th St

BAYSIDE, LONG ISLAND, NEW YORK
H. Shalat, 216-03 46th Ave.

BELLEVUE, WASHINGTON
Arch. Artist Group, 14445 S. E. 55th St.

BERKELEY, CALIFORNIA
G.M. McCue & Assoc. , 2007 Hopkins

BERKELEY, CALIFORNIA
J.W. Crisp, 1820 Spruce St.

BERKELEY, CALIFORNIA
F.S. Gerner, 1429 Grant St.

BERKELEY 4, CALIFORNIA
David Olsen, 2409 Telegraph Ave.

BIRMINGHAM, MICHIGAN
T. Lam, 1050 North Adams Rd. (with Louis F. Pacheco)

BIRMINGHAM, MICHIGAN
Begrow & Brown, 28 Maywood Rd.

BIRMINGHAM, MICHIGAN
J. Dworksi, 1080 North Woodward Ave.

BLOOMFIELD HILLS, MICHIGAN
Man. D. Dumlao, Cranbrook Academy of Art

BLOOMFIELD HILLS, MICHIGAN
M. Shiina, Cranbrook Academy of Art

BOSTON, MASSACHUSETTS
K.G. Terriss, 406 Marlborough 3rd floor rear

BRIARWOOD 35, QUEENS, NEW YORK
Herbert A. Tessler, 8416 Daniels St.

BROOKLINE 46, MASSACHUSETTS
C.E. Michaelides, 44 Stanton Rd.

BROOKLYN 5, NEW YORK
Olindo Grossi, Pratt Institute

BROOKLYN 5, NEW YORK
Wm. Breger, Pratt Institute, 215 Ryerson St.

BROOKLYN 10, NEW YORK
A.J. O'Connor, 3823 Glenwood Rd.

BUFFALO, NEW YORK
Cimini, 494 Franklin St. Rm. 7

CAMBRIDGE, MASSACHUSETTS
Alvaro Ortega, 45 Linnaean St. Apt. 2G

CAMBRIDGE, MASSACHUSETTS
The Architects Collaborative, 63 Brattle St.

CAMBRIDGE, MASSACHUSETTS
R. Gourlay, 1 Frost Terrace

CAMBRIDGE, MASSACHUSETTS
F.F. Bruck, 77 Walker St.

CAMBRIDGE, MASSACHUSETTS
D.R. McMullin, 698 Massachusetts Ave.

CHAMPAIGN, ILLINOIS
A.M. Richardson & Assoc., 117 ½ W. Church St.

CHICAGO, ILLINOIS
R.H. Zellner, 11308 S. Church St.

CHICAGO, ILLINOIS
C.S. Knight, 1240 North State Parkway

CHICAGO, ILLINOIS
Duo Assoc., 127 N. Dearborn

CHICAGO 3, ILLINOIS
Harry Weese, 104 S. Michigan

CHICAGO 14, ILLINOIS
Takeo Ito, 304 West Willow St.

CHICAGO 14, ILLINOIS
J.A. Holabird Jr., 180 N. Wabash Ave.

CHICAGO 14, ILLINOIS
R.F. Kichin, 444 Arlington Pl.

CHICAGO 16, ILLINOIS
J. Lippert, 3140 South Michigan Ave.

CHICAGO 25, ILLINOIS
J.S. Economou, 5000 N. California Ave.

CLEVELAND 20, OHIO
P.J. Hart, 12728 Woodland Ave.

COLUMBUS 3, OHIO
R. Guyer, 1688 E. Broad St.

COLUMBUS 21, OHIO
P.C. Zoelly, 2386 Dorset Rd.

CONCORD, CALIFORNIA
E. Riley, c/o Design Associates Inc. 2090 Willow Pass Rd.

COYTESVILLE, NEW JERSEY
J.E. Keegan, 2439 Second St.

CUYAHOGA FALLS, OHIO
E.K. Haag, 2765 Hudson Dr.

DENVER, COLORADO
Eugene D. Sternberg, 1930 Sherman St.

DETROIT 21, MICHIGAN
G.E. Crane, 16508 Cherrylawn

DETROIT 26, MICHIGAN
Suren Pilafien, 457 West Fort St. (with D.H. Sieg)

DETROIT 35, MICHIGAN
Berj Tashjian, 16596 James Couzens

FARMINGTON, MICHIGAN
T. Balogh, 28806 W. Eight Mile Rd.

FLUSHING 54, NEW YORK
A.J. Varnas, 30-11 Parsons Blvd.

GLENDORA, CALIFORNIA
M.H. Willson, 1018 E. Walnut Ave.

HARTSDALE, NEW YORK
J. Caponnetto, 20 Jennifer Lane

HIGHLAND PARK, ILLINOIS
P. Roesch, 2693 Sheridan Rd.

HIGHLAND PARK, ILLINOIS
Pafford K. Clay, 100 Laurel Ave.

JACKSONVILLE, FLORIDA
W.L. Stephens, 594 S. Edgewood Ave.

KALAMAZOO, MICHIGAN
D.W. Stearns, 1418 Stamford Ave.

KEY BISCAYNE, MIAMI, FLORIDA
R.C. Knight, 472 Fernwood Rd.

LOS ANGELES 5, CALIFORNIA
Maynard Lyndon, 3460 Wilshire Blvd.

LOS ANGELES 57, CALIFORNIA
John Kewell & Assoc. 1901 West Eighth St.

MINNEAPOLIS 29, MINNESOTA
Bruce A. Abrahamson, 7305 Shannon Drive

MONTGOMERY 4, ALABAMA
C.H. Lancaster Jr., 115 So. McDonough St.

NEW HAVEN, CONNECTICUT
C. Granberry, 110 Whitney Ave.

NEW YORK, NEW YORK
C.E. Tilton, 654 Madison Ave.

NEW YORK, NEW YORK
Jas. M. de Chiara, 136 West 42nd St.

NEW YORK, NEW YORK
C.C. Briggs, 104 East 40th St.

NEW YORK 4, NEW YORK
M. Blatt, c/o Th. Blatt, 32 Broadway

NEW YORK 9, NEW YORK
Ralph Myller, 645 East 14th St.

NEW YORK 10, NEW YORK
A.W. Geller, 333 East 23rd St.

NEW YORK 10, NEW YORK
Davis, Brody & Wisniewski, 220 East 23rd St.

NEW YORK 14, NEW YORK
H. Jackson, 124 Washington Place (with J. Tyrwhitt)

NEW YORK 16, NEW YORK
Leo S. Wou, 201 East 40th St.

NEW YORK 16, NEW YORK
P. Cashmore, 146 East 35th St.

NEW YORK 16, NEW YORK
P. Blake, 157 East 33rd St. (J. Neski)

NEW YORK 16, NEW YORK
B. Horvitz, 226 East 30th St.

NEW YORK 17, NEW YORK
I.M. Pei & Assoc., 385 Madison Ave. (FINALIST #8)

NEW YORK 17, NEW YORK
Moore & Hutchins, 800 Second Ave.

NEW YORK 17, NEW YORK
Cass Gilbert Jr., 342 Madison Ave.

NEW YORK 17, NEW YORK
Arch. Associated (Katz), 551 Fifth Ave.

NEW YORK 17, NEW YORK
Irving Hugh Merritt, 17 East 48th St.

NEW YORK 19, NEW YORK
G. Beiers, 250 West 57th St. (with G. Cavaglieri)

NEW YORK 21, NEW YORK
Ballard, Todd & Snibbe, 123 East 77th St.

NEW YORK 22, NEW YORK
Edelbaum & Webster, 624 Madison Ave.

NEW YORK 24, NEW YORK
W.I. Hohauser, 302 West 79th St.

NEW YORK 25, NEW YORK
Wei-fu Chun, 425 Riverside Dr.

NEW YORK 25, NEW YORK
A.G. D'Angelo, 316 West 107th St.

NEW YORK 28, NEW YORK
T.B. Gourlay, 1030 Park Ave.

NEW YORK 28, NEW YORK
N.C. Walker, 312 East 81st St.

NEW YORK 36, NEW YORK
R. Pomerance, 33 West 46th St.

NEW YORK 62, NEW YORK
L.L. Cinner, 1551 Unionport Road

PALO ALTO, CALIFORNIA
C. Arnold, 235 Webster St.

PARK FOREST, ILLINOIS
Swensson & Schaffer, 217 Indianwood

PENN VALLEY, NARBETH, PENNSYLVANIA
H.G. Egli, 28 Fairview Rd.

PHILADELPHIA, PENNSYLVANIA
H.W. Peschel, 469 Hermitage St.

PHILADELPHIA, PENNSYLVANIA
Wm. B. Hayward, 310 South 16th St.
(FINALIST #3)

PHILADELPHIA, PENNSYLVANIA
J.J. Jordan, 2020 Delancey Place

PHILADELPHIA, PENNSYLVANIA
J.A. Bardes, 2317 Waverly St.

PHILADELPHIA 3, PENNSYLVANIA
N.T. Montgomery, 140 North
Seventeenth St.

PHILADELPHIA 3, PENNSYLVANIA
R.L. Geddes, 258 S. Van Pelt St.

PHILADELPHIA 3, PENNSYLVANIA
E. Hultberg, 2049 Cherry St.

PHILADELPHIA 3, PENNSYLVANIA
R.W. Jones, 1919 Rittenhouse Square

PHILADELPHIA 4, PENNSYLVANIA
Marius Reynolds, School of Fine Arts,
University of Pennsylvania

PHILADELPHIA 4, PENNSYLVANIA
O. Ozguner, 228 South 39th St.

PHILADELPHIA 7, PENNSYLVANIA
Scottoline, Miller & Lunt, 301 Empire
Bldg. 13th & Walnut Sts.

PHILADELPHIA 46, PENNSYLVANIA
W.V. von Moltke, 415 S. Carlisle St.
(with P. Andrade)

PLEASANTVILLE, NEW YORK
Gerson T. Hirsch, P.O. Box 101,
Hardscrabble Rd.

PORT WASHINGTON, NEW YORK
A. Wood & Five Sons Inc. 1 Pleasant
Ave.

PROSPECTVILLE, PENNSYLVANIA
Leslie P. Cruise Jr. David Grove Road

SAN FRANCISCO, CALIFORNIA
P. Kirby, 21 Napier Lane

SAN FRANCISCO, CALIFORNIA
Bay Group Assoc., 304 Walnut St.

SAN FRANCISCO 7, CALIFORNIA
E.W. Hoyte, 395 Missouri St.

SAN FRANCISCO 8, CALIFORNIA
John L. King, 244 Kearny St.

SANTA BARBARA, CALIFORNIA
P. Lafond, 1345 Danielson Rd.

SCRANTON, PENNSYLVANIA
Joseph H. Young, Mears Bldg.

SEATTLE 1, WASHINGTON
Bassetti & Morse, 1602 Tower Bldg.

SEATTLE 1, WASHINGTON
J. Graham, 1426 5th Ave.

SEATTLE 5, WASHINGTON
J.R. Sprule, 1314 E. 43rd St.

SHAKER HEIGHTS 20, OHIO
W.A. Gould, 2570 Coventry Road

SOUTH PASADENA, CALIFORNIA
Simon Eisner, Community Facilities
Planners, 1136 Fair Oaks Ave.

SOUTH ST. PAUL, MINNESOTA
F. Mikutowski, 2210 Florence Lane
(FINALIST #5)

ST. PAUL 16, MINNESOTA
H.A. Magoon, 1351 E. Maynard St.

ST. LOUIS, MISSOURI
E.C. Schmidt, 9430 Manchester Rd.

ST. LOUIS 5, MISSOURI
F. Maki, School of Architecture,
Washington University

ST. LOUIS 5, MISSOURI
R. Montgomery, School of
Architecture, Washington
University

STAMFORD, CONNECTICUT
Sherwood, Mills & Smith, 65 Broad St.

TUCSON, ARIZONA
E.M. Dunham Jr., 114 Avenida
Carolina

TYLER, TEXAS
D. Wilcox, 833 South Beckham Ave.

URBANA, ILLINOIS
D.R. Dobereiner, Department of
Architecture, College of Fine &
Applied Arts, University of Illinois

WASHINGTON, D.C.
R. Brunn, 2910 Ordway St.

WASHINGTON 11, D.C.
N. Kerzman, 145 Kennedy St. N.W.

WHEATON, ILLINOIS
M.C. Price, 835 North Summit St.

WHITE PLAINS, NEW YORK
John H. Cohen, 18 Bilton Rd.

WHITE PLAINS, NEW YORK
Perkins & Will, 55 Church St. (with
J.D. Lothrop)
(FINALIST #1)

YONKERS, NEW YORK
T.R. Feinberg, 130 Colonial Parkway

WALES
CARDIFF
J.G. Hird, 65 Cowbridge Rd. E. (with
G. Brooks)

Notes

Introduction

1 Phillips, Foreword to the printed pamphlet *City Hall and Square, Toronto, Canada, Conditions of Competition* (n.p., 1957).

2 When his design won the competition, Revell spelt his name "Rewell," but he changed the spelling when he discovered that Torontonians almost invariably mispronounced it to rhyme with "jewel." Once the architect sought to formalize this change of name at home, he discovered that his ancestors had moved from Finland to Germany at one point and adopted the spelling "Rewell" so that he did not have to do anything in order to change the spelling back.

1 Beginnings
Pages 7–26

1 Born in Brockville, Ontario, in 1892 Phillips had run for both federal and provincial office three times in the 1930s and 1940s.

2 Saunders replaced Allan Lamport (who had joined the Toronto Transit Commission) as interim mayor in June 1954, having won the most votes city-wide for the four-person Board of Control.

3 John Beckwith quoted in S.J. White, "University of Toronto Exhibition, 'Architecture and You,'" *Journal* of the Royal Architectural Institute of Canada [hereafter *JRAIC*], 25, no. 5 (1948).

4 On the diffusion of modernist ideas about architecture and design in Toronto, see Christopher Armstrong, *Making Toronto Modern: Architecture and Design, 1895–1975* (Montreal: McGill-Queen's University Press 2014), passim.

5 Dickinson, "News from the Institute (Ontario)," *JRAIC*, 35, no. 5 (1954).

6 Phillips, *Mayor of All the People* (Toronto: McClelland and Stewart 1967), 110, 140; the annual term of the mayor and city aldermen was doubled in 1955.

7 Quoted in Marilyn M. Litvak, *Edward James Lennox, "Builder of Toronto"* (Toronto: Dundurn 1995), 24.

8 City of Toronto Archives [CTA], RG 242, box 253014, Report of the Civic Improvement Committee for the City of Toronto, 1911 (n.p., n.d.).

9 Mark Osbaldeston, *Unbuilt Toronto: A History of the City That Might Have Been* (Toronto: Dundurn 2008), 84–6.

10 *Report of the Advisory City Planning Commission* (Toronto, 1929).

11 CTA, Series 361, Subseries 1, Mayor's Office subject correspondence [hereafter MC], box 140525, file 612, Bland to Saunders, 20 February 1946.

12 Ibid., Planning Commissioner Tracy D. leMay to Mayor Robert Saunders, 26 March 1946; OAA chair J.A. Robertson to Saunders, 2, 13 April 1946; Saunders to Property Committee Chair Alderman W.A. Howell, 5 July 1946. The architects were principals in the well-established local firms of Marani and Morris, Mathers and Haldenby, and Page and Steele.

13 The election returns are in Toronto, *City Council Minutes (CCM)*, 1947, appendix C; CTA, Series 361, Subseries 1, MC, box 140525, file 612, memo re "The Civic Square," unsigned, n.d. [c. 1947]; Saunders to City Clerk J.W. Somers, 24 October 1947.

14 CTA, Series 361, Subseries 1, MC, box 140525, file 614, Saunders to Public Works Minister Alphonse Fournier, 2 April 1947; Fournier to Saunders, 11 April 1947; Property Commissioner G.D. Bland to Saunders, 29 April 1947; City Clerk George Weale to F.C. Hamilton, 11 May 1950.

15 CTA, Series 361, Subseries 1, MC, box 140525, file 612, Judge J. Parker to Mayor H.E. McCallum, 28 April 1948.

16 CTA, Series 361, Subseries 1, MC, box 140525, file 615, Memo re Civic Square Improvements, n.d. [August 1955]; if the new building were large enough, it could also house police headquarters, currently in the Stewart Building at College and University, which could be sold along with the Annex.

17 CTA, Series 843, New City Hall competition [hereafter NCH], box 147086, file 103, Report of Civic Advisory Council re City Hall Court House Requirements (mimeo), 15 October 1952; ibid., Series 361, Subseries 1, MC, box 140525, file 613, "Suggestions of the Committee on City Hall-Court House Requirements," n.d.; Roland Michener to Mayor Allan Lamport, 17 November 1952; F.C. Hamilton to Michener, 18 November 1952.

18 Arthur, "Editorial," *JRAIC*, 30, no. 3 (1953).

19 CTA, Series 361, Subseries 1, MC, box 140525, file 613, Jarrett to Lamport, 14 December 1952; G. Englesmith to Lamport, 15 December 1952; F.C. Hamilton to Jarrett, 18 December 1952, and to Englesmith, 19 December 1952. Englesmith also noted that a building like Lever House could be sold off later as an office building if it did not ultimately fit into the layout of the civic square.

20 CTA, Series 1512, MC, box 506521, file 45, memo from F.C. Hamilton to Lamport, 11 December 1952; ibid., Series 361, Subseries 1, MC, Thomas A. Lawrence, Toronto and York Committee on Civil Defence, to Lamport, 5 January 1953.

21 In constructing its Yonge Street subway line (which opened in 1954), the TTC provided two levels at its Queen station to accommodate the junction with the new line so that a ghostly station still exists beneath the active one.

22 CTA, Series 361, Subseries 1, MC, box 140525, file 613, OAA Secretary John D. Miller to Lamport, 1 April 1953, enclosing brief from OAA Toronto chapter to mayor and council, 14 January 1953; F.C. Hamilton to Miller, 7 April 1953; copy of Board of Control Report no. 12, 30 March 1953.

23 CTA, Series 843, NCH, box 147086, file 103, Draft Report of events re Civic Square and City Hall, 1944–55, n.d. [1955] (with notation); file 44, Agreement between City and Marani and Morris, Mathers and Haldenby, and Shore and Moffat, 8 March 1954; ibid., Series 361, Subseries 1, MC, box 140525, file 615, copy of Board of Control Report no. 21, 22 June 1953.

24 Harland Steele had been one of the architects recruited to prepare a plan for the city hall and square in 1946, but in 1954 his firm was excluded in favour of Shore and Moffat owing to pressure from the city building commissioner. When Steele protested that this was a serious blow to his firm's prestige, Mayor Allan Lamport was advised that it was city policy to try and distribute its large architectural commissions as widely as possible. Page and Steele had recently been chosen to design the "Aged Folks Home" and so was excluded from the city hall contract though the mayor assured the firm that it still had the complete confidence of the bureaucrats and could expect future work. See CTA, Series 361, Subseries 1, MC, box 140525, file 615, Steele to Lamport, 9 February 1954; F.C. Hamilton to Deputy Building Commissioner W. Holden, 4 March 1954; Lamport to Page and Steele, 17 March 1954.

25 Osbaldeston, *Unbuilt Toronto*, 88–90; CTA, Series 361, Subseries 1, MC, box 140525, file 615, Norman Barnes to Lamport, 30 April 1954, Personal and Confidential; clipping from Toronto *Star*, 13 May 1954; Lamport to M.H. Lifton, 4 June 1954.

26 CTA, Series 1512, MC, box 507969, file 205, memo re Conference with Architects for the Civic Square, 18 February 1955.

27 Matthew Lawson, city planning commissioner from 1954 to 1967, later claimed that Shore and Moffat were added to the trio of designers because the firm was seen as "young rebels" with

new ideas, but that the other two always voted together to reject their suggestions; see CTA, Fonds 388, Series 1651, Matthew Lawson fonds, box 527941, file 662, tape of interview with Lawson by Alfred Holden and Edna Hudson, 21 May 1998, two audiocassettes, side 1, counter 265–86, yet there is no evidence that S&M had any very progressive ideas and Shore's comments do not suggest otherwise.

28 Osbaldeston, *Unbuilt Toronto*, 90.

29 CTA, Fonds 1301, Philip Givens Papers, box 146331, file 25, Report from Craig and Madill re "The Existing Building, n.d. [March 1955]; Toronto *Star*, 24 March 1955.

30 The controllers were elected on a city-wide ballot and their assent was needed to place financial matters before the city council.

31 CTA, Series 361, Subseries 1, MC, box 140525, file 615, Phillips to F.H. Marani, 13 July 1955; Marani to Phillips, 15 July, 23 August 1955.

32 *Canadian Architect*, 4th Issue, April 1956.

33 CTA, Series 361, Subseries 1, MC, box 140525, file 615, George D. Gibson to Phillips, 30 November 1955; *CCM* [re plebiscite results].

34 William Dendy and William Kilbourn, *Toronto Observed: Its Architecture, Patrons and History* (Toronto: Oxford University Press 1986), 267; Phillips, *Mayor of All the People*, 141.

35 CTA, Series 361, Subseries 1, MC, box 140525, file 615, Parkin to Phillips, 8 December, 27 December (Confidential) 1955.

36 CTA, Series 316, Subseries 1, box 140525, file 616, Phillips to Norman McKibbin, 4 January 1956; Phillips to Hugh MacLean, associate editor, *Canadian Architect*, 9 February 1956.

37 Phillips, *Mayor of All the People*, 141.

38 CTA, Series 843, NCH, box 147086, file 105, Minutes of Joint Metropolitan-City Committee regarding Development of the Civic Square (typescript), 27 February 1956; memo from Peter Dobell to file, 25 March 1956; A.S. Mathers to Planning Commissioner M.B. Lawson, 29 March 1956; ibid., Series 361, Subseries 1, MC, box 140525, file 616, Civic Square Committee Report no. 1, 24 September 1956. The committee consisted of Phillips and Gardiner as joint chairs along with the four Toronto controllers and the reeves

of suburban Forest Hill, York Township, Etobicoke, and North York plus Metro's finance commissioner and the city treasurer.

39 CTA, Series 843, NCH, box 147086, file 105, "Preliminary Report on Surveys and Studies Necessary for the Preparation of a Design for the Civic Square" (mimeo), 23 March 1966.

40 CTA, Series 361, Subseries 1, MC, box 140525, file 616, Parking Authority of Toronto to city Legislation Committee, 11 October 1956; the four surface lots and the PA's own garage at Queen and Victoria streets were already operating at capacity, and a charge of twenty cents per hour was expected to recoup the capital cost of the four-level civic square garage over twenty-five years.

41 CTA, Series 843, NCH, box 147085, file 105, Gardiner to Phillips, 18 May 1956.

42 CTA, Series 361, Subseries 1, MC, box 140525, file 616, Gardiner to Phillips, 25 May 1956; Deputy Metro Clerk George M. Foster to Phillips, 12 July 1956; ibid., Series 843, NCH, box 147086, file 105, memo from B. Turner-Davis, Planning Board, to file, 17 July 1956.

43 CTA, Series 843, box 147086, file 105, Planning Board "Memorandum on Civic Square" (mimeo), 28 August 1956; ibid., Series 361, Subseries 1, A.L. Fleming to City Solicitor W.G. Angus, 22 October 1956; Fleming, Smoke, and Burgess to Angus, 18 January 1957; Angus to mayor and Board of Control, 29 March 1957; Angus to Phillips, 14 June 1957.

44 CTA, Series 843, NCH, box 147086, file 105, memo from B. Turner-Davis, Planning Board, to file, 17 July 1956; *Canadian Architect*, 4th Issue, April 1956.

45 This figure, arrived at by architect F.H. Marani without any detailed study, would continue to be bandied about for years afterwards though it bore ever less connection to reality as time passed.

46 CTA, Series 361, Subseries 1, MC, box 140525, file 616, Gardiner to Phillips, 25 May 1956; Civic Square Committee Report no. 1, 24 September 1956; ibid., Series 843, NCH, box 147086, file 106, memo by Peter Dobell, Planning Board, to file, 10 September 1966; *CCM*, 23 October 1956, and *CCM*, 1957, appendix C.

2 Competition

Pages 27–72

1 Information about Arthur's life may be found in Alec Keefer, ed., *Eric Ross Arthur: Conservation in Context* (Toronto: Toronto Regional Architectural Conservancy 2001), particularly in Keefer's "Eric Arthur's Career: An Overview," 47–80.

2 Arthur, "Editorial," *JRAIC*, 28, no. 9 (1951).

3 Toronto Reference Library, Baillie (previously Baldwin) Room [hereafter TRL, BR], Reed Collection, box Q, file "City Hall Competition Book," Introduction, n.d. [c. 1965].

4 Larry W. Richards, *University of Toronto, An Architectural Tour* (New York: Princeton Architectural Press 2009), 171–2, 88–90.

5 See, for instance, CTA, Series 1512, MC, box 507969, file 10, Arthur to Phillips, 21 May 1958, addressed to "Dear Nate."

6 Geoffrey Simmins, *Ontario Association of Architects: A Centennial History, 1889–1989* (Toronto: OAA 1989), 141–2.

7 Sara Bowser, "How to Buy a Work of Art," *Canadian Architect*, April 1959.

8 Lawson later tried to claim that it was he, not Phillips, who had suggested an international competition because the Ontario Association of Architects was blocking the city from dispensing with the three firms and retaining a new architect, so that the only way to get out of the contract was to hold a competition open to many practitioners, something that Phillips was not enthusiastic about as being too "messy"; this does not appear to square with the documentary evidence; see CTA, Fonds 388, Series 1651, Lawson fonds, box 527941, file 662, interview with Alfred Holden and Edna Hudson, 21 May 1998, two audiocassettes, side 2, counter 710–800. In this interview Lawson was also keen to promote the idea that it was he not Arthur who had really played the key role in bringing about the international competition.

9 CTA, Series 1512, MC, box 507969, file 201, Lawson to Pierre Vago, 6 November 1956; Vago to Lawson, 15 November 1956.

10 Ibid., George Y. Masson to Phillips, 8 November 1956; ibid., Series 843, NCH, box 147087, file 109, Arthur to Lawson, n.d. [December 1956].

11 CTA, Series 843, NCH, box 147081, file 45, Masson to Arthur, 18 December 1956; box 147087, file 109, OAA secretary John D. Miller to Matthew Lawson, 2 January 1957.

12 CTA, Series 843, NCH, box 147081, file 45, Masson to Phillips, 4 January 1957.

13 Bowser, "How to Buy a Work of Art"; "Institute News," Annual Meeting of the OAA, E.C.S. Cox, President's Report, *JRAIC*, 35, no. 3 (1958).

14 *CCM*, Board of Control Report no. 3, approved by council, 21 January 1957, including Lawson's report of 7 January 1957; CTA, Series 843, NCH, box 147086, file 107, Peter Dobell to Christopher Owtram, 24 January 1957 (quoted).

15 CTA, Series 843, NCH, box 147086, file 107, memo from Arthur, 11 February [1957]; ibid., Series 1512, MC, box 507969, file 205, Lawson to the mayor and controllers, 29 March 1957.

16 CTA, Series 843, NCH, box 147087, file 110, Lawson to mayor and Board of Control, 12 March 1957; ibid., box 147081, file 45, Arthur to Phillips, 25 March 1957, Personal and Confidential.

17 CTA, Series 843, NCH, box 147081, file 45, Arthur to Phillips, 28 January 1957; George Masson to W.R. Souter, vice-chair of OAA Registration Board, and its members, 29 January 1957; ibid., Series 1512, MC, box 507969, file 201, Phillips to J.D. Miller, 31 January, 8 February 1957; Miller to Phillips, 5 February, 11 March 1957; Simmins, *Ontario Association of Architects*, 144.

18 Lawson later asserted that he, in consultation with Stephenson, was really responsible for the choice of jurors, another claim not borne out by the documentary evidence; see CTA, Fonds 388, Series 1651, Lawson fonds, box 527941, file 662, interview with Alfred Holden and Edna Hudson, 21 May 1998, two audiocassettes, side 2, counter 936–7.

19 CTA, Series 843, box 147086, file 107, Lawson to Saarinen, 29 January 1957.

20 In his reply to Lawson (cited below), Saarinen asked Lawson to tell "Eric" that he had just returned from swimming in the shadow of the bathing pavilion on Manly Beach in Australia.

21 CTA, Series 843, NCH, box 147086, file 107, Saarinen to Lawson, 18 February 1957.

22 Ibid., box 147081, file 45, Arthur to Jacqueline Tyrwhitt, 8 April 1957.

23 Ibid., Tyrwhitt to Arthur, Confidential, 24 April 1957; Arthur to Martin, 7 May, 25 June 1957; Martin to Arthur, 24 May, 12 July 1957; Arthur to Sir William Holford [sic], 15 July 1957; ibid., box 147087, file 110, Holford to Arthur, 20 July 1947.

24 "Toronto City Hall and Square Competition," "The Jury," *JRAIC*, 35, no. 11 (1958).

25 CTA, Series 843, NCH, box 147087, file 110, Rogers to Arthur, 17 May 1957.

26 Douglas Shadbolt, *Ron Thom: The Shaping of an Architect* (Vancouver: Douglas and McIntyre 1995), 40.

27 CTA, Series 843, NCH, box 147081, file 45, Saarinen to Arthur, 24 June 1957.

28 Ibid., box 147087, file 110, Buildings Commissioner F.E. Wellwood to mayor and controllers, 7 June 1957; Arthur to Matthew Lawson, 19 June 1957; ibid., box 147081, file 44, Lawson to city council president, Controller Jean Newman, and aldermen, 24 June 1957.

29 *CCM*, Board of Control Report no. 21, 24 July 1957; Board of Control report no. 23, 3 September 1957; CTA, Series 1512, MC, box 507969, file 201, Arthur to Phillips, 2 August (quoted), 24 August 1957.

30 A copy may be found among other places in CTA, Series 1512, MC, box 547466, file 1013.

31 CTA, Series 843, NCH, box 147081, file 51, Arthur to Dempsey, 30 September 1957.

32 CTA, Series 1512, MC, box 507969, file 201, memo re "Number of 'Conditions' for New City Hall Competition," 28 October 1957; memo to mayor and council, 25 November 1957; CTA, Series 843, box 147086, file 108, Arthur to Nathan Phillips, 22, 28 November 1957.

33 CTA, Series 1512, MC, box 507969, file 201, L.F. K-L. to Phillips, 4 January 1958; Phillips to L.F. K-L, 20 January 1958; B.S. to "Dear Sir," 10 February, 10 March, 1 April 1958; Frederick Hamilton to B.S., 7 May 1958.

34 CTA, Series 843, NCH, box 147081, file 51, printed letter to "All Competitors, City Hall and Square Competition, Toronto, Canada, from Eric Arthur" (n.p., n.d.) [1 January 1958].

35 Bowser, "How to Buy a Work of Art."

36 CTA, Series 843, NCH, box 147087, file 111, Arthur to Lawson, 7 January 1958; Arthur to Rogers, 8 January 1958; Arthur to mayor and controllers, 10 February 1958.

37 Ibid., Saarinen to Arthur, 20 January 1958; beside Saarinen's reference to Syd-

ney, Arthur wrote, "I think he is wrong here."

38 *CCM*, Board of Control Report no. 10, approved by council 17 March 1958, and Board of Control Report no. 11, 31 March 1958.

39 TRL, BC, Reed Collection, box Q, file "City Hall Competition," outline of a proposed book by Arthur on the competition, n.d. [1964]; *Globe and Mail*, 22 April 1958.

40 CTA, Series 843, NCH, box 147081, file 43, "List of Competitors" (typescript), n.d. [April 1958]; one or two entries came from Austria, Bolivia, Cuba, Ethiopia, Finland, Greece, Haiti, Hong Kong, Hungary, Ireland, Israel, Kenya, Lebanon, New Zealand, Peru, Puerto Rico, Southern Rhodesia, Syria, and Trinidad. See appendix for list of entrants.

41 TRL, BR, Reed Collection, box Q, loose correspondence, Arthur to Pierre Vago, 27 March 1958.

42 CTA, Series 843, NCH, box 147087, file 114, clipping of "Backstage in Toronto" by Eric Hutton, n.d.

43 Interestingly, the "List of Competitors," n.d., in CTA, Series 843, NCH, box 147081, file 43, no. 254, gives Andrews's address as the Harvard School of Design, but with the addition "NOW – J.B. Parkin & Assoc., 1500 Don Mills Rd., Don Mills, Ont.," the same address as given for no.144, "J.C. Parkins [sic]." Andrews took a job with John B. Parkin Associates in mid-1958, later followed by his collaborator Macy DuBois.

44 "Odds and Ends," *Canadian Architect*, June 1958

45 Toronto *Telegram*, 22, 23 April 1958.

46 TRL, BR, Reed Collection, box Q, file "City Hall Competition," text of speech in Arthur's handwriting addressed to "Mr. Chairman, Ladies and Gentlemen," n.d. [c. 1965].

47 The following paragraphs are based upon CTA, Series 843, NCH, box 147087, file 111, Arthur and jury members to Nathan Phillips, May 1958; ibid., box 147088, file 152, envelope labelled "Content: Rough Drafts of Questions and Answers including Galley Proofs [sic]," "Notes Prepared by Eero Saarinen on Final Stage," n.d. [September 1958]; ibid., box 147082, file 62, E.R. Arthur, "Civic Square and City Hall, Competition, Toronto, Jury Criticisms of the Finalists," n.d. [September 1958].

48 CTA, Series 843, NCH, box 147082, file 56, "Statement by E.R. Arthur, Professional Advisor and Matthew Lawson, Coordinator of Competition," n.d. [September 1958], notes the unsatisfactory siting of the existing council chamber.

49 CTA, Series 843, NCH, box 147087, file 111, Arthur and jury members to Mayor Phillips, May 1958.

50 CTA, Series 843, NCH, box 147082, file 62, "Report of the Jury on Preliminary Open Competition" (typescript), 28 April 1958.

51 Arthur procured $1,000 from the McLean Foundation to have many of the models photographed, along with $3,500 from the recently created Canada Council for the Arts to microfilm the elevations and a small selection of drawings for each entry; the author recently discovered that this microfilm was among uncatalogued material in the Social Science division of the Toronto Reference Library and included a selection of drawings from each of the nearly 500 applicants, totalling about 2,500 images in all. It is hoped that the library will create a website on which these images may be displayed along with photographs of the models in the Reed Collection at the TRL. The author is also collaborating on an exhibition to be held at Ryerson University in 2015 at the time of the fiftieth anniversary of the opening of the new building which will draw upon this same material and include an illustrated catalogue. See n.40 above.

52 TRL, BR, Reed Collection, box Q, file "City Hall Competition," draft of "Comments on Design" by Arthur, n.d.

53 Ibid.

54 Horne took a particularly bold gamble by betting his supervisors in the MA program in which he was enrolled at MIT that if he was selected a finalist he could submit his entry to the university as his master's thesis.

55 Arthur later confirmed this story to Bengt Lundsten, one of the junior associates who came to Toronto with Revell to work on the city hall project; author's interview with Lundsten, Seppo Valjus, and Tuula Revell, Finnish Museum of Architecture (FMA), Helsinki, 9 October 2013.

56 Charles Jencks, *The Iconic Building* (New York: Rizzoli 2005), 30, records these events without providing any source though it also seems to have been the case

that Saarinen provided some perspectives for Utzon's sketches as required by the competition conditions.

57 CTA, Series 843, NCH, box 147079, file 23, Finalists' Registration Forms and Identification Slips, 1958, nos. 006 and 087.

58 See CTA, Series 843, NCH, box 153724, file 118, which contains 4x5 black-and-white photos of entry models 001–100; on the verso of the Lambert photo (087) his address is given as Stuttgart, but on the "List of Competitors" in ibid., box 147081, file 43, the address of "Lambard" [sic] has been corrected to Dusseldorf.

59 When one of the younger entrants subsequently asked for financial assistance to fund these activities, Arthur agreed to recommend that each of the finalists should receive $2,500 immediately since it seemed unlikely that anybody would drop out at this point; see CTA, Series 843, NCH, box 147087, file 112, Arthur to Matthew Lawson, 29 May 1958; Lawson to mayor and controllers, 9 June 1958. This was approved by council on 23 June.

60 TRL, BR, Reed Collection, box Q, file "City Hall Competition," text of speech in Arthur's handwriting addressed to "Mr. Chairman, Ladies and Gentlemen," n.d. [c. 1965].

61 TRL, BR, Reed Collection, box Q, file "City Hall Competition," "Report by the Jury on the Preliminary Open Competition," annotated in Arthur's hand "Sent to Eight [Finalist] Competitors, 28 April/58."

62 CTA, Series 843, NCH, box 147087, file 111, Arthur and the competition jury to Nathan Phillips, n.d. [April-May 1958].

63 CTA, Series 1512, MC, box 507969, file 205, Matthew Lawson to mayor and controllers, 29 March 1957; Series 843, NCH, box 1407087, file 112, City Clerk George Weale to Matthew Lawson, 14 May 1958.

64 CTA, Series 1512, MC, box 507969, file 201, Buildings Commissioner F.E. Wellwood to mayor and controllers, 6 June 1958; *CCM*, Board of Control Report no. 19, approved by council 23 June 1958.

65 CTA, Series 1512, MC, box 506521, file 45, Gardiner to Nathan Phillips, 12 May 1958, urging the mayor to use his own strong ties to the Conservatives to lobby other cabinet ministers from Toronto to support a deal.

66 CTA, Series 843, NCH, box 147087, file 112, Questions and Answers for Final Stage City Hall Competition – Second Stage, 26 May 1958.

67 TRL, BR, Reed Collection, box Q, Arthur's miscellaneous correspondence, Giedion to Arthur, 14 May 1958; see also ibid., file "Finalists-Biographies," Saarinen to Arthur, 27 June 1958, where Saarinen concurs that "a book would be an excellent thing."

68 CTA, Series 843, MC, Arthur to Phillips, 21 May 1958; TRL, BR, Reed Collection, box Q, Arthur's miscellaneous correspondence, Arthur to Marsh Jeanneret, UTP, 22 May 1958.

69 CTA, Series 834, NCH, box 147087, file 112, Arthur to mayor and Board of Control, 6 August 1958; Deputy City Clerk S.W. Eakins to Arthur, 15 August 1958.

70 TRL, BR, Reed Collection, box Q, file "City Hall Competition," Francess G. Halpenny, UTP, to Arthur, 29 July 1964; Arthur to John Fisher, 17 September 1964; Fisher to Arthur, 14 April 1965.

71 Ibid., outline of contents of proposed book by Arthur, n.d. [1964], and file "City Hall Competition Book," Introduction by Arthur, n.d. [c. 1965].

72 Ibid., Arthur's handwritten fifteen-page text, n.d. [1965].

73 These typescripts may be found in TRL, BR, Eric and Paul Arthur fonds, L52, box 14, file "Correspondence re City Hall, 1958–1978."

74 (Toronto: University of Toronto Press, 1964), 236.

75 See TRL, BR, Reed Collection, box Q, file "Finalists-Biographies."

76 See the correspondence with various finalists in ibid.

77 CTA, Series 1512, MC, Arthur to Phillips, 28 August, 5 September (two letters), 8, 16 September 1958; Series 843, box 147087, file 112, Arthur to Vincent Tovell, 8 September 1958. Arthur invited Matthew Lawson to the OAA dinner, noting that he and the president of the University of Toronto would be the only non-architects included; see ibid., Series 843, NCH, box 147087, file 112, Arthur to Lawson, 8 September 1958.

78 Ibid., Deputy City Clerk S.W. Eakins to Matthew Lawson, 14 August 1958.

79 CTA, Fonds 388, Series 1651, Lawson fonds, box 527941, file 662, interview with Lawson by Alfred Holden and Edna Hud-

son, 21 May 1998, two audiocassettes, side 2, counter 260–84.

80 See CTA, Series 843, NCH, box 147082, file 62, Eric Arthur, "Civic Square and City Hall Competition, Toronto, Jury Criticisms of the Finalists" (mimeo), n.d. [September 1958].

81 Berton, "Things I Didn't Know Till Now about the New City Hall," Toronto *Star*, 9 October 1958.

82 Author's interview with Bengt Lundsten, Seppo Valjus, and Tuula Revell, FMA, 9 October 2013; the architect's daughter, Tuula Revell, also suggested that the shift meant that visiting dignitaries (like the queen) being driven up the ramp to enter the council chamber would be able to exit the right side of a limousine opposite the council chamber doors.

83 "Toronto City Hall and Square Competition, Majority Report," *JRAIC*, 35, no. 10, (1958); see also Osbaldeston, *Unbuilt Toronto*, 94–7, and Bureau of Architecture and Urbanism, *Toronto Modern: 1945–1965* (Toronto: Coach House 2002), 78–83.

84 CTA, Fonds 388, Series 1651, Lawson fonds, box 527941, file 662, interview with Lawson by Alfred Holden and Edna Hudson, 21 May 1998, two audiocassettes, side 2, counter 156–74.

85 "Toronto City Hall and Square Competition, Minority Report," *JRAIC*, 35, no. 10 (1958). Even Saarinen admitted that installing civic workers in a building more like a filing cabinet might offer a more efficient design; see CTA, Series 843, NCH, box 147088, file 152, envelope labelled "Contents: Rough Drafts of Questions and Answers including Galley Proofs" [sic], "Notes prepared by Eero Saarinen on Final Stage, Specific Evaluation of [entry] #006," n.d. [September 1958]; Toronto *Star*, 9 October 1958.

86 CTA, Fonds 388, Series 1651, Lawson fonds, box 527491, file 662, interview with Lawson by Alfred Holden and Edna Hudson, 21 May 1998, two audiocassettes, side 2, counter 331–41, and side 3, counter 347–87.

87 The firm of which Tyrwhitt was a member was among the unsuccessful entrants.

88 TRL, BR, Reed Collection, box Q, file "City Hall Competition," text of speech in Arthur's handwriting addressed to "Mr. Chairman, Ladies and Gentlemen," n.d.; Arthur was, of course, not being

truthful about the open-minded attitude of most OAA members, who had, after all, done their best to exclude everyone except Canadians from the competition.

89 "Reflections on Monumentality"; Bowser, "How to Buy a Work of Art"; Giedion, "City Hall and Centre"; Tyrwhitt, "The Civic Square," *Canadian Architect*, April, 1959; CTA, Series 843, box 147081, file 45, Tyrwhitt to Arthur, 24 April 1957, Confidential.

90 CTA, Series 843, NCH, box 147082, file 56, Statement by E.R. Arthur, Professional Advisor, and Matthew Lawson, Coordinator of Competition, n.d. [September 1958].

91 Ibid., box 148087, file 112, Rolland to mayor, controllers, and council, 26 September 1958 (mimeo); Rolland to Planning Board, n.d. In the event, Rolland received only 5,560 votes for controller and came in last in the city-wide poll while the four elected members garnered between 55,000 and 49,500 votes.

92 CTA, Series 1512, MC, box 507969, file 201, J.W. Goodman, Goodman Food Brokers, to Phillips, 26 September 1958; Phillips to Goodman, 3 October 1958.

93 Arthur, Editorial, *JRAIC*, 37, no. 3 (1960); Zeidler, "West Ellesmere United Church and Christian Education Centre, Scarborough, Ont., Architects, Zeidler and Craig," ibid., 36, no. 4 (1959).

94 TRL, BR, Reed Collection, box Q, file "City Hall Competition," speech in Arthur's handwriting addressed to "Mr. Chairman, Ladies and Gentlemen," n.d. [c. 1965].

95 CTA, Series 843, NCH, box 147087, file 114, Hawaii Planning Director Frank Lombardi to Matthew Lawson, 12 December 1958.

96 Ibid., memo from Lawson, 23 December 1958.

97 Ibid., Lawson to Lombardi, 24 December 1958, Confidential.

98 CTA, Series 361, Subseries 1, MC, box 140525, file 617, James Lawrence, Jr, to Phillips, 18 December 1958; Phillips to Lawrence, 7 January 1959. The mayor added that the jurors had expressed the view that the Toronto competition had been the best-managed one ever held.

99 CTA, Series 843, NCH, box 147082, file 62, Toronto Planning Board, "Synopsis of the City Hall & Square Competition for Toronto, Canada" (mimeo), September 1958; ibid., Series 1512, MC, box 507969,

file 201, Arthur to Phillips, 7 November 1958; ibid., Series 361, MC, box 140525, file 617, Arthur to Phillips, n.d. [November 1958].

100 TRL, BR, Reed Collection, box Q, file "City Hall Competition," outline of contents of Arthur's proposed book, n.d. [1964].

101 CTA, Series 843, NCH, box 147087, file 114, Arthur to Matthew Lawson, 22 October 1958; draft letter from Arthur to entrants, n.d. [October 1958]; Lawson to Arthur, 28 October 1958; R.G. Ricketts, secretary, Royal Institute of British Architects, to Arthur, 24 November 1959; Pierre Vago to Arthur, 27 November 1959.

102 TRL, BR, Reed Collection, box Q, file "City Hall Competition Book," B. Turner Davis, "City of Toronto Planning Board, Points on Organization of Competition for Professor Arthur," 9 December 1959; Arthur to Edmond K. Bacon, 14 January 1960, Bacon being the person in charge of organizing a proposed competition in Philadelphia.

103 TRL, BR, Reed Collection, box Q, miscellaneous correspondence, Giedion to Arthur, 14 May 1958.

104 CTA, Series 1512, MC, box 507969, file 201, formal report of competition jury, n.d. [September 1958].

105 "Reflections on Monumentality," *Canadian Architect*, April 1959. See Stephenson to the editor, *JRAIC*, 43, no. 8 (1966); by then, Stephenson had moved from Toronto to the University of Western Australia where he could observe at first hand the travails surrounding the Sydney Opera House which was already far over budget.

3 Winner
Pages 73–92

1 The following two paragraphs are largely drawn from this document, which is to be found in TRL, BR, Reed Collection, box Q, loose correspondence, Revell autobiography, n.d. [1958], on the letterhead of Viljo Rewell Arkkitehti, Safa.

2 FMA, Revell Collection, brown envelope labelled "V. Revellin Kirjeenvaihto" [correspondence], copy of article by Kyösti Alander, director FMA, "Viljo Revell and His Studio," n.d. [c. 1962].

3 See Tuula Revell, "Viljo Revell, Biography"; Susanna Santala, "Viljo Revell

and Changing Modernism"; and Laurie Pujonen, "Viljo Revell and the New Building Technology," all in Revell et al., ed., *Viljo Revell: "It Was Teamwork You See,"* (Helsinki: Didrichsen 2009). Also, Roger Connah, *Finland (Modern architectures in history)* (London: Reaktion 2005), 149–50.

4 An undated document in Revell's papers at FMA also describes the final design of the two towers as being vertical Vierendeel trusses with the two chords being the shell and the interior line of columns, so that the differing stiffness of the two chords produces very interesting stress distribution, resulting in quite high stress concentrations at the region of the end buttresses; see FMA, VR, brown slipcase labelled "Toronto-kirjeenvaihto" [correspondence], loose letters 1961–2, memo re "The Toronto City Hall," n.d. [c. 1962].

5 Author's interview with Bengt Lunsten, Seppo Valjus, and Tuula Revell, FMA, 9 October 2013.

6 FMA, Revell Collection, black three-ring binder, "Viljo Revell / Esitelmiä-Haastatteluja-Luentoja" [Presentations-Interviews-Lectures], English translation by Fred J. Fewster of interview with VR by B. Tikkanen, *Suomen Kuvalehti*, 14 March 1959.

7 Author's interview with Bengt Lundsten, Seppo Valju, and Tuula Revell, FMA, 9 October 2013.

8 CTA, Series 843, NCH, box 147087, file 112, Arthur to Lawson, 8 September 1958; *Toronto Star*, 9 October 1958.

9 FMA, Revell Collection, brown slipcase labelled "Toronto-kirjeenvaihto [correspondence], 1958 ja 1959," 1958 letters arranged alphabetically, Arthur to Revell, 2 October 1958; Wilson to Revell, 1, 9 (quoted), 24 October 1958. Bregman and Hamman was among the firms that got in touch with Arthur; see ibid., George R. Hamman to Arthur, 7 October 1959.

10 FMA, Revell Collection, brown slipcase labelled "Toronto-kirjeenvaihto [correspondence], 1958 ja 1959," 1958 letters arranged alphabetically, Arthur to Revell, 2 October 1958.

11 Ibid., Parkin to Revell, 9 October 1958; Revell to Arthur, 15 October 1958, enclosing the requested draft; Revell to Arthur, 8 November 1958.

12 Ibid., Parkin to Revell, 15 October 1958.

13 Ibid., Arthur to Revell, 20 October 1958; Revell to Arthur, 30 October 1958.

14 Ibid., Arthur to Revell, 3 October 1958; Revell to Arthur, 8 November 1958.

15 Ibid., Revell to Parkin, 20 November 1958; Parkin to Revell, 25 November 1958; Lawson to Revell, 28 November 1958.

16 Ibid., Revell to Graham, 27 October 1958; Revell to Parkin, 3 January 1958.

17 CTA, Series 362, Subseries 1, MC, box 104525, file 617, Parkin to Revell, 8 December 1958.

18 FMA, Revell Collection, brown slipcase labelled "Toronto-kirjeenvaihto [correspondence], 1958 ja 1959," 1958 letters arranged alphabetically, Parkin to Revell, 6 December 1958. The partners were Viljo Revell and Company and the three Parkins (John B., his brother Edmund, and John C.). The letterhead of Revell-Parkin later included the words "The above firms have combined in a joint venture to carry out Toronto City Hall and Architectural Commission"; see CTA, Series 491, Bell Papers, box 140301, file 2, letter dated 1 August 1963.

19 FMA, Revell Collection, brown slipcase labelled "Toronto-kirjeenvaihto [correspondence], 1958 ja 1959," letters bound with string, 1959–61, T.R. Lovett to Revell, 17 March 1959; Revell to Lovett, 24 March 1959.

20 Author's interview with Lundsten, Valjus, and Tuula Revell, FMA, 9 October 2013.

21 Ibid.

22 Ibid.

23 CTA, Series 491, Bell Papers, box 140299, file 46, Stage I Report, Toronto City Hall, Revell-Parkin to mayor and Board of Control, 2 November 1959.

24 FMA, Revell Collection, brown slipcase labelled "Toronto-kirjeenvaihto [correspondence], 1958 ja 1959," letters bound with string, 1959–61, Revell-Parkin to Matthew Lawson, 8 June 1959; Walter F Conlin, Jr., Severud-Elstad-Krueger, to John B. Parkin Associates, 2 June 1959.

25 Ibid., Revell-Parkin to H.H. Rogers, 13 July 1959.

26 TRL, BR, Reed Collection, box Q, file "City Hall Competition Book," "The Toronto City Hall," n.d. [c. 1965].

27 Author's interview with Bengt Lundsten, Seppo Valjus, and Tuula Revell, FMA, 9 October 2013.

28 Ibid. Valjus expressed the view that this change was less desirable aesthetically

than the original concept but it satisfied the engineers.

29 FMA, Revell Collection, brown slipcase labelled "Toronto-kirjeenvaihto" [correspondence], loose letters, 1961–2, memo re "The Toronto City Hall," n.d. [c. 1962].

30 See K. Dau, *Wind Tunnel Tests of the Toronto City Hall* (Toronto: University of Toronto Institute of Aerophysics Bulletin no. 50, July 1961).

31 Toronto *Star*, 29 October 1964.

32 Author's interview with Bengt Lundsten, Seppo Valjus, and Tuula Revell, FMA, 9 October 2013; folklore later had it that Revell was so angry with the engineers that it caused him to have a stroke or heart attack at the time but this does not appear to be correct.

33 FMA, Revell Collection, brown slipcase labelled "Toronto-kirjeenvaihto" [correspondence], loose letters, 1961–2, memo from Revell to John B. Parkin, 11 September 1961.

34 Ibid., memo from Parkin to Revell, 13 September 1961.

35 Ibid., memo from Revell to Parkin, 29 September 1961, Confidential.

36 FMA, Revell Collection, brown envelope labelled "V. Revellin Kinjeenvaihto" [correspondence], Professor Arne Rekola to Bo Therman, 23 December 1959.

37 Author's interview with Bengt Lundsten, Seppo Valjus, and Tuula Revell, FMA, 9 October 2013.

38 FMA, Revell Collection, brown slipcase labelled "Toronto-kirjeenvaihto" [correspondence], loose letters, 1961–2, Revell to Anderson, 31 October 1961; Anderson to Revell, 7 December 1961.

39 FMA, Revell Collection, brown slipcase labelled "V. Revellin Kirjeenvaihto" [correspondence], brown envelope labelled "Toronto Kirjeenvaihto, 1962–5," Edmund Orlowski to Revell, 10 January 1962; memo re "Property, 95 Post Road, Don Mills," n.d. [c. 1962].

40 Author's interview with Bengt Lundsten, Seppo Valjus, and Tuula Revell, FMA, 9 October 2013; Lundsten always harboured suspicions that the officers were really casing the building since there was news during the succeeding weeks that Toronto policemen were breaking into offices to steal valuables.

41 FMA, Revell Collection, brown slipcase labelled "V. Revellin Kirjeenvaihto" [Correspondence], brown envelope labelled "Toronto Kirjeenvahto, 1962–5," Revell to Orlowski, 31 January 1962.

42 FMA, Revell Collection, brown slipcase labelled "Toronto-Kirjeenvaihto" [correspondence], loose letters, 1961–2, J.A. Renwick to Edmund Orlowski, 1 June 1962; Revell to Revenue Canada, 15 June 1962; brown envelope labelled "V. Revellin Kirjeenvaihto," Revell to Tudor, 6 July 1962; brown slipcase labelled "V. Revellin Kirjeenvaihto," brown envelope labelled "Toronto Kirjeenvaihto," 1962–5, Revell to Parkin, 23 August 1962; Revell to Renwick, 6 September 1962.

43 FMA, Revell Collection, brown slipcase labelled "Toronto-Kirjeenvaihto" [correspondence], brown envelope labelled "Toronto Kirjeenvaihto," 1962–5, Revell to Parkin, 30 January 1962; Revell to Arthur, 9 February 1962.

44 Revell family records, Helsinki, yellow box labelled "Kirietia," Parkin to Revell, Helsinki, 6 February 1962.

45 FMA, Revell Collection, brown slipcase labelled "Toronto-Kirjeenvaihto" [correspondence], loose letters, 1961–2, Renwick to Revell, 22 March 1962, Personal and Confidential.

46 CTA, Series 843, NCH, box 147081, file 45, Arthur to Phillips, 28 January 1957; OAA president Guy Masson to W.R. Souter, vice-chair, OAA Registration Board, and board members, 29 January 1957; ibid., Series 1512, MC, box 507969, file 201, Phillips to OAA secretary John D. Miller, 31 January 1957; Miller to Phillips, 11 March 1957.

47 FMA, Revell Collection, brown slipcase labelled "Toronto-Kirjeenvaihto" [correspondence], loose letters, 1961–2, Renwick to Revell, 22 March 1962, Personal and Confidential.

48 FMA, Revell Collection, brown box labelled "Toronto-Competition etc., 1958–61," file "Viljo Revell & Co.," Timothy Donohue to Revell, 5 October 1962.

49 Ibid., Manthorpe to Revell (at MIT), 29 November 1962; brown slipcase labelled "Toronto-kirjeenvaihto" [correspondence]," Manthorpe to Revell, 22 January 1962.

50 FMA, Revell Collection, brown slipcase labelled "V. Revellin Kirjeenvaihto" [correspondence], loose letter, 1961–2, Revell to Castrén, 25 January 1963 (translated from Finnish by Veli Rahala).

51 Ibid., Revell to H.H. Rogers, 30 January 1963.

52 Ibid., Revell-Parkin to Revell, 12 March 1963.

53 FMA, Revell Collection, brown slipcase labelled "V. Revellin Kirjeenvaihto," brown envelope labelled "Toronto Kirjeenvaihto," 1962–5, Revell to Parkin, 16 July 1963; Parkin to Revell, 22 August 1963; Revell to T.W. Lovett, 9 September 1963.

54 Author's interview with Bengt Lundsten, Seppo Valjus, and Tuula Revell, FMA, 9 October 2013; FMA, Revell Collection, brown slipcase labelled "V. Revellin Kirjeenvaihto [correspondence], C. Bowler, National Revenue to Viljo Revell and Company, 5 July 1963.

55 FMA, Revell Collection, brown slipcase labelled "V. Revellin Kirjeenvaihto [correspondence]," brown envelope labelled "Toronto Kirjeenvaihto," 1962–5; Edmund Orlowski to Revell, 15, 21, 28 January 1964.

4 Construction
Pages 93–120

1 CTA, Series 361, Subseries 1, MC, Lawson, Rogers, and Angus to mayor and Board of Control, 10 March 1959.

2 Phillips, *Mayor of All the People,* 145; CTA, Series 491, Bell Papers, box 140300, file 28, brief from Gardiner, 24 March 1959.

3 CTA, Series 843, NCH, box 147087, file 113, contains the minutes of these meetings headed "Interview Report, Viljo Rewell [sic] – John B. Parkin Associates," nos. 1–19, Project 5867, New City Hall, 2–30 April 1959.

4 Ibid.; see nos. 6 and 8, both 14 April 1959; ibid., Rogers to various city department heads, 5 June 1959; Rogers to mayor and Board of Control, 20 July 1959.

5 Ibid., Frederick N. Smith (for Revell-Parkin) to Matthew Lawson, 8 June 1959.

6 CTA, Series 361, Subseries 1, MC, box 140525, file 618, Lawson to mayor's executive assistant, F.C. Hamilton, 9 October 1959; Lawson to Phillips, 29, 30 October 1959.

7 CTA, Series 491, Bell Papers, box 140299, file 46, Revell-Parkin, Stage I Report, Toronto City Hall, to mayor and Board of Control, 2 November 1959; Anthony Westell, "The Mayor Has a Blind Faith in New City Hall," *Globe and Mail*, 5 November 1959.

8 CTA, Series 361, Subseries 1, MC, box 140525, file 618, Gardiner's presentation to Metropolitan Council with Respect to the City Square and New Civic Administration Building, 7 February 1960.

9 Ibid., PA Chair Ralph Day to mayor and Board of Control, 8 September 1960; H.H. Rogers to mayor and Board of Control, 3 October 1960.

10 In a project that is voluminously documented in various series in CTA, there are almost no records dating from 1960.

11 CTA, Series 491, Bell Papers, box 140299, file 46, Matthew Lawson to City Solicitor Angus, 26 January 1961; ibid., Series 361, Subseries 1, MC, box 140525, file 619, Revell-Parkin to Nathan Phillips, 1 February 1961; press release, 2 February 1961; Rogers to Phillips, 4 May 1961.

12 CTA, Fonds 1301, Givens Papers, box 146332, file 3, Rogers to Phillips and Controllers D.D. Summerville and W.E. Allen, 26 May 1961; CCM, Executive Committee report no. 32 to council, approved 13 June 1961.

13 CTA, Series 361, Subseries 1, MC, box 140525, file 619, City Solicitor J.P. Kent to J.A. Kennedy and OMB members, 1 June 1962l; OMB secretary B. Vickers to Kent, 5 June 1961; memo from Kent to Phillips, 30 June 1961, Confidential; Phillips to Leslie Frost, 4 July 1961, Confidential; file 620, Phillips to Municipal Affairs Minister W.K. Warrender, 22 September 1961; Frost to Phillips, 2 October 1961.

14 Phillips, *Mayor of All the People*, 147; CTA, Series 491, Bell Papers, box 140295, file 145, J.A. Kennedy and A.L. McCrae, OMB order 7540–57 re City of Toronto, 7 October 1961.

15 Phillips, *Mayor of All the People*, 147; CTA, Series 361, Subseries 1, MC, box 140525, file 619, memo from City Clerk G.T. Batchelor to Board of Control, 11 May 1961; Trevor C. Cox, OGCA, to Rogers, 7, 27 July 1961; Cox to Board of Control, 10 August 1961, on which Rogers noted that he telephoned Cox and told him no changes would be made.

16 E.G.M. Cape, Foundation Company of Canada, and McNamara Construction.

17 CCM, Board of Control Report no. 22, 18 September 1961; the square was originally to be called simply "Phillips," but this was later altered to "Nathan Phillips" to avoid confusion.

18 CTA, Series 491, Bell Papers, box 140299, file 50, Report of Meeting at office of City Property Commissioner Rogers, 26 September 1961.

19 CTA, Series 491, Bell Papers, box 140301, file 1, "New City Hall and Nathan Phillips Square," n.d. [October 1961].

20 FMA, Revell Collection, brown slipcase labelled "Toronto-kirjeenvaihto" [correspondence], loose letters 1961–2, Revell-Parkin to H.H. Rogers, 6 December 1961, 19 January 1962.

21 "Hogtown" was, of course, the derogatory moniker often applied to the city elsewhere in Canada; it referred to the large pork-packing enterprises located there in the nineteenth century.

22 CTA, Series 361, Subseries 1, MC, box 140525, file 621, clipping from column by Pierre Berton, n.d. [April 1962]; ibid., Fonds 1301, Givens Papers, box 145332, file 3, A.M. Linden to Givens, 3 May 1962; Givens to Linden, 9 May 1962.

23 CTA, Series 361, Subseries 1, MC, box 140525, file 621, Phillips to Johnstone, 23 May 1962; Johnstone to Phillips, 7 June 1962; ibid., Series 491, Bell Papers, box 140295, file 147, Site Report no. 18 from Revell-Parkin, 11 July 1962.

24 CTA, Series 361, Subseries 1, MC, box 140525, file 622, R.W. Johnstone to Revell-Parkin, 20 September 1962; Rogers to Revell-Parkin, 26 September 1962; memo from Board of Control Vice-Chair Donald Summerville to mayor and Board of Control, 30 October 1962.

25 CCM, Board of Control Report no. 29, approved by council 5 November 1962; Elizabeth Hulse, "Beer Precast," in Michael McClelland and Graeme Stewart, eds., *Concrete Toronto: A Guidebook to Concrete Architecture from the Fifties to the Seventies* (Toronto: Coach House and E.R.A. Architects 2007), 290; there were, however, well-founded doubts about whether the marble would continue to sparkle for very long owing to the Toronto climate.

26 FMA, Revell Collection, brown slipcase labelled "Toronto- kirjeenvaihto [correspondence]," loose letters 1961–2, Revell-Parkin to Anglin Norcross, 5 April 1962; Anglin Norcross to Revell-Parkin, 2 May 1962.

27 CTA, Series 491, Bell Papers, box 140299, file 46, Report of Property Commissioner, 30 October 1962.

28 CTA, Series 361, Subseries 1, MC, box 140525, file 622, Johnstone to Rogers, 11 December 1962.

29 CCM, Board of Control Report no. 29, approved by council 5 November 1962.

30 CTA, Series 361, Subseries 1, MC, box 140525, file 622, Anglin Norcross to Parkin-Revell, 17, 28 January 1963.

31 CTA, Fonds 1301, Givens Papers, box 146332, file 2, Anglin Norcross to Parkin and Revell, 17 January 1963.

32 CCM, Board of Control Report no. 5, approved by council 19 February 1963; Board of Control Report no. 17, approved by council 27 May 1963; CTA, Series 491, Bell Papers, box 140297, file 100, memo from George Bell to mayor and Board of Control, 15 May 1963.

33 CTA, Series 361, Subseries 1, MC, box 140525, file 622, Johnstone to Summerville, 1 February 1963, Personal.

34 CTA, Fonds 1301, Givens Papers, box 146332, file 2, Johnstone to Rogers, 1 February 1963; Rogers to Johnstone, 5 February 1963; ibid., Series 361, Subseries 1, box 140525, file 622, clipping from Ron Haggart's Toronto *Star* column of 18 February 1963, "Did Phillips Hide Facts on City Hall?"

35 CTA, Series 361, Subseries 1, MC, box 140525, file 622, draft memo from Summerville to Board of Control, 27 February 1963.

36 Ibid., Summerville to Mark Harrison of the *Star*, 4 March 1963; two memos from Rogers to mayor and controllers, 11 March 1963, Confidential.

37 CTA, Series 491, Bell Papers, box 140295, file 147, Site Report no. 38 from Revell-Parkin, 1 May 1963; ibid., box 140301, file 2, memo from Rogers to mayor and Board of Control, 13 May 1963, Confidential.

38 CCM, Board of Control Report no. 16, approved by council, 14 May 1963; and by-law 21837, ratified 27 May 1963.

39 CTA, Series 491, Bell Papers, box 140301, file 1, Bell to Vilo Revel [sic], 16 May 1963.

40 Ibid., box 140299, file 46, Report from Bell to mayor and Board of Control, 24 May 1963.

41 FMA, Revell Collection, brown slipcase labelled "Toronto-kirjeenvaihto" [correspondence], loose letters 1961–2, Rogers to Revell, 1 March 1962; ibid., brown slipcase labelled "Toronto Kirjeenvaihto," 1962–5, Revell to Parkin, 28 August 1963.

42 CTA, Series 1512, MC, box 506521, file 46, CKEY editorial, 9 July 1963.

43 A copy of this undated document printed in June 1963 may be found in CTA, Series 491, Bell Papers, box 140301, file 2; to

maintain public support, the TTC had issued a similar series of sidewalk superintendent's guides during the construction of the Yonge Street subway in the 1950s.

44 $185,000 for "solar drapes" to make the air-conditioning system effective, $115,000 for artwork (based upon a percentage of the total), $100,000 for flood-lighting the towers, and $1.04 million for furnishings plus the imposition of a new 11 per cent sales tax on any additions to the contract.

45 CTA, Series 491, Bell Papers, box 140299, file 46, Kennedy to W.R. Callow, 4 July 1963; report from Bell to mayor and Board of Control, 9 July 1963.

46 Ibid.; report from Bell to mayor and Board of Control, 9 July, 30 August 1963; ibid., Series 1512, MC, box 506521, file 46, CKEY editorial, 9 July 1963.

47 CTA, Series 491, Bell Papers, box 140295, file 148, Site Meeting Reports nos. 43, 45, from Revell-Parkin, 10 July, 21 August, 1963; ibid., box 140301, file 2, Bell to Viljo Revell, 11 July, 7 August 1963; G. Korulis to Bell, 19 August 1963; ibid., box 140297, file 101, Personnel Services Director R.G. Humphrey to mayor and Board of Control, 29 August 1963.

48 CTA, Series 491, Bell Papers, box 140297, file 97, Revell-Parkin to Bell, 5 November 1963; ibid., box 140295, file, 3, Bell to City Treasurer W.M. Campbell, 19 November 1963; *CCM*, Board of Control Report no. 30 approved by council, 12 November 1963.

49 *CCM*, Board of Control Report no. 13, approved by council, 16 April 1963; CTA, Series 491, Bell Papers, box 140300, file 24, Bell to mayor and Board of Control, 24 May 1963.

50 CTA, Series 491, Bell Papers, box 1405295, file 160, Bell to City Solicitor W.R. Callow, 21 October 1963; ibid., box 140301, file 1, Callow to Bell, 28 November 1963.

51 CTA, Series 491, Bell Papers, box 140299, file 55, Bell to PA General Manager R.G. Bundy, 27 December 1964; John B. Parkin Associates to PA, 17 February 1964; Bell to Bundy, 20 February 1964; Bundy to Givens, 26 February 1964; Givens to G.L. Olts, Perini, 27 February 1964; Olts to Givens, 4 March 1964.

52 CTA, Series 491, Bell Papers, box 140299, file 51, Revell-Parkin to Anglin Norcross, 26 May 1964; Anglin Norcross to St Clair House Wrecking, 24 June 1964; Anglin Norcross to Bell, 23 July 1964; ibid., box 140298, file 56, Bell to R.G. Bundy, 29 May, 6 July, 1964; minutes of meeting of Perini, Anglin Norcross, and Parkin Associates, 6 July 1964.

53 CTA, Series 491, Bell Papers, box 140301, file 3, Spence to Anglin Norcross, 19 December 1963; Miles to Revell-Parkin, 31 December 1963; Bell to Revell-Parkin, 6 January 1964.

54 Ibid., file 4, R.W. Johnstone to Revell-Parkin, 20 February 1964; Bell to Revell-Parkin, 11 February 1964; J.B. Mar, Revell-Parkin, to Anglin Norcross, 13 March 1964; Bell to Johnstone, 16 March 1964.

55 Ibid., D.F. Etherington, Anglin Norcross, to John B. Parkin Associates, 1 April 1964; ibid., file 5, draft letter from J.B. Mar, Revell-Parkin, to Anglin Norcross, 22 May 1964; Bell to Callow, 26 May 1964; Callow to Bell, 29 May, 22 June, 1964; Mar to Anglin Norcross, 29 June 1964.

56 CTA, Series 491, Bell Papers, box 140294, file 163, Anglin Norcross to Bell, 25 October 1963; ibid., box 140301, file 4, Ritchie to Anglin Norcross, 16 April 1964.

57 CTA, Series 491, Bell Papers, box 140301, file 4, D.G. Ritchie to Anglin Norcross, 17 April 1964.

58 Ibid., file 2, F.A. Beer, Toronto Cast Stone, Pre-Con, to D.F. Etherington, 24 September 1963; Etherinton to Bell with Bell's minute, 26 September 1963; ibid., file 5, D.G. Ritchie to Anglin Norcross, 9 July 1964.

59 Tuula Revell, "Viljo Revell, Biography," 242; CTA, Series 491, Bell Papers, box 140301, file 1, memo to file from M.F. Matthews, coordinator of services, 10 March 1964.

60 CTA, Series 1512, MC, box 506521, file 46, Board of Control Secretary G.T. Batchelor to Parkin, 8 November 1963; Revell to Givens, 2 December 1963; Givens to Revell, 9 December 1963; ibid., Fonds 1301, Givens Papers, box 146332, file 2, Revell to Givens, 31 December 1963.

61 CTA, Series 491, Bell Papers, Revell to Parkin, 4 March 1964; Parkin to Bell, 8 April 1964; ibid., Fonds 1301, Givens Papers, Revell to Parkin, 3 April 1964.

62 CTA, Series 491, Bell Papers, box 140295, file 160, Progress Report on New City Hall and Nathan Phillips Square to 31 December 1963, January 1964.

63 CTA, Series 491, Bell Papers, box 140301, file 3, D.F. Etherington, Anglin Norcross, to John B. Parkin Associates, 2 January 1964; ibid., box 140300, file 24, Bell to Board of Control, 22 January 1964.

64 CTA, Series 491, Bell Papers, box 140301, file 4, City Clerk C.E. Norris to Bell, 17 April 1964; memo from Bell to Board of Control, 27 April 1964. In fact, civic employees would later claim that the worst thing about the design was the amount of traipsing up and down required to cross between the two towers.

65 CTA, Series 1512, MC, box 507969, file 204, Givens to Vanier, 28 May 1964; Henry F. Davis to Givens, 22 October 1964; Givens to *Life*'s George P. Hunt, 23 July 1964; Givens to *Time*'s Canadian bureau chief S. Hillman, 24 July 1964.

66 Toronto *Star*, 21 August 1964.

67 Ibid., 15, 29 October 1964.

68 CTA, Series 1512, MC, box 403195, file 47, "In Memoriam, 1910–1964," in P[arkin] A[ssociates] *Review*, n.d. [June 1965], published by the firm and also containing tributes from John B. Parkin, Eric Arthur, J.B. Mar, and Nathan Phillips along with photographs of the original design model, the building under construction, and Revell with his design team of Lundsten, Valjus, and Castrén.

69 CTA, Series 491, Bell Collection, box 140300, file 28, Revell-Parkin to Bell, 16 February 1965; memo from Bell to file, 24 February 1965.

70 Vol. 9, no. 12.

71 CTA, Fonds 1301, Givens Papers, box 146332, file 2, Givens to C.L.H., 6 November 1964.

72 *Globe*, 23 March 1965.

73 CTA, Series 491, Bell Papers, box 140300, file 23, Coordinator, Progress Report on Capital Projects, 15 August 1964; ibid., Fonds 1301, Givens papers, box 146332, file 5, memo from Bell to Board of Control, "General Resumé of Matters requiring Consideration and Decision in Connection with the New City Hall and Nathan Phillips Square including Related Matters," August 1964.

74 CTA, Fonds 1301, Givens Papers, box 146328, file 10, Arthur to "Phil," 3 November 1964; Givens to Arthur, 4 November 1964.

75 CTA, Series 1512, MC, box 506521, file 46, L.N. to Givens, 30 October 1964; Givens to L.N. (and to other protestors), 2 November 1964.

76 Ibid., box PO43195, file 47, J.G. to Givens, 29 March 1965, calling for the prison sys-

tem to be expanded since this was where many of the drinkers would end up.

77 *CCM*, Board of Control Report no. 30, approved by council 26 October 1964.

78 CTA, Series 491, Bell Papers, box 140299, file 47, Johnstone to Bell, 28 January, 15 February 1965.

79 Ibid., memo from Callow to Bell with Bell's annotations, n.d.; Bell to Johnstone, 3 March 1965; Bell to Johnstone, 11 March 1965; Anglin Norcross to Bell, 18 March 1965.

80 Ibid., Bell to Anglin Norcross, 31 May 1965; OMB Secretary B. Vickers to Callow, 3 June, 5 July 1965; memo from Callow to Givens, Bell, and City Treasurer W.M. Campbell, 21 June 1965; Callow to Vickers, 24 June 1965.

81 CTA, Series 491, Bell Papers, box 140300, file 28, Anglin Norcross to Bell, 21 June 1965; box 140298, file 70, Bell to City Treasurer W.M. Campbell, 23 July 1965.

82 CTA, Series 491, Bell papers, box 140299, file 47, Anglin Norcross to Bell, 23 June 1965; Callow to Bell, 26 July 1965; box 140300, file 27, memorandum from Bell to file, 11 August 1965.

83 CTA, Series 491, Bell Papers, box 140300, file 27, memos from Bell to file, 20 August, 1 September 1965.

84 CTA, Series 1512, MC, box PO43195, file 47, Revell-Parkin to Bell, 10 September 1965; H.H. Rogers to Bell, 15 September 1965; ibid., Series 491, Bell Papers, box 140301, file 8, Revell-Parkin to Anglin Norcross, 15 September, 8 October 1965

5 Furnishings
Pages 121–42

1 The only project in Toronto during this period that qualified for this designation was Massey College at the University of Toronto, where the Massey Foundation allowed Ron Thom to design everything down to the tableware and the letterhead.

2 CTA, Series 362, Subseries 1, MC, box 140525, file 621, memo from City Hall Coordinator H.H. Rogers to mayor and Board of Control, 15 January 1962.

3 FMA, Revell Collection, brown slipcase labelled "Toronto-kirjeenvaihto" [correspondence], loose letters 1961–2, C.B.W. [illegible], memo re "New City Hall Furnishing," 4 August 1961.

4 Revell family records, Helsinki, yellow box labelled "Kirieita," Revell to Parkin, 3 January 1959.

5 FMA, Revell Collection, brown slipcase labelled "Toronto-kirjeenvaihto" [correspondence], loose letters, 1961–2, memo from Revell to Parkin, 11 September 1961.

6 Ibid., memo from Parkin to Revell, 13 September 1961. Parkin also pointed out that, since he had just been appointed chair of Canada's National Design Council, it would be most inappropriate for him to be associated with any scheme to introduce obviously foreign-designed products into the country.

7 Ibid., memo from Revell to Parkin, 29 September 1961, Confidential.

8 CTA, Series 361, Subseries 1, MC, box 140525, file 621, memo from H.H. Rogers to mayor and Board of Control, 15 January 1962.

9 FMA, Revell Collection, brown slipcase labelled "Toronto-kirjeenvaihto" [correspondence], loose letters 1961–2, memo from Revell to Parkin, 30 November 1961.

10 CTA, Series 361, Subseries 1, MC, box 140525, file 621, memo from Rogers to mayor and controllers, 15 January 1962; Revell family records, Helsinki, yellow box labelled "Kirieita," Parkin to Revell, 6 February 1962.

11 Revell family collection, Helsinki, yellow box labelled "Kirieita," Revell-Parkin, "Toronto City Hall and Nathan Phillips Square, Proposed Furnishings Program," 30 March 1962.

12 Ibid., memo from Revell to John B. Parkin, 8 April 1962 (emphasis in the original).

13 CTA, Series 491, Bell Papers, box 140300, file 34, draft agreement between Revell, the two Parkins, and the city, 21 May 1962; *CCM*, Board of Control Report no. 17, approved by council 4 June 1962; FMA, Revell Collection, brown slipcase labelled "Toronto-kirjeenvaihto" [correspondence], loose letters 1961–2, Revell-Parkin to Rogers, 9 April 1962.

14 FMA, Revell Collection, brown slipcase labelled "Toronto-kirjeenvaihto" [correspondence], memorandum from John C. Parkin to Tudor, 22 January 1963; memo from Tudor to Mar, 22 January 1963.

15 CTA, Series 491, Bell Papers, box 140300, file 34, Houghton to Lamport, 17 June 1963; Lamport to Houghton, 18 June 1963; Bell to Revell-Parkin, 12 July 1963;

box 140299, file 40, Metro Clerk W.W. Gardhouse to Bell, 11 July 1963.

16 Ibid., box 140300, file 34, Report from Bell to mayor and Board of Control, 17 September 1964; memo from Bell to controllers, 17 September 1963.

17 CTA, Series 1512, MC, box 507969, file 203, Givens to Allen Nobleston, *Telegram* editorial department, 15 October 1963.

18 CTA, Series 491, Bell Papers, box 140300, file 28, Report from Bell to mayor and Board of Control, 29 November 1963, approved by council 9 December 1963 (emphasis in the original).

19 CTA, Series 1512, MC, box 507969, file 203, Treasurer W.M. Campbell to Givens, 9 December 1963, Private and Confidential; Givens to J.A. Kennedy, 16 December 1963.

20 Revell family collection, Helsinki, yellow box labelled "Kirieita," Parkin to Revell, 10 December 1963.

21 CTA, Series 491, Bell Papers, box 140300, file 34, Bell to Revell, Bush, Chapman, and Lochnan, 8 January 1964. In the end, Carl Lochnan was told by the federal minister not to join since it would be better to have only an advisory position, though he did agree to supply a list of qualified "specifiers"; see ibid., C.M. Drury to Bell, 2 February 1964; Lochnan to Bell, 4 February 1964.

22 Ibid., excerpt of letter from Revell to Parkin Associates, 2 January 1964.

23 Revell family collection, Helsinki, yellow box labelled "Kirieita," Revell to Parkin, 22 January 1964.

24 Ibid., Revell to Parkin, 3 February 1964.

25 CTA, Series 491, Bell Papers, box 140300, memo from Bell and M.F. Matthews to file, 28 January 1964; Arthur to Revell, 29 January 1964.

26 Ibid., file 34, Revell to Bell, 3 March 1964.

27 Ibid., Arthur to Revell, 29 January 1964; Nicholas Fodor to Bell, 6 February 1964, Private and Confidential; Report from Bell to Board of Control, 3 April 1964; ibid., file 35, Revell-Parkin to Bell, 27 May 1964; ibid., Series 1512, MC, box 506521, file 46, Arthur to Givens, 6 February 1964; *CCM*, Board of Control Report no. 8, approved by council 2 March 1964.

28 CTA, Series 491, Bell Papers, box 140300, file 34, Lochnan to Bell, 4 February 1964; memo from R.M. Bremner and M.F. Matthews to Bell, 19 February 1964.

29 CTA, Series 491, Bell Papers, box 140294, file 161, Bell to Bain, 20 March 1964; ibid.,

box 140300, file 37, Bell to Arthur and to other committee members, 10 April 1964.

30 CTA, Series 491, Bell Papers, box 140300, file 35, Chapman to Bell, 7 May 1964; Bell to Chapman, 8 May 1964.

31 Ibid., minutes of FDC meeting, 29 May 1964; Arthur to Bell, 29 May 1964.

32 CTA, Series 491, Bell Papers, box 140294, file 161, Arthur to committee members, 5 June 1964, enclosing "Conditions of Competition – Furnishings for the New City Hall," n.d., Personal and Confidential.

33 CTA, Series 491, Bell papers, box 140300, file 35, Arthur to Bell, 27 June 1964; same to same, n.d. [28 June 1964].

34 CTA, Fonds 1301, Givens Papers, box 146332, file 7, City Clerk C.E. Norris to Bell, 29 June 1964; Arthur to mayor and controllers, 16 July 1964.

35 CTA, Series 1512, MC, box 507969, file 203, telegram from Givens to Ben, 23 July 1964, adding his regards to Ruby [Ben] and the kids.

36 CTA, Series 491, Bell Papers, box 140300, file 35, Arthur to mayor and Board of Control, 16 July 1964; Ben to mayor and Board of Control, 31 July 1964. Bell sought to make it as difficult as possible for Ben to substantiate his charges by refusing to give him copies of the entries or to allow him to make photostats of them on the grounds that the Board of Control had not specifically authorized this, though eventually he was allowed to bring along a dictaphone to make transcriptions. See ibid., Fonds 1301, Givens Papers, box 146332, file 7, memo to file from W.F. Matthews, 3 July 1964.

37 CTA, Series 491, Bell Papers, box 140300, file 35, Arthur to FDC members, 5 July 1964; Arthur to mayor and Board of Control, 21 August 1964; "Oral Submission of the Chairman of the Furnishings Design Committee to City Council of the Corporation of the City of Toronto," 14 September 1964; ibid., file 36, minutes of FDC meeting, 29 September 1964; *CCM*, Board of Control Report no. 27, approved by council 14 September 1964.

38 CTA, Series 491, Bell Papers, box 140300, file 36, Arthur to Bain, 24 September 1964.

39 Ibid., file 33, Conditions of Furnishing Design Competition, New City Hall, Toronto, 20 October 1964.

40 Toronto *Star*, 15, 29 October 1964.

41 CTA, Series 491, Bell Papers, box 140300, file 36, Minutes of First Meeting of Fur-

nishings Design Committee and Successful Competitors, 2nd draft, 2 November 1964. The other question that greatly exercised the entrants was whether the city would stick to its insistence on retaining the copyright to any designs submitted as mandated by the council; they were promised that this would be reconsidered at a future date.

42 It is not even clear if she ever received the promised $5,000 fee for the assigned task.

43 CTA, Series 491, Bell Papers, box 140300, file 36, minutes of FDC meeting, 16 November 1964; Arthur to J.B. Parkin, 18 November 1964.

44 CTA, Series 491, Bell Papers, Box 140298, file 70, Campbell to Bell, 27, 30 November 1964; Revell-Parkin to Bell, 30 December 1964.

45 Ibid., Campbell to Bell, 21 January 1965; Campbell to R.M. Bremner, 26 May 1965; memo from J.E. Cooke to Campbell, 29 June 1965; Campbell to Dennison, 29 June 1965.

46 Ibid., Bell to Campbell, 30 June 1965; Campbell to Bell, 2 July 1965.

47 Ibid., Dennison to Givens, 8 July 1965; Bell to H.H. Rogers, 30 July 1965; Rogers to Bell, 30 July 1965; Bell to Campbell, 17 August 1965.

48 CTA, Series 491, Bell papers, box 140299, file 47, Bell to Dennison, 20 January 1965; another $50,000 would be set aside pay the competition expenses plus up to $50,000 for incidentals and $25,000 for contingencies, or $950,000 in all.

49 CTA, Series 491, Bell Papers, box 140300, file 36, Furnishing Design Committee to Bell, 7 April 1965.

50 Ibid., Deputy City Clerk G.T. Batchelor to Bell, 8, 9 April 1965; memo from Bell to file, 9 April 1965; report from Bell to Board of Control, 12 April 1965.

51 *CCM*, Knoll to Givens, 8 April 1965, in Board of Control Report no. 15, approved by council 15 April 1965.

52 CTA, Series 491, Bell Papers, box 140300, file 36, Batchelor to Bell, 14 April 1965; ibid., box 140301, file 7, Batchelor to Bell, 13 April 1965.

53 *CCM*, Arthur to Givens, 14 April 1965, in Board of Control Report no. 15, approved by council 15 April 1965.

54 Ibid., submission from Blake, Cassels and Graydon to city solicitor.

55 Ibid., Mitchell Houghton to Orliffe.

56 CTA, Series 491, Bell Papers, box 140300, file 36, memo from Furnishings Commit-

tee Chair Eric Arthur to Board of Control, 15 April 1965.

57 Ibid., Alderman Harold Menzies to City Clerk C.E. Norris, 23 April 1965; City Solicitor W.R. Callow to Norris, 27 April 1965; Bell to Norris, 28 April 1965.

58 TRL, BR, Reed Collection, box Q, Halpenny to "Dear Eric," 19 April 1965.

59 CTA, Series 491, Bell Papers, box 140291, file 202, Irving Grossman, Henry Sears, John Sullivan, John Andrews, William Grierson, Jerome Markson, Boris Zerafa, Robert Anderson, Macy DuBois, Jack Klein, Alexander B. Leman, Peter Webb, and George Buchan to mayor and council, 28 April 1965.

60 CTA, Series 491, Bell Papers, box 140300, file 36, Arthur to Bell, 26 April 1965; ibid., Series 1512, box 507969, file 203, Chapman to Arthur, 2 May 1965.

61 CTA, Series 491, Bell Papers, box 140291, file 202, (Miss) E.C. Fairley, General Manger of the CHFI, to Bell, 24 June 1965; L. Lenkinski, UIU, to Herbert Orliffe, 30 June 1965.

62 CTA, Series 491, Bell Papers, box 140300, file 37, J.M. Houghton to Givens, 4 May 1965; City Clerk C.E. Norris to Bell, 7 May 1965.

63 Ibid., Arthur to Bell, 11 May 1965.

64 Malcolmson, "The Excited Press and a Symbol," *Telegram*, 8 May 1965.

65 CTA, Series 491, Bell Papers, box 140300, file 37, memo from Bell to Victor Portelli, 2 June 1965; City Clerk C.E. Norris to Bell, 4 June 1965; Arthur to mayor and city council, 5 June 1965; ibid., Fonds 1301, Givens Papers, box 146332, file 7, Chapman to Givens, 9 June 1965, Private and Confidential; Givens to Australian High Commissioner Sir Kenneth Bailey, 20 May 1965.

66 CTA, Series 491, Bell Papers, box 140300, file 37, J.D. Finch, Knoll, to Bell, 26 May 1965; J.R. Quigg, Knoll, to Board of Control, 14 June 1965.

67 Ibid., Bell to Knoll and Simpson's, 23 June 1965; L.E. Wicklum, Simpson's, to Bell, 23 June 1965; J.R. Quigg, Knoll, to Bell, 24 June 1965; *CCM*, Board of Control Report no. 24, approved by council 28 June 1965; ibid., Series 1512, MC, Quigg to Givens, 29 June 1965.

68 CTA, Series 1512, MC, box 507969, file 203, K.G. to Givens, 30 June 1965; Givens to Chapman, 2 July 1965; memo from Bell to Board of Control, 9 August 1965.

69 TRL, BR, Eric and Paul Arthur fonds, L52, box 14, file "ERA Correspondence, n.d.-1967," Givens to Arthur, 30 June 1965.

70 Vol. 2, no. 7, which also contains the four winning entries and photographs and drawings of "outstanding designs" from each one.

71 See Marsha Kelmans, "City Hall's Concrete Furniture," in McClelland and Stewart, eds., *Concrete Toronto*, 81–7, which contains some illustrations and notes that the city has preserved a small collection of the original furnishings in the city planner's offices. See also Sara Bowser, "Fuss over Office Furniture," clipping from [Toronto] *Star Weekly*, 8 February 1964, for the description of the panels and their purpose (quoted).

72 CTA, Series 491, Bell Papers, box 140300, file 37, Arthur to Bell, 19 August 1965.

73 CTA, Series 491, Bell Papers, box 140301, file 8, J. David Finch, Knoll, to Raymond Bremner, 3 November 1965.

74 CTA, Series 491, Bell Papers, box 140300, file 37, H.H. Rogers to Bell, 18 October 1965; Finch to Bremner, 26 October, Private and Confidential, and 2 November, Personal and Confidential, 1965.

75 Ibid., Report of meeting of Furnishing Design Committee, 22 October 1965.

76 CTA, Series 491, Bell Papers, box 140298, file 70, Campbell to Bell, 5 October 1965; Bell to Campbell, 12 October 1965.

77 CTA, Series 491, Bell Papers, box 140299, Matthews to Bell, 30 September 1965; ibid., Series 1512, MC, box PO43195, file 47, Givens to Bell, 26 October 1965; *CCM*, Board of Control Report no. 30, 27 October 1965.

78 CTA, Series 491, Bell Papers, box 140299, file 38, memo from Bremner to Board of Control, 10 December 1965; Finch to Bremner, 14 January 1965, Bremner to Finch, 20 January 1966; Contract Bond Performance Report to Western Assurance Co., 5 February 1966; ibid., file 50, 13 December 1966.

79 CTA, Series 491, Bell Papers, box 140299, file 39, Bremner to W.M. Campbell, 8 April 1968; memo from Bremner to Board of Control, 8 April 1968.

80 Ibid., file 38, Arthur to Bremner 24 December 1965; Bremner to Arthur, 28 December 1965.

81 CTA, Series 491, Bell Papers, box 140299, file 49, Notice of Service of Claim in Mitchell Houghton v. City of Toronto, 22 June 1966, City statement of defence, 13 June 1966; ibid., box 140291, file 203, transcript of deposition of Jack Houghton, 9 November 1966. The damages claimed varied from $100,000 to $55,000; the city claimed that the $5,000 fee had fully compensated the firm.

6 Opening
Pages 143–54

1 CTA, Series 1512, MC, box 507969, file 204, Norris to Givens, 8 January 1965; Givens to Vanier, 22 February 1965; ibid., Series 491, Bell Papers, Minutes of Special Committee re Opening Celebrations for New City Hall, 8 January 1965; box 140300, file 24, Esmond Butler to Givens, 15 March 1965; *CCM*, Board of Control Report no. 32, approved by council 14 September 1965.

2 CTA, Series 1512, MC, box 507969, file 204, Givens to Mitchell Sharp, 22 January 1965.

3 CTA, Series 491, Bell Papers, box 140300, file 24, Givens to Hellyer, 4 March 1965; memo from G.T. Batchelor, 31 March 1965; ibid., Series 1512, box 507969, file 204, Charles Tidy, president, 48th Highlanders Officers Association, to Givens, 16 June 1965; Givens to Tidy, 17, 30 June 1965.

4 Ibid., Givens to J.D. Arnup, 23 June 1965; ibid., Series 491, Bell Papers, Givens to Bell, 26 July 1965; box 140299, file 52, memo from D.J. McKenzie to H. Hyde, 13 August 1965.

5 CTA, Series 1512, MC, box PO43195, file 51, Mrs R.E.R.D.H. to Givens, 27 August 1965.

6 "Pomp, Pageantry – and a Touch of Confusion," *Globe*, 14 September 1965; CTA, Series 1512, MC, box PO43195, file 47, unsigned to mayor, 16 September 1965.

7 The following is taken from Arthur's draft text for his proposed book on the building, "Toronto City Hall," n.d. [c. 1965], in TRL, BR, Reed Collection, box Q, file "City Hall Competition Book."

8 CTA, Series 1512, MC, box 506521, file 45, Arthur to Metro chair and council, 1 December 1965; Norman Melnick, vice-president, Architectural Conservancy of Ontario, 2 December 1965; WebbZerafaMenkes to Givens, 4 November 1965.

9 *JRAIC*, 42, no. 9 (1965).

10 Murray, "Quartet: Four City Halls," *Canadian Architect*, 10, no. 10 (1965).

11 Thom, "Toronto City Hall: A Critique," *Canadian Architect*, ibid.

12 Shadbolt, "Toronto City Hall, Structure and Materials: A Lesson in Design," *JRAIC*, 43, no. 3 (1966).

13 Desbarats, "L'education et l'architecture symbolique," ibid.

14 Stephenson to editor, *JRAIC*, 43, no. 8 (1966).

15 CTA, Series 1512, MC, box PO43195, file 49, Property Commissioner H.H. Rogers to Revell-Parkin, 27 May 1966; ibid., Series 491, Bell Papers, box 140299, file 42, memo from Rogers to Board of Control, 14 March 1966; *CCM*, Board of Control Report no. 31, approved by council, 25 May 1966.

16 CTA, Series 491, Bell Papers, box 140301, file 10, "Concerned wife and taxpayer," 9 April 1966; memo by D.J. Batty to file, 2 June 1966; box 140298, file 74, memo from Givens to Raymond Bremner, 2 June 1966; ibid., Series 1512, MC, box PO43195, file 48, memo from Givens to Rogers, 28 February, 1 September 1966; Rogers to Givens, 8 September 1966.

17 CTA, Series 1512, MC, box PO43195, file 48, Information Sheet re Toronto New City Hall, 10 March 1966.

7 Coda
Pages 155–72

1 CTA, Series 491, Bell Papers, box 140298, file 56, City Solicitor W.R. Callow to Raymond Bremner, 22 October, 1 November, 3 December 1965; Anglin Norcross to Bremner, 2 December 1965; box 140299, file 48, Anglin Norcross to Callow, 30 November 1965; Bremner to Anglin Norcross, 3 December 1965.

2 Ibid., box 140299, file 48, Bremner to Callow, 18 January 1966; file 49, Bremner to Callow, 26 April 1966; memo from Bremner to R. Robinson, 8 June 1966.

3 CTA, Series 491, Bell Papers, box 140301, file 10, Bremner to Mar, 12 August 1966; regrettably, there seems to be no more correspondence on this subject.

4 CTA, Series 491, Bell Papers, box 140297, file 104, memo from Bremner, 10 November 1966, initialled by Bremner and Anglin Norcross president D.K. Yolles; file 97, Revell-Parkin to Bremner, 9 February 1967; file 50, memo from Bremner to Board of Control, 17 April 1967; box

140300, file 28, Bremner to Callow, 16 February 1967.

5 CTA, Series 491, Bell Papers, box 140301, file 10, Revell-Parkin to J.B. Howson, trustee, 10 October 1967; box 140299, file 50, Revell-Parkin to Bremner, 27 November 967; Bremner to Callow, 22 January 1968.

6 CTA, Series 491, Bell Papers, box 140298, file 57, A.S. Cunningham to Bremner, 13 March 1968; memo from Bremner to Board of Control, 9 August 1968.

7 CTA, Series 491, Bell Papers, box 140297, file 97, memo from Bremner to Board of Control, 3 February 1969; Bremner to Harries Houser Brown Holden and MacCallum, 30 December 1969; memo from Bremner to D.J. Batty, 21 August 1970.

8 Revell, "Viljo Revell, Biography," 241–2.

9 FMA, Revell Collection, brown slipcase labelled "Toronto-kirjeenvaihto" [correspondence], loose letters, 1961–2, Moore to Revell, 21 November 1961, 8 May 1962.

10 CTA, Series 361, Subseries 1, MC, box 140525, file 620, H.H. Rogers to Phillips, 8 December 1961, Confidential; file 621, Arthur to Phillips, 17 January 1962.

11 FMA, Revell Collection, brown slipcase labelled "Revellin Kirjeenvaihto [correspondence]," Revell to Parkin, 21 March 1963.

12 Revell family collection, Helsinki, yellow box labelled "Kirieita," Parkin to Revell, 3 April 1963.

13 CTA, Series 361, Subseries 1, MC, box 140525, file 620, Rogers to Phillips, 8 December 1961, Confidential; file 622, Rogers to Board of Control secretary G.T. Batchelor, 18 January 1963; CCM, Board of Control Report no. 17, approved by council 4 June 1963.

14 FMA, Revell Collection, brown slipcase labelled "Toronto-Kirjeenvaihto [correspondence]," 1962–5, Revell to Arthur, 27 June 1963.

15 CTA, Fonds 1301, Givens Papers, box 146332, file 6, Arthur, "Memorandum on Art for the New City Hall," 20 January 1964.

16 FMA, Revell Collection, brown slipcase labelled "V. Revellin-Kirjeenvaito [correspondence]," brown envelope labelled "Toronto Kirjeenvaihto," 1962–5, Revell to Parkin, 22 January, 3 February 1964.

17 CTA, Fonds 1301, Givens Papers, box 146332, file 6, Arthur to Givens, 20 January 1964; file 2, Arthur to Givens, 6 February 1964.

18 TRL, BR, Eric and Paul Arthur fonds, L52, box 3, file "Miscellaneous Correspondence, ERA, to 1967," Eric to Paul Arthur, 21 March 1964.

19 After further consultations with Givens, Arthur nominated the following members: William Withrow, director, Art Gallery of Toronto; Jean Boggs, curator, Art Gallery of Toronto; Mrs Harry Davidson, member of the Art Gallery's Women's Committee; Mrs T.P. Lownsbrough, past chair of the Art Gallery's Canadian-American Collections Committee; Douglas Duncan, head of the Picture Loan Society; John C. Parkin, as Revell's nominee; Leonard C. Brockington, Queen's University; lawyer Roland Michener (who resigned when appointed high commissioner to India the following July); and city council representative Alderman Horace Brown. See CTA, Fonds 1301, Givens Papers, box 146332, file 2, Arthur to Givens, 7 May 1964.

20 CTA, Series 1512, MC, box 506521, file 46, R.G. to Givens, 1 April 1964.

21 TRL, BR, Eric and Paul Arthur fonds, box 3, file "Biographical Miscellaneous Correspondence, ERA, to 1967," Eric to Paul Arthur, 12 February 1965.

22 CTA, Fonds 1301, Givens Papers, box 146332, file 2, Arthur to Givens, 7 May 1964.

23 CTA, Series 1512, MC, box PO43195, file 17, H.M. to Givens, 12 October 1965, and reply, 20 October 1965.

24 Toronto Star, 18, 19 February 1966.

25 CTA, Series 1512, MC, box PO43195, file 48, petition from M.H. to Eric Arthur, 8 March 1966; petition to mayor, n.d.; E.S.W. to mayor, 10 March 1966; L.M. to mayor, 22 February 1966; S.D. to mayor, 19 February 1966.

26 Ibid., M.D.S. to mayor, 17 March 1966; J.N. to mayor, 17 March 1966.

27 Toronto Star, 10, 16, 17 March 1966; CTA, Series 1512, MC, box PO43195, file 48, M.M. to Givens, 9 March 1966, and reply, 14 March 1966.

28 "Odds and Ends," Canadian Architect, 11, no. 4 (1966).

29 CTA, Series 1512, MC, box 547466, file 1017, Givens to P.J.B., 25 March 1966. The committee was also annoyed that city council had recently decided that a decision on a commission for a large mural inside the main entrance should be deferred a year until March 1967; see

CTA, Series 1512, MC, box PO43195, file 48, Arthur to Givens, 28 March 1966.

30 CTA, Series 1512, MC, box PO43195, file 48, Givens to J.W.P., 31 March 1966.

31 Ibid., P.J.P. to Givens, 21 March 1966.

32 At this very time Hirshhorn was in negotiation to give his art collection to the government of the United States. There had been some suggestion that he ought to donate the works to Canada, the source of his fortune, but he was told that he could not have a museum building named after him to contain his collection since it was (supposedly) Canadian policy not to have buildings named after particular individuals. In the spring of 1964 U.S. President Lyndon Johnson accepted the collection and it was agreed that the "Hirshhorn Museum" would be constructed on the south side of the Mall to contain the artwork, as indeed was done.

33 Toronto Star, 26 April 1966.

34 CTA, Series 1512, MC, box PO43195, file 49, Mrs J.P.B. to Givens, n.d. [May 1966].

35 Ibid., T.P. to Givens, 16 May 1966.

36 Ibid., Givens to Mrs J.P.B., 16 May 1966.

37 Ibid., Givens to T.P. 30 May 1966.

38 Ibid., R.E. to Givens, 21 May 1966; Givens to B.W., 24 May 1966.

39 Ibid., T.R. to Givens, 9 May 1966; Givens to T.R., 17 May 1966.

40 Ibid., telegram from Beny to Givens, 20 May 1966; Minister of National Revenue E.J. Benson to Givens, 17 May 1966.

41 Ibid., Givens to Moore, 2 June 1966.

42 Ibid., Moore to Givens, 23 June 1966; Givens to Moore, 29, 30 June 1966.

43 Ibid., memo from H. Talbot to Givens, 20 June 1966; ibid., Series 491, Bell Papers, box 140301, file 10, John C. Parkin to Raymond Bremner, 4 July 1966, Confidential.

44 CTA, Series 491, Bell papers, box 140301, file 10, Arthur to Raymond Bremner, 29 June, 12 August 1966; ibid., Series 1512, MC, PO43195, file 49, memo from City Solicitor W.R. Callow to Givens, 18 August 1966.

45 CTA, Series 491, Bell Papers, box 140301, file 10, Arthur to Bremner, 12 August 1966; memo from Vardin to Bremner, 17 August 1966; memo from Deputy City Clerk G.T. Batchelor to Board of Control, 19 August 1966.

46 Ibid., Raymond Bremner to Givens, 15 November 1966; City Works Department to Keiller Mackay, 6 December 1966.

47 Ibid., Revell-Parkin to Moore, 31 August 1966.

48 CTA, Series 1512, MC, box PO43195, file 49, Arthur to John C. Parkin, 1 September 1966.

49 Ibid., Report from City Clerk C. Edgar Norris to Board of Control, 13 September 1966; *CCM*, Board of Control Report no. 45, 14 September 1966.

50 CTA, Series 1512, MC, box PO43195, file 49, Givens to G.D.S., 6 July 1966; Givens to Mrs T.H.B. 17 June 1966.

51 Ibid., George M. Hendrie to Givens, 15 June 1966; ibid., Series 491, Bell Papers, box 140301, file 10, Raymond Bremner to D. Logan, Hendrie and Company, 21 September 1966. The company had recently overseen the moving of the Ming dynasty tomb from inside the Royal Ontario Museum to the grounds outside facing onto Bloor Street.

52 CTA, Series 1512, MC, box PO43195, file 49, telegram from Givens to Hirshhorn, 17 October 1966; telegram from Beny to Givens, 26 October 1966.

53 Ibid., Programme for Ceremony of Presentation of Sculpture to City by Keillor Mackay, 27 October 1966; Givens to Moore, 28 October 1966.

54 *Globe*, 28 October 1966; New York *Times*, 28 October 1966.

55 CTA, Series 1512, MC, box PO43195, file 49, Williams et al. to Givens, 28 October 1966; file 50, Givens to Williams et al., 10 November 1966.

56 New York *Times*, 28 October 1966; CTA, Series 491, Bell Papers, box 140301, file 10, Givens to Bremner, 3 November 1966.

57 Alderman Michael Grayson charged that the $6,000 received by Arthur's son Paul created a conflict of interest because Eric Arthur was still getting a monthly honorarium of $400 for heading New City Hall's Art Advisory Committee; see *Telegram*, 28 March 1966.

58 City Clerk C.E. Norris was instructed by Mayor Dennison's executive assistant to do the accounting and reported that Arthur had received the following: $3,000 for the architectural competition in 1957; $3,000 more the following year plus $1,500 for overseeing the judging; a balance of $5,000 in 1959; expenses of $273.99 in 1963; $3,600 for nine months' work ($400 per month) on the Furnishing Design and Art Advisory Committees in 1964 plus $83.40 in expenses; $4,800 for twelve months' work ($400 per month) in 1965 plus $97.80 in expenses; another $4,800 plus $131.57 in expenses in 1966; $2,400 for six months' work ($400 per month) in 1968: for a total of $32,685.14. See CTA, Series 1512, MC, box 508916, file 312, Norris to mayor's executive assistant, Bryn Lloyd, 27 March 1968.

59 CTA, Series 1512, MC, box 508916, file 312, R.W. Macaulay to Dennison, 16 April 1968; confidential memo from Dennison to Board of Control, 29 April 1968; memo from Bryn Lloyd to Dennison, 15 July 1968.

60 See Porteus to James Ross, 2 August 1898, quoted in Christopher Armstrong and H.V. Nelles, *The Revenge of the Methodist Bicycle Company: Sunday Streetcars and Municipal Reform in Toronto, 1888–1897* (2nd ed., Toronto: Oxford University Press 2011), 169.

Illustration Credits

Significant efforts have been made to identify, credit appropriately, and obtain publication permissions from copyright holders for illustrations in this book. Notice of any errors or omissions will be gratefully received, and the required corrections made in subsequent editions. Wherever available, the reference or file number in use in each collection appears in the following lists.

Canadian Architectural Archives, University of Calgary (Panda Collection) — **1.11**: Panda 571098-2; **2.1**: Panda 58504-3; **2.4**: Panda 58504-2; **2.6**: Panda 58564-2; **2.7**: Panda 58405-5; **2.8**: Panda 58405-5; **2.9**: Panda 581184-58; **2.38**: Panda 591161-9; **2.39**: Panda, unnumbered; **3.3**: Panda 581084-12; **3.7**: Panda 61881-173; **3.8**: Panda 61881-287; **4.1**: Panda 61881-213; **4.3**: Panda 61881-207; **6.14**: Panda 68677-1.

Canadian Institute for Historical Microreproductions (CIHM) — **1.1**: *Canadian Architect and Builder*, v.11, n.01, January 1898; artist Owen Staples.

City of Toronto Archives (CTA) — **1.2**: *Fifty Glimpses of Toronto* (1901); architect Edward J. Lennox; **1.3**: John Lyle, 1911 (redrawn); *Report of the Advisory City Planning Commission* (1929) p. 24; **1.4**: *Report of the Advisory City Planning Commission* (1929), appendix; **1.5**: *Report of the Advisory City Planning Commission* (1929) appendix; **1.6**: *Report of the Advisory City Planning Commission* (1929) p.42; **1.7**: *Report of the Advisory City Planning Commission* (1929) p.10; **1.8**: CTA Fonds 1244, Item 10092; **1.10**: CTA Series 1188 (architects Marani & Morris; Mathers & Haldenby;

Shore & Moffatt); **1.12**: CTA Fonds 1244, Item 10089; **2.5**: *City Hall and Square, Toronto, Canada, Conditions of Competition*, 1958: map insert; **4.4**: CTA Fonds 1057 Item 6478; **4.5**: CTA Fonds 1057, fl0001_id0135; **5.1**: Don Bolton, photographer; reprinted in *Concrete Toronto* (Toronto: Coach House Books 2007), 86–7); **6.13**: unnumbered (south side, Queen Street West, 1971).

Mark Fram, photographer — **title (R)**; **7.1**.

NORR Architects Engineers Planners — **3.6**: Herb Nott, photographer.

Anthony Rolph, photographer — **2.3**; **2.18**; **2.19**; **2.20**; **2.21**; **2.22**; **2.23**; **2.35**.

Ryerson University Library and Archives, *Canadian Architect* Magazine Image Collection (RUCA) — **5.0**: ruca-2009.002.2318.037; **7.5**: ruca-2009.002.2130.009; **7.8**: ruca-2009.002.2318.018.

Toronto Public Library (TPL) — **1.9**: TPL R-1100 (photographed April 3, 1955).

TPL, City Hall first-stage competition drawings, Toronto Reference Library — **frontispiece**, **title (L)**: V. Revell, architect (entry 401, m199); **2.13**: Z. Kaplan, architect (entry 329, m287); **2.24**: E. Casteneda Tamborel, architect (entry 312, m247).

TPL, Toronto *Telegram*, Baillie Room, Toronto Reference Library — **2.2**: April 12, 1958; **6.3**: September 11, 1965; **6.4**: September 11, 1965.

TPL, Reed Collection, Baillie Room, Toronto Reference Library — **0.1**; **2.11**; **2.14**; **2.15**; **2.16**; **2.17**; **2.25**; **2.26**; **2.27**; **2.28**; **2.29**; **2.30**; **2.31**; **2.32**; **2.33**; **2.34**; **2.36**; **2.37**; **2.40**; **4.2**; **6.2**; **6.5**; **6.6**; **6.7**; **6.8**; **6.9**; **6.10**; **6.11**; **6.12**; **7.2** — Revell, second-stage submission — **3.1**; **3.2**; **3.4**; **3.5**; **7.6**; **7.7** — model photographs — **2.10**: Bonner T213; **2.12**: Bonner T329.

Toronto *Star* (Getstock) — **4.6**: Norman James, photographer, published 1964-10-29 (GS2084600502); **6.1**: Dick Darrell, photographer, published 1965-09-14 (GS2084200609).

Index